D1563821

Rethinking Imperialism

Rethinking Imperialism

A Study of Capitalist Rule

John Milios

and

Dimitris P. Sotiropoulos

palgrave
macmillan

First published 2009 by
PALGRAVE MACMILLAN

Palgrave Macmillan in the UK is an imprint of Macmillan Publishers Limited, registered in England, company number 785998, of Houndmills, Basingstoke, Hampshire RG21 6XS.

Palgrave Macmillan in the US is a division of St Martin's Press LLC, 175 Fifth Avenue, New York, NY 10010.

Palgrave Macmillan is the global academic imprint of the above companies and has companies and representatives throughout the world.

Palgrave® and Macmillan® are registered trademarks in the United States, the United Kingdom, Europe and other countries

ISBN: 978-0-230-22100-0   hardback

This book is printed on paper suitable for recycling and made from fully managed and sustained forest sources. Logging, pulping and manufacturing processes are expected to conform to the environmental regulations of the country of origin.

A catalogue record for this book is available from the British Library.

A catalog record for this book is available from the Library of Congress

10   9   8   7   6   5   4   3   2   1
18   17   16   15   14   13   12   11   10   09

Printed and bound in Great Britain by
CPI Antony Rowe, Chippenham and Eastbourne

Contents

Tables

Acknowledgements

This book owes debts to several people who in international meetings and conferences have discussed our theses and/or raised questions that helped the development of our arguments when the book was still in the making. Such international events were, for example, the *Historical Materialism* annual conferences 2006 (December 8–10), 2007 (November 9–11), 2008 (November 7–9) at SOAS, London, and the 9th Annual Conference 2007 (July 13–15) of the Association for Heterodox Economics at the University of the West of England, Bristol.

The authors would like especially to thank Professor Dimitri Dimoulis (Escola de direito de São Paulo da Fundação Getúlio Vargas, Brazil) and Dr Spyros Lapatsioras (University of Crete) for having read and commented on the drafts of the book. A special mention is also owed to Wayne Hall for having corrected and taken care of the style of the manuscripts.

Introduction

For more than a century 'imperialism' has been a key concept in Left theory and politics, connoting both the aggressiveness and the overripe characteristics of modern capitalism, or at any rate of certain capitalist formations. Recent debates in Political Economy have also placed emphasis on the notion of imperialism, the reason for this being that many of Political Economy's central concerns have had to do with the regulation of the 'global' economy, capitalism's recurrent tendencies towards crisis and the centrality of the logic of capital accumulation.

But the term 'imperialism' has never denoted a single theoretical approach. From the era of classical Marxist theories of imperialism (Hilferding, Luxemburg, Bukharin, Lenin ...) to the present day, different and often conflicting theories and political strategies have been prevalent among Left intellectuals and political organisations.

A point of clarification on methodology: 'Imperialism' is one of the most widely discussed terms in Marxist theory, having entered everyday political usage and having been disseminated very widely. This acceptance may be attributed to the political-critical use to which it was put for decades, and to a large extent still is, by Leftist organizations and in particular Communist Parties. This means that imperialism belongs to Marxism as an ideology of the masses (mass Marxism), and as a practical ideology of the workers' movement (Milios 1995, Lapatsioras et al. 2008) and that to some extent it is to be included amongst common sense notions of politics and economics. The price that is paid for this is that the term becomes inexplicit, superficial and often contradictory, used mainly in denunciation of 'bad' imperialism, its 'plans' and the misery it inflicts on the world.

In the present study we clearly dissociate ourselves from this usage of the term. Our aim is to present and assess imperialism as a theoretical

1

concept, that is to say as part of Marxist theory (theoretical Marxism). At this level, however, a variety of different analyses are advanced and different definitions assigned to the concept of imperialism in the works of different Marxists. What we are seeking to do is to put to the test the rigour of these definitions, their positive and negative elements. We want in this way to arrive at a comprehensive evaluation, from which conclusions may be drawn that can be useful in political action, also re-equipping Marxism as mass ideology with a more successful and potent concept of imperialism.

Our critical evaluation of the different approaches to imperialism eschews every resort to arguments from 'authority'. No Marxist writer, however significant he/she might be from a theoretical viewpoint or on account of his/her political activity, can be regarded as being in posses-sion of all the truth in relation to imperialism (or any other concept) or at any rate enjoying any relevant advantage over other writers.

We apply three basic criteria in our assessment of the various approaches. Firstly, the internal logical coherence of the arguments in each approach. Secondly, the relationship between their coherence and fundamental concepts of Marx's, and Marxist, theory. Thirdly, the poten-tial of each approach to provide an explanation of historical and contem-porary tendencies in capitalism and, conversely, refutation of theoretical predictions and evaluations of imperialism through empirical data.

In Part I of the book (*Theories of Imperialism as a Periodization and Interpretation of Capitalism*: Chapters 1–3) we propose to conduct a criti-cal review of the various major approaches to imperialism as a point of departure for the formulation of our own theoretical analysis.

Chapter 1 (*Classical Theories of Imperialism: A New Interpretation of Capitalist Rule, Expansionism, Capital Export, the Periodization and the 'Decline' of Capitalism*) deals with the Marxist theories of imperial-ism, formulated in the years 1909–25, that is after the publication of J. A. Hobson's book *Imperialism* (1902) – above all the approaches of Hilferding, Luxemburg, Bukharin and Lenin. We argue that the theoret-ical analyses that were put forward in this period, and the controversies over the 'latest stage' of capitalism, the 'rule of the monopolies', 'global capitalism', underconsumption and crisis, capital exports, 'stagnation and decay' of capitalism, etc. retain their relevance to this day. This is so on the one hand because they comprise to a very large extent the background to present-day discussions; on the other hand, and prima-rily, because their critical assessment can make a significant contribu-tion to the further progress of Marxist theory and the Marxist critique of contemporary capitalism.

Chapter 2 (*Post-World War II 'Metropolis-Periphery' Theories of Imperialism*) includes a critical presentation of the 'metropolis-periphery' or 'centre-periphery' approaches, placing special emphasis on the notions of dependency, global capitalism, unequal exchange, development vs. underdevelopment, international division of labour, etc. on which these approaches are grounded. Following certain trends of the classical theories of imperialism, all 'metropolis-periphery' theories share the fundamental assumption that capitalism exists only as a global system, and that the locus of operations of regularities immanent in the capitalist mode of production is the international community and not the national social formation. They thus conceive the international capitalist system as a uniform global capitalist-class structure, of which national economies and national states are merely separate individual components. The theory acquires a fully elaborated expression in recent works that provide grounds for postulating a 'new international division of labour' which can help make sense of the phenomena of international restructuring of production that has become observable in recent years. In our critical presentation of these theories we stress their internal contradictions and even more so their inability to arrive at a comprehensive theory of the capitalist state and political power.

Chapter 3 (*Theories of Imperialism as Alternatives to Classical and Centre–Periphery Approaches*) investigates a theoretical tradition which, following the approaches of Schumpeter and Weber, and to some extent certain analyses of Kautsky, proposes a 'political' interpretation of imperialism, giving emphasis to the policies of the state and the interests vested in them. This tradition is partly incorporated in the modern theories of 'new imperialism' and in their endeavour to distance themselves from the reductionist perceptions of the classic and centre–periphery approaches, which perceive the state as a mirror of economic causality and economic processes. However, what is present here is less a critique of economism and reductionism and more the maintenance of a similar essentialist schema in accordance with which every social instance (the economy, the state, ideology) coexists with every other in the framework of a deeper unity which it can also fully *express* at any moment.

In Part II of the book (*Theories of Imperialism vis-à-vis Marx's Critique of Political Economy*: Chapters 4–7) we embark on a critical interrogation of all innovations introduced into theoretical Marxism by theories of imperialism (for example those concerning the capitalist state, the stages of historical evolution of capitalism, internationalization of capital, crises, etc.) thus revising or re-interpreting the theoretical system formulated by Marx, especially in *Capital* and his other mature economic writings.

Chapter 4 deals with *The State as a Vehicle of both Capitalist Expansionism and Decolonization*, touching upon both historical evidence and questions of theory. The chapter provides some preliminary illustrations of the crucial role of the state in consolidating capitalism, and in both the colonization of external territories *and* the decolonization of these territories through the creation of new nation-states.

The analysis is further developed in Chapter 5 (*Capitalist Mode of Production and Social Formation*). Some conclusions are drawn concerning the organization of capitalist power. The notions of capitalist mode of production, capitalist social formation, and capitalist state as nation-state, are all explored.

Chapter 6 (*Capitalist Mode of Production and Monopolies*) challenges a key thesis of nearly all the theories under investigation, namely that imperialism is linked to monopoly capitalism as a new stage in economic and social development. It is argued that the theory of 'monopoly capitalism' constitutes more a revision of Marx's theory of capitalism than a further development or actualization of his theoretical analysis.

Chapter 7 (*Is Imperialism the* Latest *Stage of Capitalism? Reflections on the Question of Periodization of Capitalism and Stages of Capitalist Development*) provides an alternative approach to the problem of periodization of capitalist *social formations*, of the historical forms of the capitalist state and the issue of capitalist development, also focussing on a critique of the historicist problematic.

Summarizing Part II of the book, the following conclusion might be put forward: *The nation-state's condensation of class struggle and class domination results in an internationally fragmented capitalist world.* As the setting for social relations, the territory of the state is unequivocally stamped by its national dimension, within the boundaries of each nation-state's territory. Within the framework of the social formation, it bears the mark of accumulated political power of class domination in every detail of state operations, which are the decisive factor in generating the overall conditions that are a prerequisite for reproduction of the capital relation. It is conditioned (i) by the trend towards political, administrative, judicial, institutional and cultural homogenization that is inextricably interwoven with state power and its boundaries; (ii) by the specific (national) policies for management of the workforce, incentives policies and every kind of intervention for enhancing the profitability of the (national) social capital and its expansion internationally, at the expense of other national social capitals and (iii) by the single currency and the specific institutional and legislative framework that ensures the unity and freedom of the national market and direct competition between the different capitals operating within the borders. Under these 'national' conditions there is reproduction, in forms adequate to them, of the capitalist mode of production (CMP) and the capitalist division of labour, with transformation of individual capitals into *social capital*. Global space is divided into separate (national) spaces of class domination, separate regions of expanded reproduction of *the various (national) social capitals*.

Part III of the book (*National Territory and International Space: Internationalization of Capital, Financialization and Imperialist Chain*: Chapters 8–10) deals with the interaction between the historically formed multiplicity of social capitals and capitalist states at the global level, resulting in formation of an international economic and political space (the *imperialist chain*) linking together the different social capitals and capitalist social formations. But these international integrative processes cannot go beyond certain limits. For as long as they are confronted on the global market by national capitals at unequal levels of development, the less developed nations will yield to the protectionist and equalizing reflex whose roots are in the nation-state-based structuring of every social capital.

Chapter 8 (*Internationalization of Capital*) commences with a critique of the notion of dependence as the point of departure for a theory of modification of competition on the world market, with currency parities transforming relative cost differences between competing enterprises from different countries into absolute differences in costs. On this theoretical basis an interpretation of capital internationalization and capital exports is put forward, with a corresponding refutation of the theory of unequal exchange.

Chapter 9 (*Financialization: Market Discipline or Capital Discipline?*) shows that neoliberalism (the contemporary mode of operation of markets and the economic, political and military policies of the state) neither can be interpreted as the by-product of domination by the financial sector over 'productive enterprise' (managers and workers) nor can it be seen as a symptom of the rule of the 'rentier class' over the rest of society. Neoliberalism is the strategy of the capitalist class as a whole. Its predominance is the by-product of a shift in the class relation of forces following the economic crisis of the early seventies. The present economic crisis is systemic, in the sense that it has been brought about by the elements and the relations that are at the core of the neoliberal model.

Chapter 10 (*The 'Global' Level and the Concept of Imperialist Chain*) approaches today's imperialist order through the notion of *imperialist chain*, which is formulated in accordance with Marx's concept of social capital and his theory of the capitalist mode of production. Most theories of imperialism, including historicist approaches and doctrines of 'empire', distance themselves from the Marxian problematic of social capital (defined as the expression of the causal order of capitalist rule at every level of society).

The analysis in Part III of the book defends the thesis that internal-national relationships and processes always have priority over international relations. It is precisely the fundamental discovery of Marxism that the class struggle (which is at the same time economic, political and ideological and is thus consummated within each national-state entity) is the driving force of history. The class struggle, that is to say in the final analysis the class correlation of forces within each social formation (or, otherwise expressed, the correlations inside a system of class domination), is/are the prime determinant of the developmental tendencies of the specific social formation. It is through these class correlations and relations of domination that international relations, with all the concomitant interdependence on other social formations, take effect. International relations are merely a complex of more or less significant historical determinations that act upon class correlations via the 'laws of motion' of the economy and society. In other words national processes determine the way in which the national is integrated with the international.

Finally, the *Epilogue: Rethinking Imperialism and Capitalist Rule* concludes the analysis, focussing especially on the tension between Marx's theoretical system of the Critique of Political Economy and the theory (or rather theories) of capitalist expansion and domination that emerge out of the various discourses on imperialism.

Part I Theories of Imperialism as a Periodization and Interpretation of Capitalism: Some Open Theoretical Questions

1
Classical Theories of Imperialism: A New Interpretation of Capitalist Rule, Expansionism, Capital Export, the Periodization and the 'Decline' of Capitalism

It has already been hinted in the Introduction that the questions posed by present-day analyses of imperialism and the national state, and indeed the corresponding conceptions of 'globalization', are not being raised today for the first time. They had already been introduced, in similar terms despite the different historical circumstances, in the 'classical' theories of imperialism (as they are customarily called in the relevant literature), most of which, as is well known, were formulated in the second decade of the twentieth century (in chronological order of their composition: Hilferding (1981) first published in 1909, Luxemburg (1971) in 1912, Bukharin (1972a) in 1915, Lenin in 1916).

Our view is that the theoretical analyses that were advanced and the controversies over 'global capitalism' (and indeed over the 'rule of the monopolies') that took place in the 15 years between 1910 and 1925 retain their relevance to this day. This is so not only because they comprise to a very large extent the background to present-day discussions. It is also, and primarily, because their study can make a significant contribution to the further progress of Marxist theory and the Marxist critique of contemporary capitalism.

Before proceeding with a brief and general presentation of the classic Marxist theories of imperialism, we shall make a passing mention to a writer whose intervention played an arguably significant role in the shaping of the relevant Marxist debate. This is J. A. Hobson, who was in no way a follower of Marx, but who did admire Thorstein Veblen (Hobson 1937) and won recognition (justly, as an authentic underconsumptionist) from Keynes.[1]

1.1   Imperialism is a *symptom* of the capitalist crisis in Hobson's argument

In a conjuncture of sharpening antagonism between the major capitalist powers over the colonies, the journalist and writer J. A. Hobson in 1902 coined a new popular term to describe the phenomena of his age: *imperialism*. Many of Hobson's ideas influenced the Marxist theories of imperialism that were to be formulated a few years later. In what follows we shall attempt to summarize the writer's basic theses.

(a) *Monopoly capitalism.* According to Hobson capitalism appears to have moved beyond its 'competitive' stage and entered a new phase characterized by high levels of concentration of capital in 'trusts' and 'combines' (Hobson 1938: 75–6).

(b) *Underconsumption.* Given that Keynes was most probably unfamiliar with Marxist theoretical controversies and especially the writings of the Russian *Narodniks*, he was right in postulating that the underconsumptionist theories of Malthus and Sismondi had been forgotten by the end of the nineteenth century, that is to say the date of appearance of the interventions by Hobson and Mummery (see Keynes 1973: 364).[2] What was revived with Hobson was primarily the Sismondi variant. Bear in mind that according to the latter, capitalism is characterized by an *inherent contradiction* between capitalist production and the consequent distribution of income. The growth of production is accompanied by reduction in the income of the labouring masses, in turn triggering a fall in consumption and leading to recurrent capitalist crises (Hobson 1938: 83).

(c) *Export of capital as an answer to the problem of the crisis.* Given capitalism's chronic tendency towards underconsumption, there is a permanent shortage of opportunities (investment spheres) for productive utilization of capitalist profits. The low income level of workers ultimately precludes savings from being converted into productive investments, with the result that there is a chronic *savings surplus* or *surplus of capital*. The new monopolized structure of advanced capitalism *further exacerbates* the problem rather than solving it. The reason for this is that the 'concentration of industry in "trusts", "combines", etc., at once limits the quantity of capital which can be effectively employed and increases the share of profits out of which fresh savings and fresh capital will spring' (ibid.: 76).

(d) *Imperialism is a symptom of the capitalist crisis (of underconsumption).* Imperialist policy is seen by the developed states as an answer to the problem of unutilized surplus capital:

> The over-saving which is the economic root of imperialism is found
> by analysis to consist of rents, monopoly profits, and other unearned
> or excessive elements of income [...] Thus we reach the conclusion
> that Imperialism is the endeavour of the great controllers of industry
> to broaden their channel for the flow of their surplus wealth by seek-
> ing foreign markets and foreign investments to take off the goods
> and capital they cannot sell or use at home.
>
> (ibid.: 85)

(e) *The emergence of the parasitical rentier as a consequence of the crisis.*
Hobson's analysis represents a breach with Say's Law and creates the
preconditions for the emergence of the *rentier*, that is to say the person
who converts his savings into financial assets. The latter are loans that
can be channelled *either* towards the domestic money market where
they 'stagnate', generating financial instability, *or* towards the 'international' money markets of the less developed countries (usually in the
guise of state loans). This is the origin of the idea we encounter in the
later works of Bukharin and Lenin whereby the developed states are
transformed into *rentier-states*, that is to say states that are enriched by
the debt of the underdeveloped countries (ibid.: 364–6).

We shall conclude this commentary on Hobson's intervention with
three observations.

Firstly, through his argumentation Hobson carries out a *twofold reduction*. On the one hand he reduces the phenomenon of imperialism
to capitalist crises. In exactly the same way as we see in later Marxist
analyses, the discussion on imperialism is essentially nothing more
than a sub-instance of the discussions on capitalist crises. We should
therefore not regard as exaggeration the following remark of Fieldhouse
(1961: 188–9) when he said that Hobson's conception of imperialism
'was primarily a vehicle for publicizing the theory of underconsumption'. Imperialism is defined as a *symptom* of the gradual trend towards
collapse that is inherent in capitalism: 'Imperialism is thus seen to be,
not a choice, but a necessity' (Hobson 1938: 73). On the other hand,
Hobson simultaneously reduces the political element (the state) of
a social totality to its economic element (the process of capital accumulation): the political behaviour of a state is completely dependent
on – *reflects* – the contradictions that permeate the economy. If the
survival of the advanced capitalist countries depends on the export of
capital, then, according to Hobson's argument, the state will support

this extension through imperialist policies which at their extreme can take the form of war. This is the origin of the basic idea in later Marxist theory that *competition between advanced capitals is interwoven with, and determines, geopolitical competition between states.*

Secondly, Hobson distinguished between (early) colonialism and 'imperialism' on the basis of an argument purely apologetic of colonial expansion. He claimed that pre-imperialist colonialism aimed at promoting civilisation and industry in the 'temperate zones':

> Thus this recent imperial expansion stands entirely distinct from the colonization of sparsely peopled lands in temperate zones, where white colonists carry with them the modes of government, the industrial and other arts of the civilisation of the mother country.
>
> (ibid.: 27)

Finally, one implicit precondition for Hobson's argument is not just that politics (the state) is subordinated to the economy, but also that imperialism is a *global structure*, a binding system that dictates the political and economic behaviour of individual states. Imperialism, in the form of political support for the export of surplus capital, is a global contest for hegemony presupposing one group of developed and another group of undeveloped-dependent states, common factors in an uninterrupted global continuum (core–periphery structure, the logic of dependency).

1.2 A general overview of classical Marxist approaches to imperialism: Elaboration of Hobson's thesis

Following Hobson, the Marxist theories of imperialism explicitly distinguished between *early colonialism* and the corresponding phenomena of the *'latest' phase of capitalism* to which, exclusively, they gave the name of 'imperialism'. In doing so they did not however follow Hobson's apologetic argument concerning the 'civilising effect' of early colonialism. Marxist writers claimed that the 'latest phase' of capitalism was the outcome of the 'domination of monopolies'.

Rudolf Hilferding (1877–1941), in his *Finance Capital*, was the writer who introduced into Marxist theory this idea of a 'latest phase' of capitalism, characterised by the following features (Milios 1999a, 2001): formation of monopolistic enterprises (which abolish capitalist competition), fusion of bank and industrial capital (leading to the formation of finance capital, which is seen as the ultimate form of capital), subordination of the state to monopolies and finance capital, and finally, emergence of an expansionist policy of colonial annexations and war (Hilferding 1981: 326).

The idea of a 'latest', monopolistic-imperialist stage of capitalism possessing the abovementioned features was adopted by Bukharin, Lenin, Kautsky and others (notwithstanding the disputes among them in relation to specific features of this approach or its political consequences), thus shaping what are called the Marxist theories of monopoly capitalism, which until recently dominated most Marxist streams of thought, and especially Soviet Marxism (see Abalkin et al. 1983, Brewer 1980, Milios 1988).

In her *Accumulation of Capital* (1913) Rosa Luxemburg conceived of imperialism primarily as a struggle among developed capitalist countries for the domination over still-unoccupied non-capitalist territories: 'Imperialism is the political expression of the accumulation of capital in its competitive struggle for what remains still open of the non-capitalist environment' (Luxemburg 1971: 446).

On the basis of her underconsumptionist approach, Luxemburg thought of non-capitalist territories as the major reservoir of 'third-party consumers', who alone could absorb that portion of surplus value that neither capitalists nor workers could (supposedly) realize (Milios 1994): 'realisation of surplus value requires "third persons", that is to say consumers other than the immediate agents of capitalist production[...]   there should be strata of buyers outside capitalist society [...] social organisations or strata whose own mode of production is not capitalistic' (Luxemburg 1971: 350–2). In short, 'that part of the surplus value [...] which is earmarked for capitalization, must be realised elsewhere' (ibid.: 366).

Both Luxemburg and Bukharin (in the latter's *Imperialism and World Economy*, 1915) conceived of capitalism as a *unified world structure*. In other words they claimed that in the era of imperialism, expanded reproduction of the capitalist mode of production (CMP) takes place on a world scale, not at the level of each capitalist social formation. Thus, as Bukharin put it:

> World economy is one of the species of social economy in general. [...] The whole process of world economic life [...] reduces itself to [...] an ever widening reproduction of the relations between two classes – the class of the world proletariat on the one hand and the world bourgeoisie on the other.
>
> (Bukharin 1972a: 27)

Bukharin also defined imperialism 'as a policy of finance capital', at the same time specifying that 'one may also speak of imperialism as an ideology' (ibid.: 110). The policy and ideology of imperialism are structural characteristics of modern capitalism: 'imperialism is not only a system most intimately connected with modern capitalism, it is also the most essential element of the latter' (ibid.: 139–40).

In *Imperialism: The Highest Stage of Capitalism* (1917) Lenin defined imperialism as:

> [C]apitalism in that stage of development in which the dominance of monopolies and finance capital has established itself; in which the export of capital has acquired pronounced importance; in which the division of the world among the international trusts has begun; in which the division of all territories of the globe among the biggest capitalist powers has been completed.
>
> (*CW*, vol. 22)

Lenin attributed the intensifying contradictions among imperialist powers to the uneven development of capitalism, which precluded the formation of a stable 'ultra-imperialist' alliance of capitalist powers. This in turn was giving rise to 'alternating forms of peaceful and non-peaceful struggle out of *one and the same* basis of imperialist connections and relations' (ibid. original emphasis).

In what follows we propose to embark upon a more thorough discussion of three of the main postulates introduced by theories of imperialism into Marxist theory: (1) The thesis of the global character of capitalism, (2) the idea that capitalism has been transformed into 'monopoly capitalism' and (3) the conception of capital exports as a by-product of the lack of domestic spheres of profitable investment.

1.3   Main arguments and controversies in classical Marxist theories of imperialism

1.3.1   Capitalism as a global structure

A. Luxemburg and Bukharin

As already argued, Luxemburg's and Bukharin's approach to the question of imperialism were upheld by, and introduced, a specific viewpoint on the *global character* of the capitalist mode of production. This viewpoint is precisely that the capitalist mode of production, and the fundamental structural relationships and class relations that characterize the capitalist system are reproduced in their most fully developed form only at the level of the global economy; that, accordingly, the laws and the causal relationships discovered and analysed by Marx pertain to the global economy, which is thus shaped as a single capitalist social structure.

In a manuscript published after her assassination under the title *What is Economics* (*Einführung in die Nationalökonomie*), Rosa Luxemburg puts forward the view that the national economy cannot be comprehended as a specific socio-economic structure but is simply a *section* of the *single* global economy:

> In the century and a half since the modern economy first made its appearance in England, the global economy has gone from strength to strength on the basis of the misery and ruin of the human race [...]. Nothing today plays a more important role in political and social life than the contradiction between the economic phenomena, which every day unite all the peoples into a great whole, and the structure of the states, which strive to introduce artificial divisions between people, marking out borders with posts, erecting customs barriers, inciting militarism.
>
> (Luxemburg 1925: 42–3, our translation)

This idea of the globally united capitalist structure was to be developed even further by Luxemburg in her *Accumulation of Capital*. There she was to attempt a thoroughgoing reformulation of the Marxist theory of reproduction of social capital at the global level. The extract below on the internal and external markets provides an excellent illustration of her thesis on 'global capitalism':

> At this point we should revise the conceptions of internal and external markets which were so important in the controversy about accumulation. [...] The internal market is the capitalist market, production itself buying its own products and supplying its own elements of production. The external market is the non-capitalist social environment which absorbs the products of capitalism and supplies producer goods and labour power for capitalist production. Thus, from the point of view of economics, Germany and England traffic in commodities chiefly on an internal, capitalist market, whilst the give and take between German industry and German peasants is transacted on an external market as far as German capital is concerned.
>
> (Luxemburg 1971: 288)

Bukharin put forward similar views a few years later, in 1915. He suggested that 'we may define world economy as *a system of production relations and, correspondingly, of exchange relations on a world scale*. [...] just as every individual enterprise is part of the national economy, so every one of these national economies is included in the system of world economy' (Bukharin 1972a: 27). From this point of departure Bukharin was to argue that the various national economies (which are polarized between developed industrial economies on the one hand and underdeveloped agricultural economies on the other) are *subsets* of the global economy, constituting a global capitalist division of labour, on the grounds of which the conflict between the global bourgeoisie and the global proletariat is played out:

> The cleavage between town and country, as well as the development of this cleavage, formerly confined to one country only, are now being reproduced on a tremendously enlarged basis. Viewed from this standpoint, entire countries appear today as towns, namely, the industrial countries, whereas entire agrarian territories appear to be country.
>
> (ibid.: 21)

National economies and national states were created, according to Bukharin, in a specific historical epoch, in which the level of capitalist development precluded the emergence of global economic structures. But the global capitalist economic structure is a phenomenon of the age of imperialism, so that there is now a capitalist mode of organization that 'tends to overstep the "national" boundaries' (ibid.: 74). It encounters significant obstacles, however. The development of capitalism is seen as being linked to the contradiction between the global development of productive forces on the one hand and the limitations of 'national' organization of production on the other:

> There is here a growing discord between the basis of social economy which has become world-wide and the peculiar class structure of society, a structure where the ruling class (the bourgeoisie) itself is split into 'national' groups with contradictory economic interests, groups which, being opposed to the world proletariat, are competing among themselves for the division of the surplus value created on a world scale. Production is of a social nature; [...] Acquisition, however, assumes the character of 'national' (state) acquisition [...] Under such conditions there inevitably arises a conflict, which, given

the existence of capitalism, is settled through extending the state frontiers in bloody struggles, a settlement which holds the prospect of new and more grandiose conflicts.

(ibid.: 106)

So as to be able to put forward an interpretation of the First World War, which had already broken out,[3] Bukharin evidently places greater weight than Luxemburg on the contradiction between 'global capitalism' and the 'national appropriation' of the surplus product.

B. Lenin's concept of the imperialist chain as a critique of 'global capitalism'

This is the time to mention Lenin's critique of the conclusions of the theory of 'global capitalism', which is to be found in his texts on the national question and the state. The critique that Lenin attempts to mount represents a *rupture* within the classical discourse on imperialism, leading us to crucial conclusions, which we shall further evaluate in the following chapters.

This view of capitalism as a unified global socio-economic structure predominates within the revolutionary Marxist current in the first half of the decade between 1910 and 1920. The view seems to have been adopted initially even by Lenin, as is clearly visible in the introduction he wrote for Bukharin's book on imperialism in December 1915 (*CW*, vol. 22).

During the period in question world-historical changes were taking place in Europe and in Russia. The First World War had broken out, bringing catalytic social upheavals that were tending to destabilize capitalist power in the warring countries. The popular masses were being radicalized with great dispatch: the question of social revolution was coming onto the agenda.

In the revolutionary wing of the social democracy two types of questions were being raised with the utmost urgency at that time. *First*, the question of revolutionary strategy, that is to say the question of the preconditions under which the working class might win power. *Second*, the question of political tactics, with the key problem here – apart from the stance on the war (which for the revolutionary current was not up for discussion) – being the stance of the Left towards the movements of national self-determination that were developing in various countries. On this question the viewpoints that predominated within the revolutionary wing of the social democracy all disputed in one way or another the right of nations to self-determination.[4]

These conceptions were a direct outcome of the theory of global capitalism and employed two types of arguments: firstly, that the self-determination of nations, the creation of new nation-states, had become impossible in the age of imperialism; and secondly, that the tendency of socialist revolution is necessarily towards establishing a global, or at any rate a multinational, socialist regime, a process incompatible with the demand for national self-determination. Among the theoreticians of imperialism, Luxemburg openly opposed political support for national self-determination (see Luxemburg 1961). And Bukharin too, even after the Russian Revolution, kept his distance from the demand for national self-determination.[5]

As is well known, Lenin came out against this strategy. His opposition to it led him finally to a break with the theory of 'global capitalism' and formulation of the conception of the *imperialist chain*. Lenin supported the demand for national self-determination, not from the viewpoint of nationalism but for exactly the opposite reasons, from the viewpoint of proletarian revolution.[6] As early as 1915 he was formulating the theory of social revolution as an overall outcome and distillation of social antagonisms and conflicts within a social formation, arguing that *the basic question of every revolution is that of state power* (April 1917, vol. 24). As is well known it was just a few months later, in August–September 1917, in *State and Revolution*, that he was to put forward the theory of the state as material condensation of the relationships of power and the resultant necessity for the working class *to smash and destroy the bourgeois state*.

On the basis, then, of the Marxist conception of the bourgeois state as the specific capitalist form of political organization of power, the social content of the nation becomes perceptible. *The state is a national state, the nation expresses the overall economic, social and cultural outcome of the specific (capitalist) social cohesion between the ruling and the ruled class of a social formation.* The composition of the state in the ideal case proceeds in step with the formation of the nation. As the state takes the form of the nation-state, so does the nation strive towards its political integration in an independent state. The existence, through a historical process, of other specific nationalities within a (multinational) state generally coincides with the presence of a dominant nationality (which will lend 'national coloration' to the specific state) and with the oppression by it of the other nationalities. This means that at the same time there is a tendency among the oppressed nations towards secession and the creation of separate nation-states.

Lenin's insistence on the Marxist theory of the state and of political power was to lead him to differentiate himself from the predominant conception of imperialism as a uniform global socio-economic struc-ture. He accordingly went on to formulate the *theory of the global imperi-alist chain*. The internationalization of capitalism through foreign trade and the creation of the international market, through capital exports, the creation of international trusts, etc., binds together the different capitalist social formations, creates multiform, but also unequal, con-nections between them, and in this way shapes a single global imperial-ist chain. *What this entails, however, is not a uniform global socioeconomic structure, but the meshing together at the international level of the different (nation-state) economic and social structures, each of which develops at a dif-ferent rate, largely because of the different class and political relationships of force that have crystallized within them.* This thesis has twofold theoretical consequences.

First, it leads to the formulation of the '*law of uneven development*' of each national link in the imperialist chain: 'the *even* development of dif-ferent undertakings, trusts, branches of industry, or countries is impos-sible under capitalism' (Lenin, *CW*, vol. 22). On the basis of this 'law' Lenin elaborates on an entirely new problematic: to the predominant viewpoint on the global capitalist economic structure he counterposes the imperialist chain, the links of which are not national economies (Bukharin, see above) but states. Thus what counts is not simply 'eco-nomic development' but the overall (economic, political, military) power of each state that is a link in the chain.

The *second* theoretical consequence of Lenin's thesis of the global imperialist chain involves the material (domestic and international) preconditions for proletarian revolution. This is the *theory of the weak link*. Effecting a breach with the 'imperialist economism'[7] that prevailed, in one way or another, within the international social democracy, Lenin maintained that the overthrow of capitalism would not emerge either out of the inability of the global system to reproduce itself worldwide, or out of the contradictions that are assumed to be entailed by capital-ism's excessive 'ripeness'. Socialist revolution does not take place in the most developed capitalist country but in the country that is the *weak link* in the imperialist chain: in the country where the domestic and international contradictions merge and are intensified to such a degree, at every level, as to make objectively unavoidable the clash between capital and labour and the revolutionary crisis. Lenin was to note in his 'Letters from Afar':

That the revolution succeeded so quickly and – seemingly, at the first superficial glance – so radically, is only due to the fact that, as a result of an extremely unique historical situation, *absolutely dissimilar currents, absolutely heterogeneous* class interests, *absolutely contrary* political and social strivings have *merged*, and in a strikingly 'harmonious' manner.

(Lenin, CW, vol. 24)

Lenin's theoretical intervention on the national question and the prerequisites for the socialist revolution illustrate the necessity of taking the state seriously. A theory of the state is indispensable not only for comprehending capitalist expansionism, imperialism and colonization, but also *decolonization*, through the formation of new independent capitalist states out of multinational empires or in former colonies (see Part II). Lenin's pamphlet on imperialism alone is not an adequate basis for comprehension of the range of his analysis as regards the notion and the structural characteristics of the imperialist chain (at the time of the First World War). It did not aim so much at being a theoretical intervention (this is indeed implicit in its subtitle: 'a popular outline') but an intervention primarily political in its objectives.

1.3.2   Monopoly and the decay of capitalism

Marxist theories of imperialism are by definition theories of rule by monopolies. This is perhaps the most significant thesis introduced into the Marxist problematic by Rudolf Hilferding through his book *Finance Capital*.

The basic views for which Hilferding endeavoured to provide the grounding were subsequently adopted by all the classical theories of imperialism and may be summarized as follows. The predominance of monopolies not only within the bourgeois class but also over society as a whole is the specific characteristic, indeed the distinguishing feature, of contemporary capitalism. This predominance is based on the merging of banking capital with industrial capital, under the direction of the former, and the formation in this way of a new dominant fraction of capital: finance capital. Imperialism and colonialism thus emerge as the expression and the result of competition at the international level between the dominant monopoly groups of the different countries.

According to the argumentation of Hilferding, the rule of monopolies inevitably transforms the capitalist state into a lever for the promotion of imperialist interests, the predominant interests in every developed capitalist country of the imperialist oligarchy. The result is thus the strengthening of the repressive power of the bourgeois state, policies of colonialism, exploitation by the imperialist forces of the smaller nominally independent states utilizing not only every conceivable economic means (e.g. exports of capital) but also every political means, interimperialist rivalries which can lead even to war, etc. The basis of this analysis is the hypothesis that in parallel with the predominance of monopolies goes suppression of free competition, making possible the subordination of the state to the interests of the monopolistic oligarchy. And Hilferding's problematic in relation to the state is summed up as follows:

> Finance capital does not want freedom, but domination [...] But in order to achieve these ends, and to maintain and enhance its predominant position, it needs the state [...] It needs a politically powerful state [...] which can intervene in every corner of the globe and transform the whole world into a sphere of investment of its own financial capital. Finally, finance capital needs a state which is strong enough to pursue expansionist policy and the annexation of new colonies. [...] Capital becomes the conqueror of the world, and with every new country that it conquers there are new frontiers to be crossed.
>
> (Hilferding 1981: 334–5)

These views were adopted both by Bukharin and by Lenin, in the latter case in a particularly contradictory way. Bukharin (1915) incorporated Hilferding's theses on the predominance of monopolies into his conceptions of the global capitalist economy and in this way arrived at the position on the merging of monopoly capital and the state. This merger, according to Bukharin, takes the form of a 'state monopoly trust':

> The world system of production assumes in our times the following aspect: a few consolidated, organised economic bodies ('the great civilised powers') on the one hand, and a periphery of undeveloped countries with a semi-agrarian or agrarian system on the other. [...] The economically developed states have already advanced far towards a situation where they can be looked upon as big trust-like organisations or, as we have termed them, state capitalist trusts. We may, therefore, speak at present about the concentration of capital in state capitalist trusts as component parts of a much larger socio-economic entity, world economy.
>
> (Bukharin 1972a: 73–4, 118)

Lenin similarly reiterates Hilferding's argumentation on the abolition of free competition (e.g. in the first chapter of *Imperialism*). But in addition to this, influenced by Hobson, he regards Hilferding's analysis of the *decline of capitalism* in the era of imperialism as inadequate. Thus in his notes, later published in vol. 39 of his *Collected Works* as *Notebooks on Imperialism*, he admonishes Hilferding for ignoring 'such important features of imperialism as the division of the world and the struggle for its re-division, and the parasitism and decay of capitalism' (*CW*, vol. 39), reasserting in *Imperialism* that Hilferding is 'taking a step backward compared with the *frankly* pacifist and reformist Englishman, Hobson' (*CW*, vol. 22).

In accordance with Hobson's argumentation, at this point embraced by Lenin also, capital exports and exploitation of the colonies lead to a slowing down of development of the imperialist countries. Capitalist production becomes less and less necessary for these countries, because they now feed on the exploitation of the colonies. They plunder the whole world, 'cutting coupons'. In the stage of monopoly capitalism, developed capitalism is transformed into a capitalism that is in decay. Moreover, always according to this view, the dominant classes of the imperialist countries use their colonial extra profits to buy off the upper layers of the proletariat, the workers' aristocracy. As a result, these layers become politically oriented towards opportunism, that is to say they become vehicles for a bourgeois line inside the workers' movement. Thus Hobson wrote (to quote him first and then append Lenin's detailed analysis):

> There is first the habit of economic parasitism, by which the ruling state has used its provinces, colonies, and dependencies in order to enrich its ruling class and to bribe its lower classes into acquiescence.
>
> (quotation from Hobson's book
> *Imperialism* cited by Lenin, *CW*, vol. 22)

But the argumentation adopted by Lenin was subsequently to be refuted, by himself, and indeed within the same pamphlet on *Imperialism*: 'It would be a mistake to believe that this tendency to decay precludes the rapid growth of capitalism. It does not. (...) On the whole, capitalism is growing far more rapidly than before' (ibid.).

His thesis on the continuation of technical progress will enable Lenin to relativize even the views of Hilferding on the abolition of free competition, views which Lenin himself initially incorporated into his analysis:

> Free competition is the basic feature of capitalism, and of commodity production generally; monopoly is the exact opposite of free

competition [...] At the same time the monopolies, which have grown out of free competition, do not eliminate the latter, but exist above it and alongside it, and thereby give rise to a number of very acute, intense antagonisms, frictions and conflicts.

(ibid.)

Lenin's pamphlet on imperialism unquestionably resorts to contradictory argumentation. On the one hand, imperialism is presented as decaying capitalism, a position henceforth to be a permanent motif of Soviet Marxism. On the other, it is asserted that in the era of imperialism capitalism 'is growing far more rapidly than before'. The fact that the latter thesis comprises the stronger pole of Lenin's argument does not follow only from the fact that it is put forward in his pamphlet in the form of a general conclusion. It emerges much more from the fact that in his later texts Lenin many times had the opportunity to revise the dogmatic adherence of other cadres, in the Bolshevik party, to Hobsonian positions on the parasitism and decay of capitalism. At the 8th Conference of the Russian Communist Party (Bolsheviks) Lenin said, in criticism of Bukharin:

> Pure imperialism, without the fundamental basis of capitalism, has never existed, does not exist anywhere, and never will exist. This is an incorrect generalisation of everything that was said of the syndicates, cartels, trusts and finance capitalism [...] When Comrade Bukharin stated that an attempt might be made to present an integral picture of the collapse of capitalism and imperialism, we objected to it in the commission, and I must object to it here. [...] Nowhere in the world has monopoly capitalism existed in a whole series of branches without free competition, nor will it exist. To write of such a system is to write of a system which is false and removed from reality.
>
> (CW, vol. 29)

The views on decaying capitalism have little in common with the Marxist concepts of the Critique of Political Economy. According to Marxist theory, capital is the predominant relationship, the predominant mode of organization of a bourgeois society. It is not either an object (a 'thing'), or wealth in general, which a society could indeed acquire from abroad, in this way abandoning its own 'production of wealth'. Capital is a self-valorizing value (see Milios et al. 2002: 43). It is by definition production for production's sake, accumulation on a continually widening basis.

The long-term social effect of capitalist relations is the trend towards growth in production and the productivity of labour, a tendency which is only temporarily inhibited by capitalism's cyclical crises, which function on each occasion as points of departure for a new period of capitalist accumulation:

> Productivity of labour in general = the maximum of product with minimum of work, hence, to cheapen commodities as much as possible. In the capitalist mode of production this becomes a law independent from the will of each separate capitalist [...] However, this immanent tendency of the capital relation will be only realised in its adequate form – and will become a necessary condition, also technologically – as soon as the specifically capitalist mode of production will be developed, and with it the real subsumption of labour under capital.
>
> (Marx 1969: 63, poorly translated in Marx 1990: 1037–8)

Historical evolution (that is to say the development of capitalist production in the twentieth century in the classic location for the capitalist mode of production, the capitalist industrial countries) confirms the theses of Marxist theory. In the following chapters we will have the opportunity to investigate further the question of capitalist development and growth.

1.3.3   Capital exports and the theory of underconsumption

Marxist theories of imperialism are at the same time theories of capital export. There are two predominant interpretative schemata seeking to link capital export to the formation of, and domination by, monopolies.

(a)   The *colonial extra profits* approach, which claims that colonial or low developed, low wage countries are characterized by higher rates of profit, thus attracting capital from developed countries that seek to maximize it profits:

> The precondition for the export of capital is the variation in rates of profit, and the export of capital is the means of equalizing national rates of profit. The level of profit depends upon the organic composition of capital, that is to say, upon the degree of capitalist development. The more advanced it is the lower will be the average rate of profit [...]. The state ensures that human labour in the colonies is available on terms which

make possible extra profits [...] The natural wealth of the colonies likewise becomes a source of extra profits by lowering the price of raw materials and reducing the cost price of industrial products.

(Hilferding 1981: 315, 328)

(b) The *surplus of capital* approach, the view inherited from Hobson, according to which capital exports are the outcome of restriction, in consequence of the domination by monopolies, of the sphere of capital investment in the overdeveloped capitalist countries. This is the predominant schema on the basis of which capital exports are interpreted in all the classical theories of imperialism, up to and including Bukharin's 1925 polemic against the theses of Luxemburg (*Imperialism and the Accumulation of Capital*). Hilferding was henceforth to formulate as follows the position that would deduce capital export from restrictions of the spheres of capital investment: 'Consequently, while the volume of capital intended for accumulation increases rapidly, investment opportunities contract. This contradiction demands a solution, which it finds in the export of capital' (Hilferding 1981: 234).

Both Bukharin in his *Imperialism and Global Economy* and Lenin in *Imperialism* restate Hilferding's (and Hobson's) argumentation on capital export due to an excess of capital in developed countries:

Capital export [...] does not represent an isolated phenomenon [...] is due to a certain overproduction of capital (Bukharin 1972-a: 105). An enormous 'surplus of capital' has arisen in the advanced countries [...]. The need to export capital arises from the fact that in a few countries capitalism has become 'overripe' and (owing to the backward state of agriculture and the poverty of the masses) capital cannot find a field for 'profitable' investment.

(Lenin, *CW*, vol. 22)

Luxemburg also believed that the expansion of capitalism to noncapitalist territories and social 'remnants' constituted the decisive factor which made possible the expanded reproduction of capital (which was otherwise doomed to collapse, due to the lag in society's purchasing power, compared with the supply of capitalistically produced commodities).

It is clear that classical Marxist theories of imperialism approach Hobson's argumentation, which belongs entirely in the realm of the underconsumptionist theory. In fact, the view that in certain countries there is a permanent restriction of the potential for capital investment, *permanent* meaning irrespective of the conjunctures of overaccumulation crises, and that in this way a permanent surplus of capital is created, can be justified only in terms of the underconsumptionist theory. In other words a lack of correspondence between consumption and production is created precisely because the consumption is from an economic viewpoint not in a position to absorb the continually expanding production.

However, as already pointed out (see in this chapter, note 2), this underconsumptionist approach had been refuted in mainstream Marxism following Tugan-Baranowsky's theoretical analysis at the turn of the nineteenth to the twentieth century. Here it is worth recalling that Lenin himself had the opportunity to disaffirm the basic findings of the underconsumptionist theory in the context of his polemic against the *Narodniks*, the main stream of the Russian left at the time (Milios 1999). Taking as their point of departure the small size of the home market in such a poor country as Russia, the Narodniks considered capitalist development in Russia to be an impossibility. Lenin argues that in reality (if one does not take into consideration the conjunctures of cyclical crises) there can be no 'home market question', since the concrete size of the market in a particular country is a consequence (and a form of appearance) of the level of capitalist development in the country and not a prerequisite for such development. His argument follows two lines of reasoning.

On the one hand, the appearance and expanded reproduction of the capitalist mode of production in a particular country brings into existence, and then broadens, the domestic market (in contrast to what is claimed by the Narodniks). This development coincides with the following processes: (a) creation of demand for capital goods (means of production) on the part of capital and (b) replacement of the self-sustaining precapitalist economy with the commodity economy, that is conversion of the means of subsistence of the popular masses into commodities.

On the other hand, Lenin argues that although in capitalist development both the productivity of labour and the volume of capitalistically produced commodities tend to increase at a faster rate than that of the growth in popular incomes, this does not lead to a *permanent* inability to dispose of or realize those capitalistically produced commodities, that is to say it does not inevitably lead to a permanent 'problem of markets'. Even in the absence of external markets or of 'third parties' besides capitalists and workers, the realization problem may be solved by the more rapid increase in productive consumption by capitalists (demand for means of production) than in individual consumption (Lenin, *CW*, vol. 1: 67–119; vol. 2: 117–257; vol. 3: 42 ff., 312 ff.). The whole dispute is closely related to the Marxist controversy over economic crises. Lenin unequivocally opposes all underconsumptionist approaches (Milios 1994), summarising as follows his arguments on the home market question:

> From what has been said, it follows automatically that the problem of the home market as *a separate, self-sufficient problem* not depending on that of the degree of capitalist development does not exist at all.
> (Lenin, *CW*, vol. 3: 69, emphasis added).

In contrast to these positions, the Lenin of the period of '*Imperialism*' seems to have believed that the (limited) consumption of the masses determines the course of capitalist development. What is involved here is a real turnaround in his opinions and his theoretical stance, as Brewer (1980) also correctly points out (for the same conclusion see Howard and King 1989).

But it is not only in the works of Lenin that one can find a contradictory stance towards the theory of underconsumption. In 1925, Bukharin's *Imperialism and the Accumulation of Capital* was published in Germany. This work, which is primarily a rejoinder to Luxemburg's *Accumulation of Capital*, includes one of the most profound Marxist critiques of the theory of underconsumption and so of some of the main theses that, following Hobson's original ideas, had been adopted by Marxist theories of imperialism.

Bukharin took his stand on three propositions. *First*, that the world economy cannot be comprehended as an undifferentiated whole. *Second*, that capital internationalization does not emerge from a supposed 'excess of capital' or a 'lack of investment opportunities' in capital-exporting countries, but from competition between individual capitals, in their search for extra profits on the world market. *Third*, that there is no inherent and permanently active cause of capitalist crises that could lead to the collapse of capitalism; instead, 'a unity of contradictions' exists, which may (depending on the tension of these contradictions) set a limit to the process of capitalist-expanded reproduction (which is nothing other than the 'expanded reproduction' of capitalist contradictions).[8]

Bukharin defies a taboo position of the socialist movement of that period, namely the notion that real wages cannot rise above a minimum required for the physical subsistence of the working classes.

He recognizes that aggregate real wages can increase under capitalism, to whatever level is required for the uninterrupted reproduction of socioeconomic power relations. In his words, the '"limits of consumption" are expanded by production itself, which increases (1) the income of the capitalists, (2) the income of the working class (additional workers) and (3) the constant capital of society (means of production functioning as capital).' And he continues: '(1) the increase in means of production calls forth a growth in the amount of means of consumption; (2) simultaneously, this increase creates a new demand for these means of consumption and as a result (3) a specific level of the production of means of production corresponds to a quite specific level of the production of means of consumption; in other words, the market of means of production is connected with the market of means of consumption' (Bukharin 1972b: 204, 210).

The key aim of Bukharin's criticism of Luxemburg (like Lenin's criticism of the Narodniks) was to demonstrate the necessity for abandonment of the underconsumptionist postulate of a serious immanent lag of wages behind capital accumulation; indeed, it is such a serious lag that 'it is not possible to compensate for declining personal consumption through increasing reproductive consumption' (Moszkowska 1935: 15). On the basis of this problematic Bukharin in 1925 formulated a different interpretation of capital export. He wrote:

> The expansion of capital is conditioned by the movement of profit, its amount and rate, on which the amount depends [...]. If cheaper means of production and cheaper labour are available, the rate of profit climbs accordingly, and capital tries to exploit this situation. If there are other conditions connected with the position of industry, i.e. the geographical situation, conditions which increase the rate of profit, then capital moves in that direction. Finally, if we have more advantageous conditions to realize the amount of commodities, then again the profit rate climbs, while capital increasingly orientates itself in that direction. As a result of that, the roots of capitalist expansion lie in the conditions of buying as well as in the process of production itself, and finally in the conditions of selling. [...] The gaining of a colonial 'surplus profit' explains the direction of capitalist expansion. That does not mean that the struggle only goes or only can go in that direction. On the contrary, the further it develops [...] the more it will become a struggle for the capitalist centres as well. In this case, too, the movement of profit is the main reason.
>
> (Bukharin 1972b: 256–7)

Bukharin replaces the argument about a supposed 'colonial extra profit' with the criterion of the general level of the profit rate. As noted by Busch (1974: 258–9), even if there could be surplus capital, the result would not necessarily be capital exports. This 'surplus capital' could equally well be invested in the internal market and be realized in the international market (export of domestically produced commodities). It is thus not absolutely necessary for it to be exported in the form of (money) capital.

Bukharin seems to perceive this, as he regards capital exports as one component in a broader process of 'capitalist expansion' in search of a higher profit rate. In the context of this conception, Bukharin links commodity exports to capital exports and attempts to identify the shared basis of the two processes. His analysis borrows from remarks by Marx in *Capital* according to which external trade between two countries, each with a different average productivity of labour, enables the more advanced country to derive extra profit. The extra profit is made possible by the commodity in question being produced in a country with a higher productivity of labour than the corresponding international average. Expressed differently, the commodity is sold at a higher international price than its national price.[9] So the development of foreign trade, in Marx's analysis, enables more developed states to reap additional profits and in this way raise the general rate of profit. Bukharin accordingly sees the quest for extra profits as a factor encouraging both the development of international trade and capital exports:

> Consequently: (1) if it is an occasional exchange, trade capital gains a *surplus* profit, using all means, including deceit, violence and robbery; (2) If foreign exchange becomes a regular occurrence, the country with a *higher* structure inevitably gains a *surplus profit*; (3) if capital is exported, that too happens in order to *gain additional* profit.
>
> (Bukharin 1972b: 245).

This formulation of Bukharin establishes the theoretical context for further analysis of the processes of internationalization of capital. The rate of profit and the movement of profit are the decisive 'social index' enabling analysis of the specific forms of movement of capital and of its internationalization.

Nevertheless there is a significant absence in Bukharin's argumentation: what is the real relationship between the process of appropriating extra profits through foreign trade (at the expense of a country with a lower labour productivity) and capital exports (towards that less developed country)? Or, to put it another way: Why does the capital of a more developed national economy not annihilate on the global market the capitals of less developed countries, as occurs in the domestic market, where the less developed capitals of a specific sector of the economy either modernize or are effaced? Why is it not enough for the most advanced capitals of the global market that they occupy the dominant position in international trade and resort to the practice of exporting capital? Bukharin does not pose these questions. Nevertheless, as we shall see in Chapter 8 (especially Section 8.2.2), the possibility of understanding the structural characteristics of present-day forms of internationalization of capital depends on the answer to precisely these questions.

1.4   Codification of the theoretical problematic of the classical theories of imperialism

Classical theories of imperialism do not merely introduce a new object for theoretical analysis; they also inaugurate a new problematic (constituting a new 'theoretical paradigm') within Marxist theory. At the same time, as we shall see in detail in the following chapters of Part I, they represent what is to this day the basic programmatic framework for positions related to the question. In the contemporary bibliography and discussion on imperialism, one will have difficulty finding theoretical propositions that do not have their roots in classical theories. It is here, precisely, that the great theoretical importance of these theories to contemporary Marxist thought is to be situated.

Nevertheless, these theories are not altogether unproblematic. They include more than a few contradictions or uncompleted (and undocumented) theoretical formulations, and they even to some extent flirt with bourgeois ideology, that is to say they sometimes abandon the theoretical terrain of the Critique of Political Economy. The contemporary relevance of the classical theories is thus obvious when they are considered in the light of present-day controversies over imperialism and 'globalization'.

Before proceeding with an analysis of the post-war and contemporary views of imperialism it will be necessary to summarize the basic problematic of the classical theories.

For all the classical Marxist theories there is a causal relationship between the structural characteristics of contemporary ('monopoly') capitalism and the imperialist expansion of capital. The classical theories of imperialism maintain that the specific forms assumed by the internationalization of capital and imperialist policies were in their day a necessary expression and outcome of the structural characteristics of monopoly capitalism.

The colonialism and protectionism which, as we now know, were merely historic forms of imperialist policies, forms that predominated only until World War II, were perceived by the classical theories as structural features of the 'latest phase' of capitalism, as a necessary outcome of transformation of 'old capitalism' into 'monopoly capitalism'. Lenin, for example, repeatedly asserted that liberalization of international trade was inconceivable, a 'utopia'. The thesis that 'Capitalism is growing with the greatest rapidity in the colonies and in overseas countries' (Lenin, *CW*, vol. 22) is a similar arbitrary theorization of historic epiphenomena. Of course, this thesis is confirmed by some former colonies, for example, Canada or Australia, but it proves mistaken for others such as, for example, India, or the countries of Africa.

Both political and theoretical factors, in our opinion, lie behind this arbitrary empiricist theorization of historical forms of appearance of capitalist domination.

The political factors have to do with the goals of the classical theories of imperialism: present-day capitalism had to be presented as a social system that cannot be 'improved' or reformed.

But it is the theoretical factors that are more decisive. Here what is involved is in the first instance confusion between two theoretical objects: contemporary capitalism and expansion of capital. *This confusion–conflation is a common element in all classical theories of imperialism*. Thus expansion of capitalism (imperialism in the narrow sense) is regarded not merely as an immediate and necessary result of domination by monopolies, but is often equated with the rule of monopolies itself.

Further, this *reduction of imperialism to 'rule of monopolies' downgrades (imperialist) policy to a simple reflection of the economic base*. What this does not take into account is the *relative autonomy* of the political, as for example, expressed in the historically conditioned antagonism between certain bourgeois states, and in the innate tendency towards expansion of the boundaries of sovereignty of the bourgeois state, particularly when the 'national questions', etc. remain open. National antagonisms are indeed typically the factor that *overdetermines* the developmental tendencies at the economic level leading, sometimes, to imperialist wars.

When the role of politics is not given its due weight, the theoretical analysis veers off into *economic reductionism*, making it impossible for there to be a reliable approach to the characteristics, the developmental tendencies and the contradictions of modern capitalism. Lenin, for instance, is right when he says that the basis for the division into spheres of domination and influence of the different imperialist countries can be nothing other than the overall power of each one of those countries. But this general formulation is insufficient in the absence of supplementation by concrete analysis of the international political conjuncture, so that the specific form of the interimperialist contradictions, which are different in each case, can be identified.

After the First World War, to give an example, the United States had already emerged as the most powerful imperialist country, both economically and militarily. This shift in the international balance of forces to the advantage of the United States did not lead to this country challenging British global imperialist hegemony in a politico-military manner. The United States did emerge finally as the hegemonic imperialist power, displacing Britain, but after an imperialist war in which the US not only did not take the initiative but on the contrary allied with Britain against the German–Italian endeavour to establish a "new order" in Europe. It is therefore necessary at all times to avoid the economic schematization entailed by a mechanistic equation of the process of internationalization and international expansion of capitalistic dominance with the developmental process of the forms of capitalist domination itself.

Our discussion of classical Marxist theories of imperialism opened up some important theoretical issues that can be summarized as follows:

(1) Imperialist internationalization of capitalism is to be approached not as a 'global capitalist structure' but rather from the starting point of Lenin's notion of the imperialist chain.
(2) The view of imperialism as 'decaying capitalism' or capitalism 'in its death agony' has very little connection either with Marxist theory or with empirical reality.
(3) The notions of domination by monopolies introduced by the classical theories of imperialism must be subjected to more rigorous analysis.
(4) Finally, capital exports and the resulting internationalization of capital are not explicable by the existence of surplus capital in developed capitalist countries. They are linked to international differentiations in the rate of profit and commercial capitalist competition on the international market.

We propose in the following chapters to include questions such as these in our investigation.

2
Post-World War II 'Metropolis-Periphery' Theories of Imperialism

2.1 Introductory comments: The issue of dependency

After World War II and the national liberation movements which followed, most former colonies won their national independence, leading to the dissolution of empires and the end of colonialism. Most post-war Marxist approaches to imperialism take it for granted, however, that *ex-colonies and developing countries are still subordinated to imperialist countries through relations of dependency*. For instance, as Popov stated: 'a special type of development of the countries dependent on imperialism is characteristic of the international capitalist division of labour within the framework of the world capitalist system. The dependence created by colonialism is still manifested in all the key spheres of the developing countries' economic life' (Popov 1984: 119).[1]

The notion of *dependency* played a key role in most post-World War II approaches to capitalism, imperialism and the state. Together with the related concept of world capitalism, it is to be found not only in the centre–periphery theories but also in the most heterodox versions of the political economy of development. The dependency theory assumes that despite the fall of colonialism after World War II and the creation of dozens of new states in former colonies, the periodization of capitalism, as proposed by classic theories of imperialism, is still an intellectually valid hypothesis.

Shaped in the context of classical theories of imperialism, the concept of 'global capitalism' underlay, after the Second World War, all theoretical approaches that perceive international economic relationships as relationships of exploitation and polarization between a developed imperialist centre and a dependent periphery. Because of their shared theoretical conclusions, to which we have just referred, these approaches are called *'metropolis-periphery' theories*.

We propose in this chapter to give a presentation of these metropolis–periphery theories, placing primary emphasis on those that have tended to predominate in this international current. We will accordingly be paying particular attention to the Latin-American approaches to dependency, the theory of unequal exchange, the theory of global accumulation, the views of the '*Monthly Review School*', and the theory of the new international division of labour. Finally, we will be presenting the views of two Latin-American theoreticians of the metropolis–periphery current, Córdova and Cardóso, who attempted to refute some of the basic theses of the '*Monthly Review School*'. Our aim is to advance our critique by presenting the key points of the theories under investigation in such a way as to highlight their internal contradictions.

2.2   The traditional approach

Within the framework of the dependency and centre–periphery approach two complementary orientations have developed. The key focus of the *first* is on the study of the global economy, highlighting the imbalance in global production and international trade, international capital movements, etc. It thus identifies and describes a continuing transfer of resources from the Third World to the metropolis, a draining of raw materials from the periphery – in short, the 'exploitation of the periphery' by imperialist capital. This 'plunder' of the countries of the periphery by imperialism, a by-product of their dependence, is considered to be the cause of their underdevelopment. *Dependence is thus, according to all the theories we examine here, the key term for interpreting the development and the character of the periphery.*[2]

The second orientation within the framework of traditional analysis, and also the most prevalent, focuses above all on the effects of dependence on internal structures at the periphery (predominance of foreign capital, economic, political, technological, cultural dependence, etc.). Dependence, it is asserted, creates the underdevelopment. Underdevelopment is closely linked to social inequality, unemployment, marginalization and the impoverishment of a great part of the population. Social marginalization and poverty keep the consumer potential of the population at a low level, placing parallel constraints and limitations on economic development. Imperialist dependence at the same time distorts the peripheral economy, imposing on it the requirement to specialize in a limited number of low-technology products, which are manufactured at a relatively low cost on account of the low wages, and are exported to the metropolis. The peripheral economy is thus characterized by distortion and introversion. The industrial development that has been observed in recent years in certain Third World countries is in no way incompatible with the basic characteristics of dependent and marginalized development.[3]

All these features of the periphery are regarded, as we have said, as the result, first and foremost, of imperialist dependence and exploitation. They are, that is to say, a by-product of the global capitalist division of labour, of 'global capitalism', one of whose aspects is development and the other underdevelopment. *Underdevelopment is thus not an early stage in development. It is, in the context of the global capitalist system, the necessary and permanent consequence of the predominance of metropolitan capitalism.* Underdevelopment results from 'innumerable exogenous factors, which are nevertheless to be considered to be endogenous in the context of the international capitalist system, of which our communities comprise only a part' (Córdova 1973: 13). Samir Amin summarizes the theses of the traditional approach as follows:

> Despite their different origins, the peripheral formations tend to converge towards a pattern that is essentially the same. This phenomenon reflects, on the global scale, the increasing power of capitalism to unify. All peripheral formations have four main characteristics in common: (1) the predominance of agrarian capitalism in the national sector; (2) the creation of a local, mainly merchant, bourgeoisie in the wake of dominant foreign capital; (3) a tendency towards a peculiar bureaucratic development, specific to the contemporary periphery; and (4) the incomplete, specific character of the phenomena of proletarianization.
>
> (Amin 1976: 333)

The traditional approach is the basic matrix out of which most analyses of peripheral capitalism will emerge.

2.3   Deformation of the socio-economic structure: Dualism, disarticulation, structural heterogeneity

The *theory of dualism* is the oldest and has been comprehensively elaborated by the Hungarian economist Tamas Szentes (1974, 2003). Szentes maintains that as a result of dependence, the underdeveloped countries are composed of two self-contained sectors: a 'modern', that is to say capitalist and relatively developed sector of the economy, and a 'traditional' sector with exceptionally low productivity, based on precapitalist modes of production and exploitation. These two sectors remain, according to this theory, separate. Dualism thus also implies inner disarticulation in under-developed countries, which essentially comprise 'two communities'. One consequence of their disarticulation is that the effects of any development in the modern sector are not passed on to the rest of the community. On the contrary, this sector retains its basic links only with the foreign factor, the global economy. It has been created as a result of dependence and it perpetuates that dependence. It serves the needs of the global market, not the internal-national market, which remains narrow and without dyna-mism. The modern capitalist sector is in no way incompatible with under-development. It simply assumes the character of an enclave within the peripheral communities. Dualism therefore implies inner disarticulation. This disarticulation is in turn directly linked to outer-directedness.

Theorists of peripheral capitalism modify to a greater or lesser extent the theory of dualism, selecting certain elements and rejecting others.[4]

Theorists of one tendency in Latin America would maintain that the predominant element is inner disarticulation of the peripheral economy in consequence of the developed sector's being oriented chiefly towards the global market. This disarticulation however, they continue, does not create 'two communities', as is maintained by the theory of dual-ism. It simply weakens the internal cohesion of the single peripheral community (Cardóso 1973, 1974).

But the theory of dualism is subject to criticism from another view-point also, which maintains that inner disarticulation of the peripheral economy is so pronounced that

> [O]ne ought not to speak of underdeveloped *national* economies, but to reserve the adjective 'national' to the autocentric advanced economies [...]. The underdeveloped economy is made up of sectors, of firms that are juxtaposed and not highly integrated among them-selves, but are each of them strongly integrated into entities the cent-ers of gravity of which lie in the centres of the capitalist world. What we have here is not a nation in the economic sense of the word, with an integrated internal market.
>
> (Amin 1976: 238)

This approach rejects the theory of dualism for another reason as well. It maintains that in the periphery there are no non-capitalist modes of production (a hypothesis in which the theory of dualism is grounded), in that all 'sectors' of the periphery are considered capitalist once they begin to produce for the market. The question of pre-capitalist modes of production and their expanded reproduction owing to dependence recalls the theory of 'structural heterogeneity' propounded by Córdova:

> The term 'structural heterogeneity' should not be confused with the familiar thesis on economic and social dualism. In Latin-American countries there are not two communities one next to the other as maintained by this thesis. By the term heterogeneity of the socio-economic structures of an entity we understand the existence of economic sectors in which relations of production are predominant that are based on different property relationships among the agents of production. A heterogeneous socio-economic structure entails a heterogeneous class system. Heterogeneity in the socio-economic and class structure produces a corresponding heterogeneity at the different levels of the superstructure.
>
> (Córdova 1973: 26–7 and 64)

At the same time, it is asserted that the 'structural heterogeneity' causes a 'structural deformation', that is to say, capitalist development acquires an unbalanced and deformed character. Structural deformation is not however regarded as the result of a disarticulation of the capitalist sector under the influence of non-capitalist sectors of the economy but as an outcome that emerges from the specific mode of articulation of these sectors between themselves. Naturally for Córdova too, structural heterogeneity is no more than the necessary result of the predominance of metropolitan capitalism over peripheral social formations on account of the splitting of 'global capitalism' into an imperialist metropolis and a dependent (and heterogeneous) periphery.

2.4   The theory of unequal exchange

The theory of unequal exchange was developed in France by Arghiri Emmanuel (1972). Emmanuel maintains that in the context of the global market, developed and underdeveloped countries become differentiated from each other, forming two entirely separate groups, which are basically non-antagonistic towards each other because they are specialized in the manufacture of different products. Exchanges between these two groups of countries are *unequal*, that is to say, they involve a continuous transfer of resources from the underdeveloped countries to the group of developed countries. It is this inherently unequal exchange that sustains and reproduces the polarization between development and underdevelopment. Unequal exchanges, it is asserted, are attributable to a radically unequal level of wages as between the two groups of countries.

Emannuel starts from three basic hypotheses. *Firstly*, in consequence of the international mobility of capital, an international average rate of profit is generated. At the same time international production prices are established on the global market. *Secondly*, wages at the national level, though different from country to country, have the tendency to polarize finally at two global levels: high wages in the countries of the centre and much lower wages at the periphery. This polarization stems from the 'immobility of the labour factor' on the global market (Emmanuel 1972: xxxv). *Thirdly*, in the system of international exchanges, the independent variable is wages, which are set not on the basis of some 'economic laws' but by historical and social factors (Emmanuel 1972: 64 ff.).

The fact, then, that on the global market a single rate of profit is established, while polarization is perpetuated at the level of wages (which is 'in the immediate sense, *ethical*', ibid.: 120), results in unequal exchange, in the sense of an exchange of unequal quantities of labour, expended in the production of internationally traded commodities. So 'wealth begets wealth' and 'poverty begets poverty' (ibid.: 214–15) in a system, however, where 'development is represented not as a cause but as a result of high wages' (ibid.: 254). Accordingly, 'if we suppose that for some reason, political, syndicalist or otherwise, wages in the Third World were suddenly made five or ten times higher and wages in the developed countries fell to the same level, the greater part of today's international division of labour would be bankrupted, although no objective factor of production would have changed' (ibid.: 131).

Commencing from the thesis that wage differentials in the global economy are huge, in contrast to rates of profit, which fluctuate around comparable levels, Emmanuel pursues his train of thought within the framework of the ('classical', see Milios et al. 2002: 13 ff.) labour theory of value, to come to the conclusion that the process of equalizing rates of profit on a global scale will transfer profit continually from low-wage countries to high-wage countries. The basic presupposition of such a notion is that all countries have access to the same technology. It is thus assumed that both the low-paid and the high-paid workers produce almost the same amount of value per hour, whereas prices in the low-wage countries are lower because of the lower production costs. 'Unequal exchange' is thus defined as 'the proportion between equilibrium prices that is established through the equalization of profits between regions in which the rate of surplus value is 'institutionally' different – the term 'institutionally' meaning that these rates are, for whatever reason, safeguarded from competitive equalization' (Emmanuel 1972: 64).

Emmanuel deduces from his theory a number of political conclusions. The basic one is that unequal exchange and international specialization *establish a system of exploitation of some countries by other countries*. It is not a question therefore of the popular classes of the countries of the Third World being exploited by imperialist capital (in parallel with exploitation by 'their own' national capital). It is a question of joint exploitation of the periphery by the developed countries. International solidarity on the part of the workers' movement no longer serves any purpose. On the contrary, the working classes of the centre have been transformed into the workers' aristocracy of the global system, enjoying the benefits, together with the capitalists of the centre, of exploitation of the underdeveloped countries (ibid.: 179).

2.5   Bettelheim's intervention and the theory of accumulation on a global scale

In his *Theoretical Comments* that were published as Appendix I together with Emmanuel's essay, Charles Bettelheim subjected *unequal exchange* to criticism from the viewpoint of the concepts and categories of Marxist theory. Bettelheim made it clear at the outset that in the Marxist view 'commodity exchange necessarily takes the form of *equal exchange*' (Bettelheim 1972: 272), so that it is inappropriate to maintain, as Emmanuel essentially does, that 'there exists "independently of and prior to" imperialist exploitation (in the sense of exploitation through capital investment) a "commercial exploitation" of the colonial or semi-colonial countries' (ibid.: 275).

Bettelheim was even to maintain that Emmanuel's thesis on wages constituting an independent variable is totally without foundation. Low wages correspond to certain socio-economic structures with a low level of development of the productive forces and low organic composition of capital. *They are however in the final analysis determined by the overall structure of each specific social formation* (ibid.: 291). The term 'exploitation' denotes certain class relations of production, referring to a specific social-class structure in the context of each specific country. Henceforth:

[I]t is necessary to think of each 'country' as constituting a social formation with a specific structure, in particular because of the existence of *classes* with contradictory interests. It is this structure that determines the way in which each social formation fits into international production relations.

(ibid.: 300)

Presenting exploitation of countries by other countries, Emmanuel remains at the level of the outward effects that the social relations of production have on exchange, in this way concealing those relations. This is tantamount to concealing imperialist exploitation.[5] Summarizing these conclusions, Bettelheim argued that Emmanuel's analysis is 'pre-critical', which is to say that in the realm of theory it lags behind the gains of the Marxist critique of political economy.

Emmanuel's theory was to be accepted by a considerable number of exponents of the metropolis–periphery current. The best known of them was Samir Amin, who undertook the defence of the Marxist character of this theory from Bettelheim's criticism (and also from criticism by others). Amin (1976: 138 ff.) adopted the main theses of the theoretical schema of unequal exchange but modified it in order to moderate its extreme theoretical and political implications, which as we have seen Emmanuel did not hesitate to emphasize.[6]

To be more specific, Amin endeavoured to rescue the theory of unequal exchange by means of his theory on accumulation on a global scale. According to this theory the polarization of wage levels that characterizes the global capitalist system arose out of the different types of development pursued by the metropolis and the periphery, correspondingly. This implied acknowledgement that wages are not an 'independent variable'. High wages are the result of the developmental model pursued at the centre, the model of 'autocentric' development. Correspondingly, the low wages of the periphery derive from the model of 'extraverted' capital accumulation and development imposed on the periphery by imperialism. In other words, unequal exchange is less the cause and more an effect of the deformation and underdevelopment of the Third World.

Thus, according to Amin, in an autocentric system it is presupposed that there is simultaneous existence, close interconnection and parallel development, of the sector that produces goods for mass consumption and the sector that produces capital goods. It is for this reason, he concludes, that accumulation requires continual expansion of the internal market and so of the wages on which the expansion of the market for consumer goods depends. By contrast, development at the periphery does not require expansion of the internal market and so of wages, because the system is extraverted. Therefore, while we have *one value of labour power*, which is its *global value*, according to Amin two different prices are imposed for the labour power, one above the value and the other beneath it.[7] It is from the polarization of wages that unequal exchange then arises, according to the schema formulated by Emmanuel.

However, Bettelheim had even prior to this voiced his disagreement with the theory of international value of labour power that underlies Amin's analysis: 'The law of value [...] tends [...] to reproduce the conditions of reproduction specific to each of the different social formations, which means that the wage level 'proper' to each social formation cannot be determined by the 'world level of development of the productive forces' (which is merely a false abstraction in a world system made up of distinct and opposed social formations), but that it is fundamentally linked with the specific combination of productive forces and production relations characteristic to each social formation' (Bettelheim 1972: 296).

2.6   The theory of surplus

In 1966 Baran and Sweezy were to write *Monopoly Capitalism* (Baran and Sweezy 1968). In this book the authors put forward the view that 'the economic surplus [...] is the difference between what the society produces and the costs of producing it' (ibid.: 23). The term 'surplus', to reiterate, can be applied in the context of any mode of production in any society. Nevertheless, it is worth noting that in their subsequent analyses the authors adopt a new definition which appears to correspond to the Marxist category of surplus value (or of surplus product, in the case of non-capitalist modes of production). But Baran and Sweezy say that

> [I]n a highly developed monopoly capitalist society, the surplus assumes many forms and disguises, [...] the revenues of state and church, the expenses of transforming commodities into money, and the wages of unproductive workers. In general, however, he [Marx] treated these as secondary factors and excluded them from his basic theoretical schema. It is our contention that under monopoly capitalism this procedure is no longer justified, and we hope that a change in terminology will help to effect the needed shift in theoretical position.
>
> (ibid.: 23)

The basic thesis of Baran and Sweezy is that it is a law of monopoly capitalism that the surplus has the tendency to rise both absolutely and relatively. To quote:

> This law immediately invites comparison [...] with the classical-Marxian law of the falling tendency of the rate of profit. [...] By substituting the law of rising surplus for the law of falling profit [...] we are simply taking account of the undoubted fact that the structure of the capitalist economy has undergone a fundamental change since that theorem was formulated. What is most essential about the structural change from competitive to monopoly capitalism finds its theoretical expression in this substitution.
>
> (ibid.: 80–1)

The main conclusion to be derived from this 'law of rising surplus' is that monopoly capital strives continually to find outlets for this surplus in order to keep the system from sinking into economic crisis, as all traditional domestic spheres of capitalist consumption and investment fall short. Military spending and imperialist expansion were thus regarded by the authors as countervailing tendencies to the inherent tendency towards stagnation in developed monopoly capitalism.[8]

2.7   The global (capitalist) economy, underdeveloped capitalism and the semi-peripheral countries

All the metropolis–periphery theories presuppose, as we have said, the priority of the global economy, and global and economic and social relations over the economic processes and social relations that govern the national social formations. Global processes, in other words, override processes taking place within each social formation and predicating the evolution of the latter. Underdevelopment is primarily the result of dependence and of the division of labour imposed by global capitalism. As Córdova has already informed us (Córdova 1973: 13), it arises out of 'innumerable exogenous factors that are nevertheless endogenous in the context of the international capitalist system'. This formulation expresses the inner 'logic' of the theories we are examining here.[9]

An analysis of the global capitalist economy and underdeveloped capitalism has been elaborated from this common starting point, with Frank and Wallerstein as the key exponents.[10] According to it, from the moment that the global market was created, that is, roughly from the sixteenth century onwards, humanity as a whole (that is to say all the areas linked to or comprising the global market) has been capitalistic, polarized between metropolis and periphery and pervaded by monopolistic structures. The global economy and (global) capitalism are, by this logic, synonymous terms. In Wallerstein's (1979: 44, 47) formulation capitalism is 'a mode of production in which the objective is to produce profit on the market. Capitalism has from the outset been a matter of the global economy, not of national states.' So it is pointless, and mistaken, to speak of other, pre-capitalist modes of production, or of socialism, employing as one's criterion the relation between producers and the means of production, the form of the state, etc. (ibid.: 63).

Within the parameters of the same schema, Frank (1969) was to assert that capitalist development and underdevelopment is predicated on three fundamental antitheses: extraction/appropriation of the economic surplus, polarization between metropolitan and satellite countries, and the conflict between continuity and development. On the basis of the assumption that all productive processes that involve the market are capitalist, Frank was to come out in opposition to all the theories that link the underdevelopment of the periphery to domination by, or even preservation of, expanded reproduction of certain pre-capitalist modes of production. As part of the global system, he would assert, the periphery has always been capitalistic. The capitalism of the periphery is simply different from the capitalism of the metropolis. It is an underdeveloped capitalism. What takes place at the periphery is 'the development of underdevelopment' (Amin 1976: 198 ff.).[11] Similarly, the toiling and exploited masses belong to the (global) proletariat, but again this proletariat is different from the proletariat of the metropolitan centres.[12]

The global system finally takes shape, according to Frank, as an integrated colonial system whose structure may be compared to that of a solar system of planets revolving around a sun. The metropolitan centres are enriched by the satellites. But there may be other satellites revolving around a satellite, dependent on it. This is a fundamental and permanent feature of the global system.[13] One consequence of this solar structure of the global system is however that some intermediate regions inevitably come into existence between the metropolis and the periphery: the *semi-peripheral* or *sub-imperialist states*. As Wallerstein (1979: 50–2) explains:[14]

[T]he structural differentiations between the centre and the periphery cannot be explained adequately if we do not take it into account that there is a third structurally determined position: the position of the semi-periphery. The semi-periphery is necessary for the global economy to be able to function without friction. This semi-periphery is to some extent accorded a special economic role, which however is more necessary politically than economically [...] the absence of a semi-periphery would imply a polarized international system.

Frank (1984: 91–3) explained at the same time that the term sub-imperialism or semi-periphery was a way of describing countries that 'participate in a different way' in the international social division of labour, that is to say, they export not only raw materials and light industrial products but also products derived from heavy industry.[15]

Semi-peripheries or sub-imperialist countries are terms which allow dependency theoreticians to incorporate into their models the historical processes of capitalist development of certain Third World countries. It is therefore understandable that the content of these terms should continually change in step with the changing economic reality. In 1982 Amin formulated, as follows, his theses concerning semi-peripheries and the centre–periphery polarisation:

[I]n the mercantilist and competitive capitalist stages, there were many semiperipheral situations (using the term as Wallerstein does) that could have risen to the rank of the core. But by the end of the nineteenth century the extent of world domination of core capital was already such that it precluded this possibility from then on. In other words, there is not and *there never will be* a 'new Japan' after Japan.

(Amin et al. 1982: 168, emphasis added)

Two decades later he modified his view as follows:

During the 'Bandung period' (1955-75), Third World countries practiced self-reliant development policies with the aim of reducing global polarization ('catching up') [...] The uneven results of this industrialization, imposed upon dominant capital by social forces issuing from national liberation victories, allow us to distinguish today between first-rank peripheries, which have managed to build national productive systems capable of competing in the framework of global capitalism, and marginal peripheries, which have not been able to achieve this.

(Amin 2003: 13)

2.8 The 'new international division of labour'

Most of the writers in the centre–periphery current of thought adopt the problematic of Wallerstein, namely that since the time of its establishment, the global economy has been polarized between a capitalist metropolis and a capitalist periphery, along with the existence in parallel of a few intermediate 'semi-peripheries' and dominated by monopolistic structures. However, as already suggested in the previous section of this chapter, capitalist development of certain countries in the 'periphery' necessitates constant expansion of this 'intermediate space' of the 'semi-periphery'. So, from the viewpoint of this theoretical perspective on the 'global economy', the capitalist restructuring that is observable in different countries in recent decades is a matter of simple sub-instances of transformation of the global capitalist system, leading to a 'new international division of labour'. As Fröbel et al. (1983: 30–1) explain:

> For the first time in the last five hundred years of history of the global economy it is possible today for a rentable manufacturing industry in the framework of world economy to develop on a large and expanding scale in the developing countries. [...] We call this qualitatively new development in the global economy 'the new international division of labour'.

On these assumptions the 'new international division of labour' arose out of global capitalism's tendency to maximize its profits. It is the procedure by means of which global capitalism attempts to overcome its crisis. Through the shifting of production of certain commodities to the Third World, the cost of producing them is reduced precisely because wages in the Third World remain exceptionally low. The 'inexhaustible dynamic' of cheap labour power is the key factor behind the shift of production to the Third World. It is moreover facilitated by a breaking down of the productive process into separate procedures through the introduction of new technologies. Many of these procedures can be carried out by a non-specialist workforce. Developments in transport and communications make it possible for the overall production process to be spread over a greater number of countries.

The analysis of Lipietz (1983) is informed by a similar problematic. Starting again from the position that 'the general laws of the capitalist mode of production are valid only at the level of the global system' (ibid.: 56), he takes the position that

[I]n order to emerge from the crisis, imperialism must construct a new division of labour that will relegate countries to one of three categories:

> * A metropolis that will dispose over the most advanced technology and the strategic products: the USA.
> * Countries engaging in special construction work.
> * Countries for assembly and non-specialized mass production.

(ibid.: 95)

Lipietz then surmises that the 'international division of labour' schema can also be implemented inside the metropolitan social formations, where, as a result of the articulation of a variety of modes of production, different types of 'periphery' are created.

2.9   The metropolis–periphery current and the *Monthly Review School*

The theories we present here are certainly distinct from each other, but all in all not mutually contradictory. We have already identified an obvious antagonism between theories of dualism, and of structural heterogeneity, and the theory of underdeveloped capitalism that precludes the existence of non-capitalist modes of production at the periphery. But we shall concern ourselves with matters of this kind in the immediately following section of this chapter. What concerns us here is the predominant element, the element of convergence. It is this convergence that makes the metropolis–periphery theories into a single current. There are two intermediate elements that sustain this convergence of all the theories into one strand:

1. A conception of the global capitalist system. From this conception, as we have already noted, it transpires that *the global processes have priority over the national processes,* and that development (and the underdevelopment of the periphery) is determined by the development options of the imperialistic metropolis, with the result that *the key fact about social relations at the periphery is their dependent character.*
2. A conception of imperialism in which the predatory rule of the metropolis over the periphery is seen as the essential characteristic of the global system. This conception rediscovers common ground with the positions on imperialism formulated, above all, by Rosa Luxemburg.

These two conceptions evidently establish the basic profile of the metropolis and the periphery, that is to say the two poles, the two key structures of capitalism in the light of all the theories we examine here. They are the framework of shared assumption behind every theory of the metropolis and the periphery. We do not intend to go into the details of the abovementioned controversy, but will focus on some shared viewpoints, irrespective of whether the writers adopting them think that they characterize global history for 500 or 5,000 years. In these theories the concept of *imperialism* is linked to the relations of dominance that characterize in the most general sense the relation between the developed countries of the *centre* and the developing countries of the periphery. From this viewpoint imperialism embodies the structural (global) relations of dependence (or, to put it differently, 'hegemony') and so constitutes an organic (and probably insurmountable) element of the global system.[16] It could of course be argued that it is a precondition for establishment of the individual states and a dominant contradiction above and beyond the other political and social contradictions: the imperialism of dependence is at the heart of global capitalism. It is its key element. The powerful economies of the centre shape the relations under which production in the peripheral economies is carried out, continually absorbing surplus value from them. International organizations, such as the World Bank and the International Monetary Fund, operate under the control of the countries of the centre, promoting their specific vested interests. The capitalist centre is responsible for the underdevelopment of the periphery.

It is in the context of the metropolis–periphery current that a narrower convergence is effected between a number of theories, a convergence that finds expression in the so-called *Monthly Review School* (from the journal of the same name which the chief representatives of the school publish and by means of which they make their interventions).[17]

The convergence involves on the one hand the theories of Emmanuel and Amin of unequal exchange and global accumulation, and on the other Baran–Sweezy's theory of surplus and Wallerstein and Frank's theory of underdeveloped capitalism. Some elements of the traditional analysis of the periphery are necessarily adopted. As for distorted development at the periphery, this school maintains, as we have said, that there are different categories of peripheral country and that each tends to be linked in its own particular way to the metropolis, so that it is not appropriate to speak generally of national social formations at the periphery. Worth noting here are two ideological elements that characterize the '*Monthly Review School*':

The first has to do with a peculiar attitude towards the market and in particular the world market. This 'market' is identified as the distinguishing, and predominant, characteristic of the CMP (every type of production that is oriented towards the market is capitalism, without any reference to the specific relation of labour to the means of production and their economic owners. Increased wages, that is to say, the expanded domestic market for consumer goods, is the decisive criterion for 'autocentric development'. Exploitation of the periphery arises out of instances of unequal exchange on the world market, etc.).

The second appears to have been influenced by the view, first formulated by Bukharin, that the global capitalist system is a single uniform class structure, within the framework of which the ruling bourgeois classes unite in a single hierarchically organized bloc, notwithstanding the intra-bourgeois contradictions, in exactly the same way as occurs with the bourgeois classes of an individual capitalist country. Amin (1976: 360, 196) comments characteristically:

> The contradiction is not between the bourgeois and the proletariat of each country considered in isolation but between the world bourgeoisie and the world proletariat. [...] [T]he world bourgeoisie consists principally of the bourgeoisie of the center and, secondarily, the bourgeoisie that has been constituted in its wake, at the periphery. The bourgeoisie of the center, the only one that exists at the scale of the world system, exploits the proletariat everywhere, at the center and at the periphery, but [...] it exploits the proletariat of the periphery even more brutally.

It is from this schema that the school's 'Third Worldist' political conclusions emerge: it is almost exclusively at the periphery that social change can come into existence. But what kind of change will it be, given that the main, the real 'enemy', is not there, at the periphery, but at the centre? Obviously the revolutionary masses of the periphery can strike at the 'enemy' only indirectly. And in any case the desideratum for them cannot be to crush 'their own' bourgeois state but to fight for 'national independence' and 'autocentric' development. The theory of the global bourgeoisie that the school has adopted supplants the Marxist theory that the state is the level *par excellence* at which bourgeois class (political) domination is concentrated (see Part II of the book).

2.10   The critique of Córdova and Cardóso

The theoretical disagreements between the '*Monthly Review School*' and some Marxists of the metropolis–periphery current who support different viewpoints are not limited merely to questions pertaining to deformation of social and economic life at the periphery. On the contrary, the discussion and the critique have been expanded to some broader theoretical questions with a bearing on the internal coherence of the theories presented here.

Of particular significance in this respect are, in our opinion, the theoretical interventions of two Latin American theorists of the metropolis–periphery current, Córdova and Cardóso. The former directed his critique primarily against the theory of 'underdeveloped capitalism' as formulated by Frank (but also against the theory of surplus), the latter against the theories that deal with the (non) expansion of the domestic market.

Córdova (1973) opens his analysis with references to the concepts of surplus introduced by Baran and deployed by Frank. He reaches the conclusion that given the way these concepts are formulated for society as a whole, they tend to conceal the specific class-exploitative character of the relations of production. By contrast, the concepts of surplus value, of land rent, of surplus product, etc. introduced by Marx illuminate precisely these specific exploitative relationships, that is to say the class struggle.[18] Córdova (ibid.: 124) thus concludes: 'there is no reason to replace the Marxist categories of surplus value, surplus product, surplus labour, etc., with the term "social surplus"'.

He was subsequently to maintain that the process of 'extraction/appropriation of the economic surplus' was not, as Frank believed, the specific characteristic of capitalism but rather the basic contradiction in every mode of production and every class society. The distinguishing feature of capitalism is production and abstraction/appropriation of the surplus value of the free worker by the capitalist, possessor and owner of the means of production. But Frank and Wallerstein see only the market, deploying a definition of capitalism that conceals precisely this relationship between capital and labour.

Córdova rejects both the thesis that the societies of Latin America were fully capitalistic as early as the sixteenth century (as they contained relations of slavery and forced labour, etc.), and the thesis that they have been monopolistic since that time. Thus, in the societies of the periphery there is not a homogeneous 'underdeveloped capitalism' but 'a complex mosaic of relationships and accordingly of ways of extracting surplus labour' (ibid.: 136). Dependency at the periphery, Córdova was to assert, allows for expanded reproduction of the pre-capitalist relations that are associated with underdevelopment. He was in fact to argue as follows: 'although the extreme dependence of Canada on the USA is today obvious, nobody would say that Canada is an underdeveloped country. Why? Because in Canada the network of pre-capitalist relations, with which capitalism has been associated in our countries, is absent' (ibid.: 148). Frank, Córdova continues:

> [A]bdicates consideration of the role of social class, because clearly it is unnecessary. In his system of metropoles and satellites, exploitation is not exploitation of certain classes by other classes, but is a consequence of the hierarchical levels whereby each sector alienates its immediate inferior, to be alienated in turn by its immediate superior.
>
> (ibid.: 150)

Marxist analysis is obliged (contrary to Frank's theory that the only 'totality' is the global economy) to take into account the class relations and the economic structure of each specific social formation:

> Because colonization takes place on the basis of certain economic motivations, the key to understanding the resultant relations is to be found in the economic structure of each society. [...] We must in any case take it as our starting point that it is the class structure that creates the colonial system and rules over it, and not the opposite.
>
> (ibid.: 153, 155)

The theory of the world capitalist system eschews concrete analysis, so that the conclusions it comes to on the periphery have very little connection with what actually happens there. But Frank's philosophical background, too, is unrelated to Marxism, as Córdova argues:

> The concept that Frank has of history is nothing other than the result that emerges, with the passage of time, from the determinate influence exercised by the system of colonial relations, which is presented in the form of an idea (in the Hegelian sense) on the social whole. The economic structure as well as the technical, political, legal and ideological structure, is presented as the reflection of this idea at the different levels of social life.
>
> (ibid.: 165)

The critique of Cardóso (in Sonntag 1974), by contrast, typically targets the theories focusing on the narrowness of the market at the periphery. He notes that the development of capitalism is not linked in the first instance to expansion of the market for consumer goods, and so to the size of wages, but primarily to the expansion of productive consumption of capital, and that in any case the problem of the market is not posed as a problem sui generis, unrelated to capitalist development itself.[19] And he concludes that 'behind the apparent logic of such an interpretation there hide mistakes which have to do with the nature of the capitalist production process' (Cardóso ibid.: 53).

Examining the case of Brazil, he in fact argues against the thesis of the (inevitable) extraversion of the peripheral countries: 'All the data we have so far cited has been aimed at showing that today's economic expansion is not attributable to exports but to growing domestic demand. Brazil appears as anything but a sub-imperialist country' (ibid.: 60–1). Cardóso effectively refutes the thesis that a strong local bourgeois is not constituted at the periphery, with all important decisions being made by imperialistic capital. He argues that 'to assert that capitalist accumulation truly takes place and at the same time to deny the significance of the bourgeoisie is a characteristic contradiction' (ibid.: 45). His conclusion is as follows:

> All the theoretical and analytical endeavours to demonstrate the specific, and new, element in present-day forms of dependence have rapidly disintegrated, leaving vague turns of phrase embroidering deceptive basic principles: the development of underdevelopment, sub-imperialism, the lumpen bourgeoisie, revolution at the periphery, etc.
>
> (ibid.: 37)

In another work of Cardóso there is questioning of the thesis that the development of the metropolis is based on plunder of the periphery. 'The idea that the development of capitalism depends on the exploitation of the Third World should be scrutinized more carefully. In reality, the basic tendencies in recent years indicate that Latin America's share of the expanding international trade, and of investments [...] the relations between the developed capitalist countries and the dependent nations lead rather to a marginalization of the latter within the global system of economic development' (Cardóso 1974: 217).

2.11 Epilogue

We shall present a more comprehensive critique of metropolis–periphery theories in the next chapters. Of course the interventions we have introduced here, of Córdova and of Cardóso (which although they are to be included in the metropolis–periphery current, revise basic assumptions of the '*Monthly Review School*'), and Bettelheim's intervention on the theory of unequal exchange, do in themselves represent a preliminary, and partial, critique.

The theoreticians of dependency continue to reproduce their arguments in theoretical discussion, indeed with a considerable number of followers, with one basic difference: the discussion on dependency has retreated backstage and emphasis is now placed on investigating the historical development of the 'global system' (see, for example, Wallerstein 1998; Frank and Gills 1996; Modelski 1987; Arrighi 1996, Amin 1989). Certainly one reason for this displacement is the radical change in the theoretical and political conjuncture (the fashion of globalization). We nevertheless believe that the most important factor is historical and empirical refutation of all the dependence arguments utilized in the 60s and 70s (for more on this see Part II and III, Willoughby 1986, Howard and King 2000).

Dependency theorists also fail in their effort to explain contemporary developments in capitalism. For example, Wallerstein (1998, 1999) argues that capitalism is no longer tenable as a system. He believes that the capitalist economy is trapped in a fatal contradiction. While sovereign states provide the basis for every capital accumulation, for the first time in 500 years they are on a downward slide in terms of their inner and outer sovereignty: 'This is the primary sign of the acute crisis of capitalism as an historical system' (Wallerstein 1999: 33). Arrighi (1996, 1999), by contrast, sees the modern neoliberal organization of capitalism as a subversion of the hegemonic position of the USA, in a similar cyclical pattern to that experienced in the past by Genoa, Holland and Britain. Faced with a setback in commodity markets, with profit opportunities for its capitals beginning to decline, a hegemonic power switches to financialization: financial capital flows elsewhere in search of profits.

Any comprehensive critique of the above argumentation must start from a specific nodal point: critique of the hypothesis that global capitalism functions as a uniform class structure or, at any rate, that the international processes and relationships have priority over processes and social-class relationships inside each social formation, and indeed determine the latter's evolution. One crucial issue in this context is the theory of the state. Can, in the context of the 'global economy', the state be regarded as an instrument in the hands of international corporations or monopolies, or is it a condensation of the class power of a (national) capitalist ruling class associated with other coterminous capitalist ruling classes (and, respectively, capitalist states) through relations on the one hand of class solidarity and on the other of economic, political or other ('cultural', 'ethnic' etc.) competitiveness? More precisely, can capitalist states in the so-called Third World be regarded as an appurtenance or accessory of the developed capitalist states? These theoretical problems will be tackled in Parts II and III.

3
Theories of Imperialism as Alternatives to Classical and Centre–Periphery Approaches

3.1   Introduction: In search of a non-reductionist analytical framework

In Chapter 2 we found that the centre–periphery problematic and the relevant discussion conducted after the Second World War was in reality largely based on arguments from the classical theories of imperialism. Some of the basic findings from this discussion might be summarized as follows:

(1)   Development of the productive forces leads to monopoly production structures (concentration and centralization). This process creates surplus capital.

(2)   Production is internationalized. Individual 'national' capitals develop on a geographical terrain that greatly transcends national borders. Capitalism becomes a global system; that is to say the 'laws' of the system now operate on a world scale.

(3)   The state in developed capitalist countries provides geopolitical *support* through (colonial) imperialism for movement of capital. In reality it becomes merged with the monopolies. The world is divided into spheres of influence. Competition between individual 'national' capitals takes the form of geopolitical competition between the powerful states. The state in the 'dependent' countries becomes a tool in the hands of imperialism and the monopolies.[1]

It is worth noting that from the very outset there have been endeavours to mount a critique of the economic reductionist conception imposed by point (3). Indicative in this connection have been the interventions by Weber and Schumpeter who, however, as we shall establish below, subsequently converge in their theoretical problematic. Apart from other similarities, they also put forward a different conception of the state, which ceases to be conceived of as an *inert instrument* in the hands of individual monopoly capitals, acquiring its own autonomous dynamic.

There are a number of other contemporary analyses that speak of a *new imperialism* and whose stance on the same point (3) is critical. Some of them accept point (1). Others do not. The basic point of convergence is acceptance of (2), a view that enables individual capitals to distance themselves from the national space without losing their national 'identity'. Individual capitals with different national origins compete in the international sphere. Following the end of colonialism the powerful states, then, seem to have been confronted with the problem of solving a very difficult 'equation': *how is it possible to safeguard the outflow of their individual capitals that are being invested in places outside the range of their political influence?* Everything, therefore, starts from the fact that 'imperialist capital' is traversing a politically fragmented world. The 'new imperialism' (in many variants depending on the author) is the solution to this difficult equation, expressing the political aspect of a basically economic relationship. It is the political solution for the consolidation of economic hegemony.

We do not propose to embark upon further elaboration of questions that will be discussed below. Let us merely note that the attempt to achieve differentiation from the economic reductionism of point (3) often occurs without specific reference either to the structure of the state or to the mode of organization of class domination within capitalist social formations (or, even worse, sometimes the discussion implicitly accepts the mainstream argumentation on 'modern' sovereignty). It seems, finally, that the key absentee from the discussion, again, was Marx.

3.2 The 'political' approach to imperialism: Some notes on a long theoretical tradition

3.2.1 Introduction: Imperialism as an 'autonomous' policy of the State

As aptly noted by Callinicos (2007), both Weberian historical sociologists, such as Anthony Giddens, Michael Mann and Theda Skocpol (see below), and international relations theorists in one or the other realist tradition have criticized classical Marxist analyses for their failure to perceive that the kind of competition specific to inter-state systems is a more or less *transhistorical phenomenon* governed by a logic *irreducible* to that of class exploitation. The problematic in question takes us back a very long way, even before the time of Max Weber. In what follows we shall focus on some moments (or aspects) of this – unquestionably *non-homogeneous* – theoretical tradition.

It is worth noting that reductionist-type *biological* (and not economic) theories of imperialism were formulated well before the turn of the twentieth century. It is then that we encounter a number of extreme racist approaches, chiefly in England (in the works of Benjamin Kidd and Karl Pearson) and Germany (in the works of Friedrich Naumann, Friedrich von Bernhardi and Houston Stewart Chamberlain). Influenced by the logic of social Darwinism, these analyses did not seek out the origins of imperialism in the economic sphere. On the contrary, they judged that since the white race is 'superior' to the other, coloured races, its destiny and duty is to exercise dominion over them. Imperialism is portrayed in essence as a purely *biological* (in the racial sense) phenomenon: it has to do with the struggle for the survival of the most powerful 'race'.[2]

Among the first writers to incorporate systematically into their analysis a *purely* political definition of imperialism was the Austrian theoretician, Heinrich Friedjung. According to his argumentation, imperialism should be regarded *as a phenomenon of power politics in which the state is the decisive agent of history*.[3] What we see formulated, in other words, is an *intellectual orientation* that much later came to be associated primarily with the so-called *realist approach*.

This is in reality a suitably theorized systematization of views that were widespread in public debate. Many theoreticians and politicians of the time were in the habit of viewing the imperialistic expansion of the great European powers as an *ineluctable* political process: the world of the future would be dominated by great empires, and any nation-state which did not join their ranks was condemned to an inferior status.[4] In a speech in 1897, Chamberlain, for example, reaffirmed the above assertion in the most unambiguous way: 'it seems to me that the tendency of the time is to throw all power into the hands of the greater empires, and the minor kingdoms – those which are non-progressive – seem to be destined to fall into a secondary and subordinate place' (quoted in Mommsen 1982: 6).

3.2.2   Imperialism as the fusion between independent political and economic factors: Brief comments on Weber's argumentation

In a general sense Weber's analysis moved within the parameters of the abovementioned current. In late nineteenth century Germany, with the exception of the circles of revolutionary Marxism, the 'bourgeois' intelligentsia did not make any particular effort to analyse the phenomenon of imperialism (Mommsen 1982, Koebner 1949).

It was after 1880 that the idea of a German colonial empire began to acquire momentum among the intelligentsia. All of bourgeois science rose to the occasion in response to the invitation to establish a dynamic German *Weltpolitik*. Weber was one of the important supporters of this new ideological line. In a lecture at the University of Freiburg in 1895 he said categorically:

> Also crucial for *our* development is the question of how long-range policy can highlight the significance of great issues of political power. We must become aware that the unification of Germany was a youthful folly pursued by the nation in its maturity and that it would have been better for it to have been avoided, taking into consideration how much it has cost us, if it is destined to be the culmination and not the point of departure for German policies of power on the global level.
>
> (quoted in Mommsen 1977: 128)

According to Weber, state political structures are characterized by a specific *internal logic* that is linked to expansion and war, and is in no way to be reduced to economic interests. The emphasis here is placed on the *prestige aspect* that induced the great powers to engage in overseas expansion. What is involved is an unavoidable 'dynamic of power', which evidently underlies the *immanent expansionist* 'behaviour' of the powerful capitalist states:

> The power of political structures has a *specific internal dynamic*. On the basis of this power, the members may pretend to a special 'prestige', and their pretensions may influence the external conduct of the power structures. [...] The prestige of power means in practice the glory of power over other communities; [...] The Great Powers are very often expansive powers. *Yet, Great Powers are not necessarily and not always oriented towards expansion. Their attitude in this respect often changes, and in these changes economic factors play a weighty part.*
>
> (Weber 1978: 911–12, emphasis added)

Weber seeks to emphasize the fact that it is not enough in itself to note the autonomous expansionist logic of the state if one is to account for all of the factors that give rise to imperialism. Specific structures at the economic level *co-determine* the extent and the manner of political expansion. Concerning the economic motives of imperialism, Weber's line of thought could also be summarized as follows: the predominantly sociological motive for imperial expansion 'was especially likely to appeal to ruling élites', and this 'was usually associated with specifically economic interests, particularly those of groups which sought monopoly profits instead of being content to manufacture and exchange goods in a formally free market. Monopolistic concessions of all kinds were especially likely to occur in the context of imperialist policy, and consequently financial groups and enterprises who were interested in this type of opportunity – among whom armament manufacturers were not the least important – could be relied on to support imperialist expansion' (Mommsen 1982: 19–20). Imperialism is the product of a concrescence of political and economic factors in a single current.

It is also noted by Weber at a number of points that imperialism entirely corresponds to the interests of the ruling élites given that the expansion of the boundaries of state jurisdiction typically entails an augmentation of their social prestige, making a decisive contribution to consolidating their rule over the subjected classes.[5]

Weber concludes his argument with the observation that liberal competitive capitalism can curb the expansionist drive of the state, to a significant extent limiting the phenomenon of imperialism. In this way he introduces a fundamental distinction which – as we shall see below in the resultant theoretical debate – was to win many later followers. The imperialist 'predatory' form of capitalism, mainly associated with monopolistic economic interests, is nothing more than a deviation from free trade, privately oriented capitalism. Pursuing a different line of argument, Weber appears to some extent to share the conclusions of the classical theories of imperialism: he accepts the notion of a *partial* connection between imperialism and the monopolistic organization of the economy, at the same time considering, however, that the potential for reversion to a peaceful liberal capitalism should by no means be excluded. The 'pure' normal form of capitalism, considered as an economic system based on the production and rational exchange of goods within a market framework, is an impediment to the manifestation of autonomous state expansionism and thus *is not necessarily to be linked to the phenomenon of imperialism* (Weber 1978: 913–21).

To recapitulate: Weber regards imperialism as a *permanent potential within capitalism*, associated with a specific expansionist dynamic of the capitalist state as well as with economic domination by monopoly interests.

3.2.3 The vacillations of Kautsky and his flirtation with Weberian logic

The previously mentioned key distinction between normal free-market capitalism and the predatory monopolistic form of capitalism based on imperialist expansion into overseas territories brings to mind the work of a German Marxist of the same period: Karl Kautsky.

As is well known, Kautsky was the most distinguished Marxist theoretician of the German Social Democracy after the death of Marx and Engels. He contributed to the spread of Marxist ideas through popularization of many of the texts of the latter, from 1883 onwards editing the theoretical journal of Social Democracy, *Die Neue Zeit*. Arguably, it was he more than anyone else who determined the party's political orientation. On the question that interests us it should be noted that he was probably the first Marxist theoretician to pay serious attention to the phenomenon of imperialism (through a series of articles beginning around 1884), without his work as a whole reflecting any coherent relevant theory. Kautsky's ideas on imperialism were fruitful but profoundly contradictory, containing 'the germ of every significant view expressed by anti-revisionists before 1914, as well as anticipating the non-Marxist model of imperialism advanced by Joseph Schumpeter' (Howard and King 1989: 92). In fact, certain moments of his work argue for a conception of imperialism that moves within the parameters of the more generally institutionalist theoretical strategy pioneered by Weber which to a great extent – as we shall see below – presented ideas that later reappeared in the work of Schumpeter.[6] We shall subsequently endeavour to pinpoint these moments in Kautsky's thought (without, however, referring to his intervention in its entirety).

In his early texts Kautsky adopted the underconsumptionist viewpoint considering that the Great Powers' expansion into their overseas colonies was a policy that satisfied the economic interests of the bourgeoisie as a whole. His analysis in *The Class Struggle*, published in 1892, is indicative. It was in this work that he undertook to explain (for an international audience) the Sozialdemokratische Partei Deutschlands 's (SPD's) Erfurt Programme. Kautsky thought that the territorial expansion of the developed industrial states was basically a race to secure markets, which, because of underconsumption by the masses, were necessary for capitalist development. Notwithstanding the possibility of channelling the surplus commodities as exports into international markets, 'the domestic market is the safest for the capitalist class of every country, [...] it is the easiest to maintain and to exploit' (Kautsky

1892, iv: 3). The political expansion of the state in the context of expanding internal markets through the widening of borders is thus in the economic interest of the bourgeoisie as a whole: 'in proportion as the capitalist system develops, so also grows the pressure on the part of the capitalist class in every nation for an extension of its political boundaries' (ibid.). It is precisely from here that there emerges that political competition for colonies which contributes to militarism and gradually turns Europe into an armed camp. According to Kautsky, there are two possible outcomes:

> The colonial policy of these states affords inadequate relief to the need of expansion caused by their capitalist system of production. [...] *There are but two ways out of this intolerable state of things: either a gigantic war that shall destroy some of the existing European states, or the union of them all in a federation.*
>
> (Kautsky 1892, iv: 3, emphasis added)

In his exposition Kautsky largely enlists arguments that a decade later constituted the core of Hobson's analysis, and also the analysis of numerous Marxists. *Imperialism is a political phenomenon whose foundations are unequivocally economic.* The contradictions between the great imperialist powers will either lead to an outbreak of war and violence or will be settled peacefully. We thus see that Kautsky had quite early arrived at the idea of *ultra-imperialism*, to which he was to return – with modified argumentation – some years later.

We do not propose to elaborate on every twist and turn in Kautsky's thought on the subject of imperialism.[7] Suffice it to say that shortly before the turn of the century, in 1897–8, Kautsky appears to have flirted with the notion that 'pure' industrial capitalism has no need of imperialism for its reproduction. Consequently, it is the pre-industrial structures that are responsible for the explosion of imperialist contradictions.[8] The argumentation is unmistakably present in the long article titled 'Colonial policy old and new' (1898). Let us pause briefly to consider it.

Kautsky is now clearly performing an *about-face* in relation to his previous views. The colonialism of the seventeenth and eighteenth centuries can in no way be regarded as the outcome of industrial capitalism. The colonies served the interests of the 'pre-industrial' classes of traders and bankers and no one else. Industrial capitalists had no interest in them because industrial capital needed purchasers of commodities, something which could naturally not be provided by colonies. The commercial and financial fractions of capital were inherently monopolistic and militaristic. By contrast, industrial capital sought peace and unimpeded free trade. It was thus *intrinsically anti-imperialistic*: 'the more industrial capital, and particularly production for export, advances into the foreground, the greater the capitalist nations' need for peace' (Kautsky 1898: 804–5).

But how in the context of the above logic could one interpret the intensity of colonization at the end of the nineteenth century and the return both to formal forms of domination and to protectionist practices? According to Kautsky these processes were the effects of political reinforcement of pre-industrial reactionary social forces (merchants, financiers, state bureaucrats) whose interests in no way favoured capitalist economic development:

> [I]t was not the needs of industrial development that brought on the latest phase of colonial policy, but, on the one hand, the needs of classes whose interests are opposed to the requirements of economic development and, on the other hand, the needs of states whose interests are opposed to those of advanced civilization. *In other words, the most recent phase of colonial policy is, like protectionism, a work of reaction; it is by no means necessary for economic development, often even harmful.* It originates, not in England, but in France, Germany and Russia.
>
> (Kautsky 1898: 806, emphasis added)

This argumentation of Kautsky seems to have constituted something of a deviation from the mainstream logic of his work. Four years later in the pamphlet titled *Commercial Policy and Social Democracy* he reverts to his familiar viewpoint (imperialism as a battle for foreign markets in a situation of overproduction), largely foreshadowing the later analyses of Lenin and Hilferding 'by pointing to the connection between the formation of cartels, industrial capitalists' demands for protection, and the growth of militarism which threatened to spark off a world war' (Howard and King 1989: 94).

But the 1898 problematic did not entirely disappear from Kautsky's thinking and this may be useful when it comes to venturing an interpretation of the argument on ultra-imperialism. In 1914 Kautsky maintained that although developed capitalism has a need for colonies, it is essentially peaceful in nature. Not free trade but the multiplicity of the destructive consequences of war impels the great powers into a 'holy alliance'. They had the capacity to collaborate in the exploitation of the world without powerful conflicts manifesting themselves between them, on condition that they divide up the economic space in accordance with the balance of (international) forces.[9] According to this logic, it would be possible to attribute the outbreak of the First World War to the transitory political ascendancy of the abovementioned 'pre-industrial' and predominantly militaristic social forces.[10]

3.2.4   Imperialism as the outcome of the survival of pre-industrial political structures in Schumpeter's analysis

As we saw above, Weber's general conception of imperialism involves two basic theses. *First*, imperialism reflects the immanent expansionist logic of the capitalist state. It can simultaneously serve the economic interests of the commercial and monopolistic segments of capital while contributing in parallel to reproduction of their political predominance within their respective social formations. *Second*, pure liberal capitalism has no need of imperialist expansion for its reproduction. Indeed for precisely that reason, it is opposed to, and is ultimately capable of curbing, the expansionist dynamic of the state. Consequently, imperialism is basically a *political phenomenon*, even when it succeeds in co-opting the ambitions of the monopolistic economic elites (to the extent that they exist). This current of thought – not of course with all its wealth of elaboration – is embodied in the argumentation of Schumpeter.

On the issue of imperialism Schumpeter was the first theoretician to clearly differentiate himself from Hilferding and all other Marxist approaches that conceived of imperialism as an indispensable trend of the 'latest phase' of capitalism. He at once limited the field of discussion by defining imperialism as the 'objectless disposition of a state toward unlimited and violent expansion' (Schumpeter 1951: 6). Schumpeter considered imperialism to be an obsolete policy and regime, that is, an absolutist remnant, which was bound to fade away with the development of modern capitalism. Indeed, he regarded imperialism as an 'old' inheritance from pre-modern capitalist eras, which was going to disappear; in contrast to Hilferding, who regarded imperialism as a 'new', inherent characteristic of capitalism in its 'latest', monopolistic stage: 'a purely capitalist world [...] can offer no fertile soil to imperialist impulses. That does not mean that it cannot maintain an interest in imperialist impulses' (ibid.: 69).

Schumpeter not only regarded expansion and war as a possible outcome of intra-state (imperialist) rivalries but also identified the variety of forces that are opposed to militarism and war. He claimed that the socialist perspective could be comprehended as an attempt to find a solution to the problem of imperialism. Schumpeter (ibid.: 296–7) gave Hilferding credit for coming to grips with such problems, but believed that factors impeding imperialistic policies are not lacking in capitalist society. Liberal capitalism was 'by nature anti-imperialist', so 'we cannot readily derive from it such imperialist tendencies as actually exist, but must evidently see them only as alien elements, carried into the world of capitalism from the outside, supported by non-capitalist factors in modern life' (ibid.: 96). Imperialism should thus not be described as a necessary phase of capitalism, but as a *transitional phenomenon pending the final triumph of capitalism.*

He finally remarked, however, that many elements (for example, tariffs, cartels, trusts, monopolies), which were analysed as a part of the 'economic' framework of imperialism, were political and, possibly, pre-capitalist in origin (ibid.: 295). Schumpeter wrote further:

> It was neo-Marxist doctrine that first tellingly described this causal connection (Bauer) and fully recognized the significance of the 'functional change in protectionism' (Hilferding) [...]; Thus we have here, within a social group that carries great political weight, a strong undeniable, economic interest in such things as protective tariffs, cartels, monopoly prices, forced exports (dumping), an aggressive economic policy, an aggressive foreign policy generally, and war, including wars of expansion with typically imperialist character.
>
> (ibid.: 79, 83–4)

Schumpeter regarded that monopolistic structures and protectionist policies had deeper political and social causes.[11]

Schumpeter wrote his essay on imperialism (1919) when historical events (World War I) seemed to have verified the hypothesis of Marxist authors (for example, Hilferding, Bukharin and Lenin) that modern capitalism included imperialism as one of its indispensable features. Therefore, his approach may be regarded as a critique of this hypothesis (Taylor 1951: 546). Sweezy claimed that Schumpeter's essay on imperialism was a corrective supplement to his own *Theory of Economic Development*, repairing his omission of any explanation of 'imperialism' (Schumpeter 1951, preface by Sweezy).

In one sense this analysis of Schumpeter is a powerful interpretation of imperialism from within the parameters of liberal economic thought. The 'invisible hand' (Smith), in international markets transformed into the theory of comparative advantage (Ricardo), has difficulty reconciling imperialism – the logic of state expansionism – with the 'normal' functioning of capitalism. If we accept Smith's basic thesis, that if left free from artificial interference natural economic forces will prove stronger than any political or legal 'obstacles' (Rubin 1989), then imperialism can be understood as an exception to the rule, attributable to political structures that do not accord with the real nature of capitalism. Later neoclassical approaches share the same viewpoint. According to neoclassical economists 'the use of force brings deadweight losses – net costs for which there are no corresponding net benefits. Consequently, rational decision makers will recognize the superiority of contract as a means of acquisition because all parties may benefit more through voluntary exchange than through violent conflict. Thus, while the reality of imperialism has rarely been denied, it has been widely thought to be outside the boundaries of orthodox economic analysis, which limits itself to the logic of the rationally acquisitive action' (Howard and King 2000: 19).

3.2.5   Theories of imperialism as 'political discontinuity': A general assessment

The abovementioned tradition of thought obviously did not stop with Schumpeter. It was disseminated via a whole range of later analyses and to a certain extent has currency even to our day. It is a view which testifies to great confidence in the democratic and peace-loving character of liberal capitalism. It receives theoretical inputs from the liberal tradition of free trade, emphasizing the internationalist character of the present-day capitalist system. It 'over-politicizes' the phenomenon of imperialism, attributing the imperialist aggressiveness of capitalism (where it exists or has appeared) more to traditionalist remnants within industrial societies or to phenomena not compatible with the 'normal' structure of the capitalist system as such.

One indicative example is a memorable intervention by Arendt (1951). Placing particular emphasis on the link between fascist and imperialist ideology, she maintained that racist ideologies of imperialism and the anti-liberal structures of imperialistic politics sooner or later lead to fascism. Indeed she reached the same conclusion as Schumpeter: in the final analysis imperialism is the effect of residual elements of pre-democratic social structures that have survived in modern industrial societies. Therefore, pure liberal capitalism has no need of imperialism for its reproduction.

Schumpeter's argumentation was taken over in its entirety by Winslow (1931, 1972) who, distancing himself both from classical Marxist viewpoints and from Hobson's analysis, extols the analysis put forward by the former: 'one of the most ambitious and noteworthy attempts to give an entirely new and positive orientation to the theory of imperialism without completely abandoning the economic interpretation is found in Professor Joseph Schumpeter's "sociological" theory of imperialism'(Winslow 1931: 749). In the same line of argumentation, he conceived imperialism as an outcome of 'pre-capitalist' structures. He thus believed that 'a purely capitalistic world could never give rise to the imperialistic impulse' and that 'imperialism had its beginning before, not after, the industrial revolution' (ibid.: 751). Therefore, the content of imperialism is political and not economic. Economic competition is peaceful and 'co-operative'. Political rivalry, by contrast, takes the form of nationalism, imperialism and militarism. Imperialism is a phenomenon that tends to disappear to the extent that, with the development of capitalism, pre-industrial political institutions are replaced. It is in the nature of capitalism not to generate phenomena such as imperialism (Winslow 1931, 1972).

Similar views are to be found in the more comprehensive exposition by Rostow (1960), who undertook to present a theoretical proposal on historical development that could be an alternative to Marxism (or at least to Marxism as he himself had understood it). On the question of imperialism the writer accepts that in all their developmental stages, industrial societies have sought to satisfy their economic interests through establishment of overseas territories. Nevertheless, and contrary to the views of the classical theorists of imperialism, imperialist expansion is of slight significance for the development of modern industrial societies. The latter have no need of imperialism for their reproduction.[12] Of course it may frequently be the case, according to Rostow, that the great differences between countries in levels of economic development, which in turn can often be reflected as significant differences in military potential, can give rise to aggressive imperialistic policies (of a regional or global nature). However, for one more time, imperialist expansion is in his view by no means peculiar to industrial capitalism, but is generally due to non-economic and, especially, political factors (Mommsen 1982: 84).

We do not propose here to go into great detail concerning every aspect of a problematic whose origins are in the theoretical interventions of Weber and Schumpeter. Undoubtedly, the ultimate inheritors of the abovementioned reflections are today's representatives of the school of *political realism*. According to this line of thought, imperialist expansionism and inter-state antagonisms are not reducible (or not exclusively reducible) to the economic sphere but reflect (or mainly reflect) the logic of *states acting as states* (Howard and King 2000: 30), that is representing an internal expansionist dynamic as such, or better, *an internal logic of power*. As has been widely commented in the relevant literature, this is a view that has gained wide acceptance in the works of well-known historical sociologists who have been influenced by Weber, for example, Giddens (1981, 1987), Mann (1986, 1988) and Skocpol (1979).

The argumentation of this paragraph would be incomplete without a mention of the *deeper similarity* that exists between the theoretical moments examined above and classical Marxist analyses. Although the former have often emerged in the course of attempted criticism of the latter, in reality they achieve nothing more than rearrangement of an argumentation that always unfolds within the same wider problematic. Let us pause for a little to reflect on the preceding assertion.

As can be easily observed, there is a notable convergence towards the view that imperialism corresponds to forms of capitalism that are different from its liberal variant. In the analyses of classical Marxism, imperialism was linked to monopoly capitalism as a new stage in societies' economic development. In analyses following the Weber–Schumpeter logic, on the other hand, imperialism was interpreted as the result of politico-economic structures (pre-industrial or otherwise) that were in any case entirely unrelated to the deeper logic of liberal industrial capitalism. In the Lenin–Hilferding analyses, liberal (and more or less peace-loving) capitalism was represented as something irrevocably past, while in the texts of Schumpeter it was portrayed as an ineluctable future (sooner or later the monopoly structures would be eliminated as the capitalist system became more democratic and liberal). But in all instances the phenomenon of imperialism retained *structural discontinuities* which in extreme cases could be 'guaranteed' up until the time of their disappearance (a contingency in no way excluded even by Weber).

Even though we propose in Part II to conduct a detailed examination of the constitution of power relations within a social formation, we should note that the above perspectives deviate significantly from the way in which Marx himself regarded the social totality, that is to say the complex structural and decentralized coexistence of the economic, political and ideological levels. Both in classical Marxist analysis and in analyses along the lines of the Weber–Schumpeter intervention, the *coexistence* of the three social levels is *synchronic*, in the sense that the evolution of one plane directly reflects the development of the others. This is the well-known *essentialist schema* according to which all the social moments are organized in a framework of the deeper unity which they can also *express* at any moment (a Hegelian conception of social whole, for more details see Part II and Althusser and Balibar 1997).

In the economistic analyses of classical Marxism everything starts from the transformations on the economic plane. Subsequently, the entire politico-ideological organization of the capitalist states (the 'superstructure') – always contemporaneous with these transformations – adapts to them. Imperialism is thus a *stage*, reducible to the movement of maturation of the productive forces and reflecting the mode of existence of monopoly capitalism. On the other hand, the Weber–Schumpeter approach does not in any way constitute a refutation of the aforementioned (Hegelian) conception of the social whole. It *simply posits a different way of organizing the contemporaneous coexistence of the different social planes*. The entire critique amounts to a simple reversal of causality, which now passes from the level of the economy to that of politics. In Schumpeter's conception monopoly capitalism was nothing more than a 'departure from the pure liberal form of capitalism, which was possible because the capitalist class, influenced by survivals of pre-industrial social structures of an aristocratic type, was corrupted into monopolistic practices' (Mommsen 1982: 26). Here the economic movement reflects the pace of the political. As long as pre-industrial or pre-capitalist (aristocratic) structures prevail or are reproduced in the latter, social organization will systematically deviate from the pure liberal form of capitalism, and imperialism will be the inevitable consequence.

What Schumpeter ultimately achieves is to counterpose to the economism of the Marxist classics a naive and simplistic historicism, without modifying in any way his general manner of apprehending society. Imperialism is always a manifestation of the contemporaneous coexistence of the different social planes, externalising their essential inner unity. History is thus portrayed as a succession of 'essences' and the corresponding forms of expression that are assigned to them. Irrespective of whether it is to be dated *prior* to or *subsequent* to the liberal 'pure' capitalism, *imperialism is nothing more than a developmental stage*. It expresses either the 'end' of capitalist history or one phase before the 'end'.

3.3   Setting the base of recent discussions on capitalist imperialism: The kernel of the Schumpeterian–Weberian approach

As already mentioned, Schumpeter (and, in his way, Weber) shaped what we might call the 'liberal' approach to imperialism. But there is unfortunately still an element in their analyses that has passed unnoticed in contemporary discussions: the non-economic-reductionist theoretical agenda. Many recent heterodox and Marxist works construct their argumentation around this broader Weberian problematic.

Let us for now attempt to follow Schumpeter's argument. His basic aim was evidently to criticize the dominant classical analyses of imperialism (above all Hilferding's and Lenin's). To accomplish such a task he introduced an argument comprising *two distinct moments*.

On the one hand he firmly believed that capitalism was 'by nature anti-imperialist' in the sense that in a purely capitalist world imperialism is an *irrational process*. Capitalism 'can offer no fertile soil to imperialist impulses' (Schumpeter 1951: 73, 69). On the other hand imperialism pertains to the *conduct of the state*, perceived as an *end in itself*: 'expansion for its own sake' (ibid.: 6). Imperialist state policy is thus perceived as otiose, if regarded from a purely capitalist standpoint. Schumpeter believed that he was living in a *transitional phase* of capitalism, which was the unique outcome of the *coexistence* of 'two different epochs': capitalism and absolutism. Present-day capitalism existed alongside feudal remnants (with the bourgeoisie partially subject to the power of imperialist autocracy).[13]

This transitional social regime could be given the name of *imperialist capitalism* to differentiate it from *anti-imperialist pure capitalism*, a theoretical construct designating a hypothetical gradual countertrend extrapolated into the future (ibid.: 98). Imperialist capitalism in Schumpeter's conception is the temporary outcome of the *fusion* between two distinct 'logics of competition': the inter-state 'political' competition of absolutism (objectless state expansion) and the inter-enterprise 'economic' competition of capitalism (free trade). Schumpeter's argumentation is of course more complex than what might be suggested from this schematic summary. He analyses not only the peculiar historical form taken by the inter-connection between these two different forms of competition but also the way they change over time.

We are thus confronted with *two different logics of competition*, an economic and a political one. Economic competition and political competition operate at different levels, which must not be confused. According to Schumpeter, confusion of the two levels (economic reductionism) is the key mistake of Marxist theories. Imperialist capitalism can take different forms depending on the proportions of the mix between 'absolutist' political rivalries on the one hand and capitalist competition on the other.

Capitalism and *autocratic territorialism* as defined by Schumpeter do not operate in isolation from one another. Imperialist capitalism is a fact, but also represents a significant deviation from what is implicit in the logic of both capitalism and territorialism in the abstract. This problematic allows the formulation of many contemporary approaches which stress the 'tension' between the political and the economic 'logics' of capitalism.

For example, all that would be needed would be a slight *shift* in the Schumpeterian way of thinking – such as that formerly proposed by Löwe (1926) – in order to arrive at the argument that imperialism is a *constant* and not a temporary attribute of capitalism. Capitalism would now represent a permanent fusion between the two abovementioned logics of competition, with inter-state political competition (the territorialist logic) being not a feudal remnant but a rather stable way of organizing political space under capitalism as well. The capitalist state would, to use the well-known formulation proposed by Giddens (1987), approximate the Weberian conception of the 'container' of its own *autonomous* power (and so, as indicated, of its own 'expansive dynamic').

Following the same line of argumentation, Arrighi (1996: 32–4) remarked that under capitalism the *historical connection* between the two different 'logics' of competition can lead to two opposite 'modes of rule or logics of power'. In his analysis:

> Territorialist rulers identify power with the extent and populousness of their domains, and conceive of wealth/capital as a means or a by-product of the pursuit of territorial expansion. Capitalist rulers, in contrast, identify power with the extent of their command over scarce resources and consider territorial acquisitions as a means and a by-product of the accumulation of capital. Paraphrasing Marx's general formula of capitalist production (MCM´), we may render the difference between the two logics of power by the formulas TMT´ and MTM´, respectively. According to the first formula, abstract economic command or money (M) is a means or intermediate link in a process aimed at the acquisition of additional territories (T´ minus T = +ΔT). According to the second formula, territory (T) is a means or an intermediate link in a process aimed at the acquisition of additional means of payment (M´ minus M = +ΔM).
>
> (ibid.: 33)

We quote the above passage because we believe that it embraces a theoretical speculation more or less characteristic of the relevant contemporary literature. Apart from the authors already discussed, Wood (2005), for example, tends rather to agree with Arrighi, arguing, however, that the abovementioned formulations apply more properly to pre-capitalist empire building (a view approximating Schumpeter's). In the following sections we propose to examine some modern analyses that share the same general theoretical assumptions. Before embarking on this examination, here are two points of criticism to be made in relation to this *quasi-Schumpeterian* or *quasi-Weberian* problematic.

It must be admitted that there are several different ways of conceiving the 'inner logics' or social natures of a capitalist society, whether at the economic or at the political level. In our view the recent literature fails to elaborate a consistent theory of the state. The whole discussion appears to be trapped in a pseudodilemma between on the one hand viewing the state as a *thing* or an *instrument* and on the other conceiving of it as an *autonomous Subject*.[14] In the immediately following section we shall concern ourselves with some rather representative moments of these conceptions, contrasting them with the Marxian approach to the State. In Part II of this book we will have the opportunity to outline a Marxist conception of the state, according to which, unlike in the instrumentalist conception, class contradictions are not taken as being external to the state. But, by the same token, in contrast to the conception of state as a subject, in the view that we propose to outline, the contradictions within the state cease to be external to class struggle. In other words, We must not think the relationship between the economic and the political levels as a relationship of *externality*, with the state appearing as an autonomous entity to be counterposed to economic vested interests, sometimes capable of resisting them and at other times obliged to subordinate itself to them entirely. It is therefore advisable to exercise a certain amount of caution in our approach to those who seek to criticize the classical Marxist theories of imperialism adopting the Weberian logic. Unfortunately there is a whole constellation of contemporary analyses that move in this direction (see below).

3.4   Modern theories of 'New imperialism'

3.4.1   Imperialism as a symptom of capitalist crises: Short notes on Harvey's approach

Harvey's analysis of the 'New Imperialism' is ambitious and includes a wealth of information and insight. It is no accident that it has been at the centre of such wide-ranging discussion in the relevant contemporary literature.

The writer seeks basically to arrive at an interpretation of imperialism from the 'dialectical relationship between the politics of state and empire on the one hand and the molecular movements of capital accumulation in space and time on the other' (Harvey 2003: 89, also see p. 26). In this fashion, Harvey insists on regarding the economic ('movements of capital') and political ('politics of state and empire') levels as *autonomous and independent moments within the social totality*. Hence, 'the fundamental point is to see the territorial and the capitalist logics of power as distinct from each other' (ibid.: 29).

One of the basic consequences of the above is that the *state* and *capital or the fractions of capital* are represented as autonomous *agents* (ibid.: 89–91), whose actions 'intertwine in complex and sometimes contradictory ways' (ibid.: 29) because their 'motivations and interests' *differ* (ibid.: 27). This is of course the Weberian premise of the two interconnected logics of power. In this way Harvey defends the institutionalist problematic that portrays the state as entirely independent of (and so external to) the class struggle, pursuing its own 'territorial logic of power' at the initiative of state managers (ibid.: 29–30).

However, as we shall discover below, this thesis is, in the course of analysis, often subject to challenge and the state treated as if it is a tool in the hands of multinational corporations and finance capital (ibid.: 188–9, 135–6). Brenner (2006: 80–6) charges Harvey with failure to follow his own methodological premises consistently. Such inconsistency is in our view explicable from *his having embarked on his analysis without any clearly defined theory of the state*. Brenner is right when he argues that Harvey 'never tells us why he expects the territorial logic of power and the capitalist logic of power to come into conflict' and that 'his illustrative examples do not make his case' (ibid.: 81). Harvey's basic approach to imperialism moves along the same trajectory as the previously mentioned classical theories. Let us be more concrete.

Imperialism is characteristically linked to capitalist crises (Harvey 2003: 124, 126) and there are detectible links between the new imperialism and the overaccumulation crisis that developed capitalism has been embroiled in since the early 1970s. There are evidently two possible escape routes from the crisis. The first route enables capitalism to survive through 'a series of spatio-temporal fixes that absorb the capitalist surpluses in productive and constructive ways' (ibid.: 135). But of course this is the hard way, necessitating infrastructural reorganization in core capitalist countries. The second route requires the use of political and military means to turn international competition to the advantage of the more powerful states, not to mention financial means 'to rid

the system of overaccumulation by the visitation of crises of devaluation upon vulnerable territories. [...] Like war in relation to diplomacy,
finance capital intervention backed by state power frequently amounts
to accumulation by other means. An unholy alliance between state
powers and the predatory aspects of finance capital forms the cutting
edge of a "vulture capitalism" that is as much about cannibalistic practices and forced devaluations as it is about achieving harmonious global
development' (ibid.: 134, 136). In the absence of any other solution, the
'new imperialism' is what emerges from the second route to escape from
capitalism's declining profitability.

On this point the writer adopts – admittedly after complex
ratiocination – the traditional problematic of Hobson (ibid.: 126), having first introduced a Hegelian interpolation. In two brief paragraphs
in the *Philosophy of Right*, the German thinker outlines what amounts
to the classic underconsumptionist interpretation of imperialism.
The inner contradictions of bourgeois society impel it in this way to
seek solutions through external trade and colonial/imperial practices
(Hirschman 1976, Harvey ibid.).

What Harvey finds interesting in the above is the idea that in periods
of crisis 'capitalism must perpetually have something "outside of itself"
in order to stabilize itself' (ibid.: 140). This is why he also returns to
analysis of Luxemburg's theories with a view to refuting them. *In the
face of stagnant effective demand, capitalism can achieve accumulation not
only when it is able to find purchasing power in 'non-capitalist territories' (as
Luxemburg maintained) but also when it takes purchasing power away from
them (dispossession).* It therefore begins to appear plausible that some
sort of 'outside' is necessary for the stabilization of capitalism. This is
the source of the basic idea of 'accumulation by dispossession':

> Access to cheaper inputs is, therefore, just as important as access
> to widening markets in keeping profitable opportunities open.
> The implication is that non-capitalist territories should be forced
> open not only to trade (which could be helpful) but also to permit
> capital to invest in profitable ventures using cheaper labour power,
> raw materials, low-cost land, and the like. [...] Overaccumulation
> [...] is a condition where surpluses of capital [...] lie idle with no
> profitable outlets in sight. [...] What accumulation by dispossession
> does is to release a set of assets (including labour power) at very low
> (and in some instances zero) cost. Overaccumulated capital can seize
> hold of such assets and immediately turn them to profitable use.
>
> (ibid.: 139, 149)

Marx's fundamental mistake, according to Harvey, is that he relegates primitive accumulation, that is accumulation based upon predation, fraud and violence, to an 'original stage' that is considered no longer relevant (ibid.: 144).[15] But by the same token, Luxemburg too is partially wrong when she understands this 'outside' of capitalism as a closed system (ibid.). For Harvey, the idea that some sort of 'outside' is necessary for the stabilization of capitalism has of course some relevance. But capitalism can either make use of some pre-existing outside or it can actively create it (ibid.: 141). In the former case, the pre-existing outside is to be identified primarily with the public realm. The neoliberal logic of privatizations makes a pre-existing outside available for surplus capital: 'assets held by the state or in common were released into the market where overaccumulated capital could invest in them, upgrade them, and speculate in them' (ibid.: 158). But the same goal can be achieved when the outside is created through crises, which result in devaluation of existing capital assets and labour power: 'regional crises and highly localized place-based devaluations emerge as a primary means by which capitalism perpetually creates its own "other" in order to feed upon it' (ibid.: 151).

The capitalist state, which proves an indispensable tool at the disposal of capital (ibid.: 154), obviously contributes with all its might to this process. 'One of the prime functions of state interventions and of international institutions is to orchestrate devaluations in ways that permit accumulation by dispossession to occur without sparking a general collapse' (ibid.: 151). Although he many times asserts the contrary, in elaborating his argument Harvey has no qualms about reducing his 'political agent' to the intentions of the economic agents, implying that the state functions (perhaps willingly) as a helpful tool in the hands of financial rentiers and multinational corporations (ibid.: 184–6, 189, 147).

We do not intend to try to put forward a comprehensive critique of the weaknesses of the preceding train of thought. *The basic problem is that the profitability of capital and production of surplus value are treated as questions of income redistribution.* It is for this reason that the solution to the crisis of overaccumulation is also relegated to the status of *plunder*, which is nothing more than income transfer for the benefit of capital. The accumulation of capital is represented as being spatially *extensive* because it is based on a devaluation of the productive inputs that capital is able to impose. In this sense the neoliberal movement of capital is based on the *plundering of income*, situating Harvey rather closer to the problematic of Ricardian socialists. The solution to the problem of profitability is, again, *unequal exchange, permanent theft, dispossession.* His argument could probably also be read as a generalization of the theories of unequal exchange if the concept can be made to apply to the movement of capital in general and not to the economic relations between the individual states.

Still, the solution to capitalism's crisis cannot just come from some 'outside'. It must be *intensive* in the sense of presupposing a total reorganization of the conditions of exploitation and production of surplus value, that is to say an overall reconstitution of the movement of M-C-M´ inside the capitalist 'core' countries (a prospect that Harvey (ibid.: 108–24) takes into account in a way that excludes the consideration of class struggle). Harvey's essential argument has to do, quite directly in the final analysis, with the problematic of classical theories on imperialism. Capitalism cannot find domestic outlets as a solution to the economic crisis and accordingly 'exports' capital, imperialism and, on occasion, wars (ibid.: 180–2). Consequently, capital's contemporary strategy is accumulation by dispossession, which of course lies at the heart of imperialist practices:

> The rise in importance of accumulation by dispossession as an answer, symbolized by the rise of an international politics of neoliberalism and privatization, correlates with the visitation of periodic bouts of predatory devaluation of assets in one part of the world or another. And this seems to be the heart of what contemporary imperialist practice is about.
>
> (ibid.: 182)

The main elements of the traditional theories are preserved intact. The discussion on imperialism is transformed into a discussion on capitalist crises. Imperialist policies serve the neoliberal requirements of capital export from the strongest countries. Ultimately imperialism appears as a characteristic or a power that is possessed or preserved as a privilege by the powerful developed states (often as a symptom of crisis). From this viewpoint Harvey's intervention is symptomatic of the research strategy that seeks out the causes of imperialist policy in the structural crises that appear inside the developed capitalist economies.

3.4.2   How new is 'new imperialism'? Short comments on Callinicos' argumentation

Callinicos makes persistent references to a Marxist approach to imperialism. Unlike Harvey, he intentionally takes as his theoretical starting point the interventions of Lenin and Bukharin (coming to conclusions similar to those of Harvey). However, he does not dispute the fact of their having noteworthy limitations, demanding criticism, revision and refinement (Callinicos 1994; 2005; 2007: 537). He makes it clear that his own argumentation is based on a reorganization of, and not a mere reproduction of, classical theories of imperialism (ibid.). He classifies himself together with Harvey as one of the 'theorists of the new imperialism' (in accordance with the suggestion of Kiely 2005a: 32–4):

> Both Harvey and I have independently developed very similar conceptions of capitalist imperialism as constituted by the intersection of, respectively, capitalist and territorial logics of power and economic and geopolitical competition. One of the attractions of this approach is that it avoids any attempt to reduce the geopolitical strategies of states to economic interests [...]. The Marxist theory of imperialism analyses the forms in which geopolitical and economic competition have become interwoven in modern capitalism, but does not seek to collapse these analytically distinct dimensions into one another. [...] The real challenge to Harvey's and my position is not that it is economic reductionist, but rather precisely the opposite.
>
> (Callinicos 2007: 539)

The above quotation gives a concise summary of Callinicos' viewpoint, which (like that of Harvey) amounts to a return to the well-known Weberian problematic. On the question of 'geopolitical competition' Callinicos frankly admits that he is influenced by contemporary analyses of the neo-Weberian historical sociologists (Callinicos 2006). The following brief comments may be helpful in highlighting the overall logic of the writer's viewpoint.

Firstly, following the same line of argumentation as Harvey, Callinicos sees capitalist imperialism as the result of a historic encounter between *two different forms of competition*, (i) economic competition between capitals and (ii) geopolitical competition between states. Moreover, these two forms of competition begin definitively to merge only towards the end of the nineteenth century. Callinicos is here reiterating the well-known argument of Hobson and the classics of Marxism, regarding present-day imperialism as a relatively recent historical phenomenon that emerges somewhere around the end of the nineteenth century (Callinicos 2005; 2007: 540–1).

Callinicos' view is that up until that point political competition was something separate from economic competition. Following Brenner (see below) – and up to a point Schumpeter – he falsely believes that during the phase of transition from feudalism to capitalism, that is to say the period of military expansionism and constitution of states, geopolitical competition is imbued with feudal elements (Callinicos 2005), with the result that this transitional phase of capitalism is extended into the early twentieth century. But his finding also betrays a conviction that in this transitional phase the dimension of politics is something entirely separate from the overall changes at the economic level, retaining conspicuous feudal features or residues.[16] We propose to embark on a more comprehensive critique of these views in Part II. For the moment suffice it to say that the initial stage of transition to capitalism already *presupposes a state with manifestly capitalist characteristics* (notwithstanding the fact that the bourgeoisie may not yet have attained full political supremacy), meaning that the specifically capitalist conjoining of economic and political 'competition' has been accomplished in the structural sense long before the turn of the twentieth century (see Chapter 4, also Poulantzas 1973: 157–67, Foucault 2007).

Secondly, Callinicos (2007: 545) does in fact try to avoid reproducing the logic of economistic reductionism: 'capitalist imperialism is best understood, I claim, as the intersection of economic and geopolitical competition. But, since (*per hypothese*) these forms of competition differ in structure and are (immediately at least) supported by the interests of different actors, how they interrelate is historically variable.' Evidently, in order to differentiate his own position from that of the writers who would reduce geopolitical competition to economic competition, he reverts to a problematic of institutional historicism (a conception which as we saw before notably pervades Harvey's analysis also). According to it, the relations between the various levels of a social formation can be reduced to malleable interpersonal relations between independent agents belonging to different social groups. As Callinicos (with Ashman (2006)) characteristically notes, 'the interrelation of economic and geopolitical competition must be grounded in an account of the rules of reproduction of *two groups of actors*, capitalists and state managers.' These social groups are distinct both in their collective motivations and in their vested interests. Thus, it is ultimately the historical form of these interests that will shape the form of the interrelation between capital (economic) and the state (political).

Thirdly, the definition of capitalist imperialism as the historical outcome of an interconnection between capital and the state means, according to Callinicos (2007: 541, emphasis added), that '*the process of inter-state competition became subsumed under that between capitals.*'

The sentence just quoted is already reproducing the *reductionist* logic that characterizes the traditional theories of Marxism. But the state is not subordinating itself to capital as an inert instrument. It is a *free agent*, whose interests harmonize with those of capital.[17] In any case, the upshot is that Callinicos' analysis in the end suffers from the same problems as Harvey's: the state becomes dependent on capital because the securing of its '*own interests*' depends on the promotion of capitalist profits and capital accumulation.[18]

Fourthly, the aforementioned institutional view of the *collective agents* enables Callinicos (1994, 2005, 2007) to proceed with the following periodization: Not only does capitalist imperialism get underway at the end of the nineteenth century but it may be divided into two separate phases depending on the relations between economic and geopolitical competition. During the first period, covering the twentieth century up to the Second World War, 'economic and geopolitical competition were mutually reinforcing' (Callinicos 2007: 546). This provides a retrospective vindication of classical theories of imperialism because even if they do not succeed in providing us with a comprehensive position on imperialism, they nevertheless do succeed in conveying an accurate picture of their times, placing emphasis on the link between state and capital. During the second period, by contrast, 'the second half of the twentieth century was [...] marked by a partial dissociation of economic and geopolitical competition' (ibid.). We are now in the era of the Cold War, when the United States 'was able simultaneously to integrate all the regions of advanced capitalism into a single transnational political and economic space' (ibid.). In this instance the competition between capitals did not have the same potential for transformation into military conflicts as it occurred in the preceding period (for more on this see Callinicos 1994).

There is nothing surprising about the criticism to which both Callinicos and also Harvey have been subjected as a result of being identified with the traditional reductionism and economism of classical Marxist theories (Kiely 2006) and/or, effectively, with the positions of Weberian historical sociologists and theoreticians of the realist school of international relations (Pozo-Martin 2006). In reality, as can be seen from the abovementioned periodization, Callinicos' methodological historicism enables him to shift at will in either direction. What is most important, however, is that the prerequisite for the previous shifts has been a failure to comprehend the specifically capitalist character of the state.[19] This is a misunderstanding that stems from the historicist way in which he examines society as a whole. We shall return in detail to this in Part II.

3.4.3   The new imperialism as an 'economic relation'

Harvey's intervention should perhaps be recorded within a broader frame of reference, which in a relevant extension of classical Marxist theories seeks out the roots of 'Western imperialism', and in particular that of the United States, in phenomena of (economic) crisis making their appearance inside developed capitalist societies. However, it could be understood as an *extreme variant* of the abovementioned train of thought (such as that put forward by Callinicos) that 'Western capital' moves beyond the political boundaries of the West in an international (global) quest for privileged spheres of profitability, without this necessarily being linked with crisis processes or crisis phenomena. On the contrary, it could be *a necessity imposed by the very nature of capitalism*. This notion is also very much present in the relatively recent intervention of Wood (2005) to which we now propose to devote some attention (as representative of a broader literature).[20]

We do not here propose to expand the discussion into all aspects of Wood's analysis. We will confine ourselves exclusively to the question of defining *the new imperialism* and the presuppositions that accompany it. According to the writer, the term 'new imperialism' denotes the form of imperialism that emerged after the Second World War in conjunction with the economic and political-military hegemony of the United States. The new imperialism is basically an 'economic relationship' and requires 'brutal force to implant and sustain it' (ibid.: 153). It is out of this that there emerges the differentiation between the 'new' imperialism and other older historical forms assumed at various times by imperialism (capitalist or otherwise).

To better understand Wood's argument we should note that capital becomes more comprehensible if seen as an *autonomous entity* which, while *always* retaining a specific national *origin* (ownership), can expand into a *geographical space* which much transcends national boundaries (of the state in question). From this viewpoint capital cannot in any sense be comprehended as a social relationship of exploitation within the community in which it is operating, with the result that we are now embarking on *radical* differentiations from Marx's theoretical system. In fact Wood's analysis is entrapped in what Marx called *fetishism of capital* focusing on the fact that the 'social relation' of capital appears to everyday experience 'as the mere fruit of property in capital' (Marx 1991: 516, 497). Individual 'capital' as 'thing' seems to be moving away from its national basis, expanding into a politically fragmented international space, discovering fields of application, and producing profits which however never cease to refer the capital to an 'ethnic' entity (that is to say to its origins at the *centre*).[21] As we propose to argue in detail in Part II of the book, such a conception fails to capture the reality of actual capital movement. Capital that crosses national borders is incorporated into a different process of capitalist accumulation, in accordance with the terms that prevail within the recipient country. It 'represents' on each occasion different conditions of class exploitation, irrespective of who possesses the 'legal right' to the surplus value produced.

Manifestly flirting with the dependence theory, Wood (2005: 154) moreover considers that global geopolitical space is divided up between 'imperial powers' and 'subordinate states'. The problem of the new imperialism can thus be formulated as follows: *if the economic hegemony of 'imperial capital' is extended beyond the range of efficacy of its nation-state, the latter is obliged to resort to political imperialism of a type appropriate to developed capitalism, so as to secure from a distance the specific legal and political order that is required in its everyday transactions.* The method of positing the question is reminiscent of a logic corresponding to that found in classical Marxist analyses. 'Western capital' or 'imperialist capital' functioning in straightforward accordance with the 'operations of the market' is able to engage in limitless exploitation of the 'subordinate economies' (ibid.: 20), thereby imparting to the developed capitalist centre a power of 'imperial domination far beyond the capacities of direct political rule or colonial occupation' (ibid.: 21). 'Actually existing globalization, then, means the opening of subordinate economies and their vulnerability to imperial capital, while the imperial economy remains sheltered as much as possible from the obverse effects' (ibid.: 134).

It thus becomes comprehensible why the new imperialism is regarded as a 'directly economic relationship' (ibid.: 153). The extension of 'imperialist capital' prescribes relationships of global economic domination, which in turn comprise the domain of a new empire. More concretely:

Not only imperial powers but subordinate states have proved necessary to the rule of global capital. [...] The 'globalized' world is more than ever a world of nation states. The new imperialism we call globalization, precisely because it depends on a wide-ranging economic hegemony that reaches far beyond any state's territorial boundaries or political domination, is a form of imperialism more dependent than any other on a system of multiple states [...] Imperial hegemony in the world of global capitalism, then, means controlling rival economies and states without going to war with them.

(ibid.: 154, 157)

In contrast to current theories of globalization, Wood's version highlights an imperialism in which nation-states retain their significance as intermediate links in the moment of 'global capital' (ibid.: 154).[22] Present-day wars are of a different character to those of the past. They do not correspond to a regime of generalized conflict between the dominant imperialist powers, but have to deal with the 'constant threat of force' (ibid.: 164) based on the military power of the new empire of the United States: 'this endless *possibility* of war that imperial capital needs to sustain its hegemony over the global system of multiple states' (ibid.: 165).

If we have chosen to refer to Wood's intervention, it is because we regard it as representative of a general framework of thought whose influence, embodied in a number of different variants, is still very much in currency in the present-day discussion. As may be readily understood, these views reflect a logic which, to a greater or lesser extent, characterized both classical Marxist theories and post-war neo-Marxist approaches to dependence. The central idea is reducible to a *scheme for income redistribution*. Whether through trade flows or through financial flows (within a neoliberal framework), the capitalist 'centre' always appears to be extracting surplus value from the 'periphery' and it is precisely this form of economic 'exploitation' that comprises the core of today's new imperialism.[23] The latter is politically supported by the action of the hegemonic imperialist states (though not to the same extent). It is a conception that comes very close to the conclusions of the world-system(s) theory.

If we accept the significance of the nation-state in contemporary 'globalized' capitalism (a notion that represents a blatant breach with analyses that speak of a globalized bourgeoisie freed from attachments to specific states so as to be able to create the prerequisites for a global authority (for more on this discussion see Chapter 10)) the above line of argument may lead to either of two different intellectual stances in relation to the links between the new and the old imperialism. All this takes us a long way back in time, to a dilemma with which the thought of Kautsky was required to grapple.

3.4.4   Once more on Kautsky's dilemma: Different conceptions of 'new imperialism'

The dilemma of 'inter-imperialist conflict vs. global imperialist coalition', that is the dilemma on the subject of ultra-imperialism that plagued Kautsky from very early on, bore within itself the logic of *reformism*. It was this that attracted Lenin's harsh criticism. Kautsky's line of thought came up against the following dilemma. Although he himself never ceased to believe that developed capitalism needed to be able to expand abroad in order to survive (seeking raw materials and outlets for capital), at the same time, he thought that intra-imperialist conflicts and military confrontations were contrary to the long-term interests of the bourgeoisie. This was because the latter was faced simultaneously with opposition both from the metropolitan working class and the national liberation movements in the colonies. This contradiction could be resolved only through a peaceful ultra-imperialism (a notion which effectively detached the abolition of imperialism from the tasks of the revolution, see Kautsky 1914; Lenin, *CW*, vol. 22). What was necessary was the creation of a 'holy alliance' between the great capitalist powers, a collaborative imperialism (albeit not of equals) by means of which the differences in imperialist power could be incorporated internally without the outbreak of violent antagonisms.

In the present-day discussion the same question, along with its variations, comes back again and again. There are accordingly a number of analyses which, while agreeing on the logic of the new imperialism, differ on the question of how the form of inter-imperialist contradictions is to be interpreted. Some of these approximate Lenin in his analysis of the imperialist chain, placing particular emphasis on the contradictions between the great imperialist powers, while others are more receptive to the problematic of Kautsky.[24] The line of thought is essentially familiar. Competition between individual national capitals in the international sphere draws in and transforms the politics of the corresponding national states, which notwithstanding the assessments of the supporters of globalization have not lost their salience. The imperialism of the capitalist centres is either collaborative in character or otherwise this 'collaboration' could perhaps be regarded as a brief respite between the inevitable sharpened inter-imperialist contradictions. The following comments will necessarily be brief (with all the dangers inevitably entailed in presenting a summary account of a massive volume of writing).

Many theoreticians of the new imperialism attach particular importance to the fact that inter-imperialist rivalries persist, or at least that there is the permanent potential of their coming back. Imperialism is a game of economic hegemony *also* played between the states of developed capitalism, and all present-day political conflicts and wars may be situated to a greater or lesser extent within such a framework.[25] According to Rees (2006: 37) it is in the 'critical meeting point between overwhelming military strength and relative economic decline' that 'we can best see the motivation of the US increasingly to rely on its military capacity to discipline both its allies and its competitors on the world stage' (for more see Kiely 2006: 210–11).

On the other hand, several commentators share Kautsky's problematic, being more inclined to see the contradictions between the imperialist powers as subordinated to a logic of *collaboration* at least during the period that followed the end of the Second World War.[26] According to these writers the new element characterizing imperialism today, by contrast with classical imperialism, is that *there is no unequivocal relationship* between 'imperialist capital' and the countries in which it is invested. With the collapse of colonialism there is a new type of association between capitalism and imperialism, the key element of which is: 'that *the densest imperial networks and institutional linkages, which had earlier run north-south between imperial states and their formal or informal colonies, now came to run between the US and the other major capitalist states'* (Panitch and Gindin 2003). This 'does not mean that capital is no longer tied to particular nation states, but it does mean that the world cannot be divided into *exclusive* blocs. [...] As things stand we have an international order in which competition exists alongside high levels of cooperation between the major states, led by the US [...], but other states are happy to cooperate in this order provided some gains are made for all' (Kiely 2006: 213, 211–12).

It is also worth noting that in the most recent analyses one frequently sees great emphasis on the role of the United States as the *driving force* behind global development. Without wishing to ignore the importance of the American economy, we should emphasize that this is a conception that underestimates the role of class struggle in the mode of organization of capitalist development inside nation-states. It is in any case for this reason that the same analyses share the view of Kautsky, which they have arrived at *from a different route*. Kautsky considered that it was the resistance of the workers that had forced the imperialist powers to avoid sharpening the conflicts between themselves. By contrast, in the preceding analyses co-operation between the imperialist states of the capitalist centre emerges from the growth of an increasingly integrated world market.[27]

The basic element linking together all the above approaches of the new imperialism is in the final analysis the non-acceptance of the concept, central to Marxist thought, of *social capital* or *collective capitalist*. We will have the opportunity to concern ourselves with the details of this question in Parts II and III of this book. The individual capitals that are introduced into a social formation are seen as foreign 'things' that *either* are unable to be integrated into the elements of social capital and so persist in functioning antagonistically vis-à-vis 'domestic' capital in the first case, *or* are included in social capital so as to decompose it. In one case 'imperialist capital' exploits the 'subordinate economies' (Wood 2005: 20), while in the other 'domestic capital' tends 'to be "dis-articulated"' as a coherent and independent national bourgeoisie' (Panitch and Gindin 2003).

3.5   Geopolitical competition as a remnant from the pre-capitalist past: Recent echoes of Schumpeter's thesis

As ascertained previously, Callinicos' analysis (and that of Wood as well) of the origins of present-day imperialism is undoubtedly influenced by the arguments we meet with in the work of Brenner (1976, 1982, 2001).

   In the analysis of Brenner (1982: 16) each historical period is characterized by its own *property relations* which, once established, impose narrow boundaries on every form of economic development. This means that property relations limit and shape the behaviour of economic actors, who are on each occasion in a position to pursue rigorously specific strategies for reproduction of the social and economic positions they occupy. One of the basic corollaries of such a thesis is that it imposes a *mild historicist problematic*[28] on the investigation of capitalism, particularly on the investigation of the latter's early phase during the period of its transition from feudalism. Consequently, one of the most conspicuous peculiarities in the analysis of Brenner (1982, 1976) has to do with the reappraisal of absolutism. According to the latter, the social property relations accompanying the period of absolutism are not yet capitalistic but neither are they any longer specifically feudal. Exactly the same is true of the character of the absolutist state, in the sense that it is caught up in the maelstrom of *geopolitical accumulation* (Brenner 1982: 36–41) that generally characterizes pre-capitalist periods (for more in this connection see Lacher 2005, Teschke 2003, Pijl 2006, Wood 2005).

   In pre-capitalist periods – always according to the logic of Brenner (ibid.) – for a number of reasons there was no incentive for increasing production through the introduction of technology. As a result, the basic means at the disposal of the ruling class for improving its own material situation (apart from through collecting land rent from the peasants) was through *territorial expansion*. This involved a number of prerequisites, such as, for example, expenditure on military forces and armaments, but also more effective political organization of the feudal domains with a view to concentrating resources to finance military operations. Pre-capitalist social organization thus necessarily included a dynamic of territorial expansion and constitution of states, within which the dominant process is that of geopolitical accumulation through the conquest of new territory. This process is essentially accumulation through redistribution of wealth,[29] and to some extent resembles the Schumpeterian logic.

The above train of thought can lead us to some general conclusions, which come into conflict with our theoretical orientation as we shall have the opportunity to demonstrate in Part II.

It is surely no surprise that not only Callinicos who, as we have already ascertained, draws on the problematic of Brenner but also Lacher (2005) and Teschke (2003, 2007), whose work is an immediate extension of the logic of the latter, should more or less share the neo-Weberian notion that geopolitical competition between states preceded capitalism and is not at all linked to the particular logic of social organization that corresponds to it. It is a view that leads inevitably to the conclusion that 'capitalism [...] came to exist, politically, in the form of a system of territorial states – a historical legacy of the post-feudal period that continues to structure capitalism until the present day (though perhaps not beyond)' (Lacher 2005: 34; see also Teschke and Lacher 2007). In the same train of thought Brenner (2006: 84) concludes:

> Abstractly speaking, a single state governing global capital is perfectly conceivable and probably most appropriate from the standpoint of capital. [...] That capitalism is governed by multiple states is the result of the historical fact that it emerged against the background of a system of multiple feudal states, and, in the course of its development, transformed the component states of that system into capitalist states but failed to alter the multi-state character of the resulting international system.

In the opinion of the writers, absolutism did not promote a capitalist bourgeoisie, so that the absolutist state failed to become a modern state. It was not even a precursor of, or a transitional stage towards, a modern state (Teschke 2003: 189–93). Mercantilism was a rationalization strategy of absolutist rulers who were failing to promote capitalist industry. Mercantilism's social rationale was based on the persistence of non-capitalist social property relations, which necessitated the internal and external accumulation of surplus by political means, either through direct political coercion of direct producers or through a politically maintained unequal exchange, that is through political accumulation (ibid.: 210). Hence, according to Lacher:

> The argument outlined above does *not* imply that the international relations of capitalist modernity are somehow marked by a persistent logic of absolutist geopolitics. To be sure, during the 19th century, and even into the 20th, there were absolutist remnants that continued to exert influence over the politics, economy and culture of capitalist societies [...]. Still, if absolutism bequeathed capitalism a territorial framework, if the products of the logic of political accumulation that had operated in the absolutist period continued to structure capitalist modernity by imparting to it an inter-state dimension, that does not mean that the *absolutist* international system persisted.
>
> (Lacher 2005: 34)

A Schumpeterian logic echoes in the above formulations. We do not propose to embark on a detailed commentary of these views because it would divert us from our purpose. Let us focus on the basic position that until recently the dynamic of imperialist competition has not entailed anything specifically capitalistic: to a significant extent it is an inheritance from absolutism.[30] From this viewpoint the traditional periodization of imperialism (which we have already noted) continues to apply, while the distance from the neo-Weberian analysis is not ultimately so great: for a significant part of its history (until recently), capitalism has coexisted with a geopolitical competition that is foreign to its specific historical character.

3.6 Social imperialism theories: Back to the 'prestige' aspect of political power

A number of other interesting analyses share a similar non-reductionist theoretical orientation with the theoretical framework mentioned above. However, and this is the striking difference, these analyses place a greater emphasis on *internal* class factors, totally politicizing the phenomenon of imperialism. Mommsen (1977: 28; 1982: 93–9) calls this the orientation of *social imperialism*. The position of Wehler in his early writing (1970) is characteristic in this line of argumentation. Imperialism is treated as a means to the end of keeping the traditional elites in power over a community in rapid change.[31] Evoking an 'endogenous' theory of imperialism (Mommsen 1982: 99), Wehler's argumentation echoes some of the (interesting) ideas expressed earlier by Weber.

Mommsen partially disagrees with the above conception, considering that imperialism cannot be the only material underpinnings for processes of political manipulation by the dominant elite. An approach that sees imperialism as an *instrument* in the hands of specific social groups, given that imperialist passions have acquired such broad resonance among the broad masses of the population (Mommsen 1977: 28), is very one-sided. By contrast, he thinks that greater emphasis should be placed on linking classical imperialism to the rising middle classes and most certainly to the rising upper bourgeois class. 'These groups use imperialism both as a vehicle for ideological emancipation from the traditional ruling classes, above all from the aristocracy, and as a defensive strategy against the rising lower classes, that is to say the organized working class supporters of socialism' (ibid.: 28). This is perhaps the most important 'reason why imperialism has always been represented as closely interwoven with nationalist ideology' (ibid.). In this sense nationalism, which sooner or later is converted into imperialism, has functioned as an aggressive ideology against anachronistic ruling classes, while at the same time comprising a means of mobilization for the rising bourgeois fractions of the passive lower social classes (ibid.: 29).

Always, according to Mommsen, economic factors are not losing their significance, but *they are being reduced to the level of politics*. Imperialism serves the long-term 'economic' interest of the ruling classes, which have no other objective than to preserve the existing social hierarchy. It is only as one of their secondary and non-determinant aspects that imperialist rivalries serve economic interests at the level of the individual, that is to say interests linked to minority groups of capitalists and speculators (Mommsen, ibid.).

In a very interesting intervention Willoughby (1986) argues along similar lines. At the end of an extensive and very well-documented analysis of the relevant literature he highlights the basic weakness of both post-war and pre-war classical theories of imperialism. On the one hand he perceives the economic *reductionist* character of the latter and consequently the vulnerability that is entailed by their not really being anything more than 'a radical theory of capital expansion' (ibid.: 8). On the other he presents a very pertinent critique of the parasitical (and no doubt equally reductionist) later Marxist approaches, considering that 'it is not true that global capitalism must coerce the Third World into a position of permanent economic backwardness. On the level of the abstract theory of capital expansion and exploitation, it is not possible to argue for the inevitable necessity of the North-South divide' (ibid.: 54, emphasis in the original text).

According to Willoughby if there is something that should be retained from the classical Marxist theories of imperialism, it is the investigation of 'the ways in which the international economy's evolution affects the economic and political reproduction of social relations in the advanced capitalist center' (ibid.: 18). He thus establishes as a central element of his analysis the 'attempt to link capitalist evolution to political and social structures', providing 'a meeting ground for Marxist and non-Marxist theories of imperialism' (ibid.). This aspect of the question too contributes to turning his interest towards Veblen, together with Weber and even Schumpeter, who seek out a primarily *social* framework for the interpretation of imperialism. From this viewpoint his theoretical strategy is closely linked to the corresponding strategy of Mommsen.

In his argumentation international coercion and conflict is not optimally functional for the reproduction of global capitalism. 'It is not even necessary to assume that the ultimate result of imperialist behaviour is rational from the perspective of capital' (ibid.: 57). 'Understanding why capitalist imperialism is *not* an *economic* inevitability is the key to determine why imperialist coercion and conflict are such inevitable features of the capitalist global economy' (ibid.: 45). For Willoughby this makes investigation of the *social factors* contributing to the development of imperialist policy and ideology within the developed capitalist nation-states (ibid.: 59) a subject of particular interest.

Within this framework, his analysis is guided by the view that the imperialist process is in essence a means of political and ideological incorporation (with the potential to fail) of the population of the developed states into existing power structures:

> [T]he real benefits that individual corporations and institutions receive from capital expansion are transmitted politically and culturally to the population as a whole. State agents, often utilizing racially and sexually charged rhetoric, are able to induce large sectors of the population to support the politics of oppression. [...] The expansion of capital, by permitting the integration of large sectors of the populace into metropolitan-sponsored foreign activities, makes large sectors of the population susceptible to this politics.
>
> (Willoughby 1986: 62)

The interesting element in this approach (both of Mommsen and Willoughby) is that in its interpretation of imperialism it places emphasis on *internal* social processes. This distinguishes it in two ways both from the classical and from the post-war approaches to imperialism. The inner dynamic of social formations takes precedence over whatever influences derive from the international environment. At the same time imperialism appears to be a 'quality' of all states without exception and not a structural element in a global system that imposes the political geography between the powerful metropolitan states and the dependent states of the periphery.

Part II Theories of Imperialism vis-à-vis Marx's *Critique of Political Economy*

4
The State as a Vehicle of both Capitalist Expansionism and Decolonization: Historical Evidence and Theoretical Questions

4.1 Introduction

Following the general conclusions of Part I it is argued that Marxist theories of imperialism embody a certain specific interpretation of Marxist theory, or of a theoretical paradigm in Marxism, vis-à-vis the primary objects of analysis of the said theory, that is capitalism, its stages of historical evolution, its internationalization, its expansionism and its crises.

Theoretical discussion of the main theses put forward in these approaches has exposed certain contradictions, drawing attention also to a theoretical void: *the lack of a coherent theory of the CMP, the capitalist social formation and the capitalist state*.

As a result, writers in this tradition are frequently unable to provide a coherent interpretation of historical development. Why do certain former colonies, such as the USA, Canada or Australia belong in the category of 'central' capitalist social formations and states (in accordance with centre–periphery theories), while others continue to be regarded merely as peripheral appurtenances of the central formations? Is there a theory of the capitalist state to justify the thesis that the collapse of colonialism after World War II is so insignificant to the periodization of international capitalist relations (or 'global capitalism') that the 'final stage' of capitalism commencing in the last decades of the nineteenth century is arguably still continuing? To pose the same question differently: on what theoretical grounds, apart from the theory of 'monopoly capitalism', can the expansionism and colonialism that preceded the period of so-called imperialism, as opposed to the late colonial era (from the late nineteenth century to World War II), be bracketed off as a distinct period in the history of capitalism? On grounds of Marx's theory of the CMP this period now has to be revisited. Why does the second colonial period have more affinities with the present-day non-colonial post-war era than with the era of early colonialism? Last but not least, is there a tendency towards expansionism that is innate in every form of capitalist domination, that is also in the less developed capitalist states that are not to be classified as being in the supposedly 'ripe' or 'monopoly capitalist' stage? Witness the Iran–Iraq war. Or should all national and intra-state antagonisms – in the former Soviet Union, in former Yugoslavia, in Cyprus – be understood only as the result of 'imperialist interventions' by the capitalist 'Great Powers'?

In this introductory chapter to Part II we attempt further to clarify the abovementioned questions, so as to better plot the course of our analysis. Starting from some preliminary definitions, drawn on the one hand from Marx's *Critique of Political Economy* (mainly developed in *Capital* and his other mature writings), and on the other from selected historical evidence, we will focus on the blind spots in the theories of imperialism that impede comprehension of present-day capitalist relations of class exploitation and political domination.

4.2   Capitalism

One comprehensive introductory definition of capital could be the following: a historically specific social relation that expresses itself in the form of 'money as an end in itself' or 'money that creates more money', in accordance with the formula M-C-M′ where M stands for money and C for commodity. Marx has shown that this formula of money circulation is actually the expression of capitalist economic and social relations, incorporating as it does the process of direct production, which now becomes production-for-exchange and production-for-profit. A historically specific form of exploitation then emerges: capitalist exploitation of the labouring classes. Money has now become the most general form of appearance of value and thus of capital (for more on this, see in the following chapters).

In the context of capitalist economic and social relations the movement of money as capital binds the production process *to* the circulation process: commodity production becomes a phase or moment (and indeed, for the whole valorization process, the *decisive* moment) of the circuit of social capital:

$$M - C_{Mp}^{Lp} \ldots P \ldots C' - M'$$

The capitalist appears on the market as the owner of money (*M*) buying commodities (*C*) which consist of means of production (*M*p) and labour power (*L*p). In the process of production (*P*) these commodities C are productively used up so as to generate an output of other commodities, a product (*C'*) whose value exceeds that of *C*. Finally, he/she sells that output to recover a sum of money (*M'*) higher than (*M*). In Marx's own words: 'Capital is money; capital is commodities. In truth, however, value is here the subject of a process, in which, while constantly assuming the form in turn of money and of commodities, it at the same time changes in magnitude, throws off surplus-value from itself considered as original value, and thus valorizes itself independently. [...] *The circulation of money as capital is an end in itself*, for the expansion of value takes place only within this constantly renewed movement. *The circulation of capital is therefore limitless*. [...] As the conscious bearer of this movement, the possessor of money becomes a capitalist [...] it is only insofar as the appropriation of ever more and more wealth in the abstract is the sole driving force of his operations that, he functions as a capitalist, i.e. as capital personified and endowed with consciousness and a will' (Marx 1990: 255, 253–4, emphasis added).

4.3   Early forms of capitalism and primitive accumulation

For labour power to constitute a commodity it must have undergone a long historical process of social transformation and revolution from which there emerges the free worker. The formation of the capital–wage labour relationship is thus a historically specific form of class power inseparable from the institutional, legal and ideological structure of the 'free individual' and of equality. As already stated, Marx describes the internal interdependencies which condition this historic social order of things as the CMP. The *CMP* (and not 'the economy' in general) is thus constituted as the pre-eminent object of Marxian theory:

> One thing, however, is clear: Nature does not produce on the one side owners of money or commodities, and on the other men possessing nothing but their own labour-power. [...] Had we gone further, and inquired under what circumstances all, or even the majority of, products take the form of commodities, we should have found that this only happens on the basis of one particular mode of production, the capitalist one.
>
> (Marx 1990: 273)

Capitalist economic relations become stabilized for the first time in the form of commercial capital in the city-states of Italy, starting from Amalfi as early as the ninth century.[1] From the thirteenth century onwards the two glorious rival city-states of Venice and Genoa take the lead. As Braudel notes:

> The really crucial turning-point was the terrible Fourth Crusade which began with the capture of the Christian stronghold Zara (1203), and ended with the sack of Constantinople in 1204. Until then, Venice had been a parasite on the Byzantine Empire, eating it from within. Now it all but became her property. But all the Italian cities benefited from the collapse of Byzantium; similarly they all benefited from the Mongol invasion which after about 1240 opened up for a century or so a continental route from the Black Sea to China and India, one that had the inestimable advantage of by-passing the Islamic barrier.
>
> (Braudel 1984: 109–10)

This early capitalism was based on the big trading and finance company, which dominated production of saleable goods, turning it into capitalist production. Capitalist merchant companies constantly spread commodity relations not only by expanding their own economic activity (in the context of which labour is directly subordinated to capital as wage labour) but also by transforming and indirectly absorbing production processes that had previously been mediated through non-capitalist social relations.

This conclusion is predicated first and foremost on the finding that under certain circumstances commodity production becomes synonymous with indirect subordination of labour to capital. As the non-capitalist ruling classes disintegrate, with the feudal estates eliminated and the state operating in the interests of capital, artisans and farmers are transformed into market producers and manufacturers of commodities.

So long as the artisan or the farmer could sell his commodities to different merchants, he could retain the economic status of an independent commodity producer. But the diversification of demand and consequently of production, along with the need to produce not for a local but for various distant markets (both tendencies created by the increasing division of labour and the increasing significance of market relations), made the producer increasingly dependent on one specific merchant, who would supply him with raw materials and become the *buyer-up* of the producer's total output. Since the buyer-up is now the economic agent who places the product on the different markets he determines the type of product and the quantity of products that each artisan or farmer working for him is to produce. He places advance orders for the wares he requires and in many cases begins to supply the direct producer with raw materials.

In this way the buyer-up in effect acquires control over the production process of the individual producers, that is of their means of production. It is he who decides the extent of output and its degree of diversification as well as establishing the division of labour among the separate producers under his control, in accordance with productivity criteria that he sets, and changes in demand to which he adjusts. The buyer-up can now lower the prices of the commodities he purchases (buys up) from direct producers to a level which yields for the producer an income not higher than a worker's wage. The system that now emerges is what Rubin (1989: 159) calls 'the cottage or domestic or decentralized system of large-scale industry', which 'paved the way for the complete reorganization of industry on a capitalist basis'. The farmer or artisan becomes a form of façon worker remunerated by a 'piece-wage'.

By the late fifteenth century the new economic relations had spread throughout Europe from the Baltic and North Sea city-states and the Hanseatic League (twelfth to sixteenth century) to Portugal and Spain, Holland, Flanders, England and France, thus giving rise to a 'world capitalist economy'.

The process of social transformation that led to the formation and gradual predominance of the capitalist social order is described by Marx as 'primitive accumulation'. It entails on the one hand private appropriation of feudal or common property by the landlords, who are now transformed into modern 'rentiers' – appropriators of capitalist land-rent,[2] and on the other the creation of masses of proletarians, who were 'freed' from all forms of proprietorship over the means of production. It entails establishment of a centralised state power (the absolutist state) capable of upholding[3] the new capitalist social order that emerges from appropriation of property and proletarianization while at the same time legitimizing it as a regime of 'freedom and equality'.[4]

According to Marx (1990: 878–9, emphasis added): 'the prelude of the revolution that laid the foundation of the capitalist mode of production was played out in the last third of the fifteenth century and the first few decades of the sixteenth. A mass of "free" and unattached proletarians was hurled onto the labour-market by the dissolution of the bands of feudal retainers [...]. Although the *royal power, itself a product of bourgeois development*, forcibly hastened the dissolution of these bands of retainers in its strife for absolute sovereignty, it was by no means the sole cause of it. It was rather that the great feudal lords, in their defiant opposition to the king and Parliament, created an incomparably larger proletariat by the forcible driving of the peasantry from the land, to which the latter had the same feudal right as the lords themselves, and by the usurpation of the common lands. [...] The old nobility had been devoured by the great feudal wars. The new nobility was the child of its time, for which money was the power of all powers.'[5]

4.4   The absolutist state as a vehicle of capitalist transition and the rise of colonialism

The first form of capitalist class power to emerge in the course of historical development, pre-industrial-commercial capitalism, is thus linked to the emergence of the absolutist state. The *absolutist* state is a *bourgeois state*. It comprises the type of political power that safeguards the transition from feudalism to capitalism, subsequently stabilising the social power of capital. But state power is imposed not only internally, within the bounds of its own territory. It is also projected outwards to safeguard the conditions for expanded reproduction of 'national' capitalist relations, and the resources that are required for it to become possible. What emerges, in other words, is a tendency in *every* capitalist social formation to expand beyond its boundaries:

> What [...] took place in the age of merchant capital (the 16th and 17th centuries) was the accumulation of huge capitals in the hands of the commercial bourgeoisie [...]. The transition from feudal to capitalist economy enjoyed the active promotion of *state authorities*, whose increasing centralization ran parallel with the growing strength of merchant capital [...]. To smash through the privileges of the estate holders and towns, a strong crown was essential. But the bourgeoisie also needed a powerful state to protect its international trade, to conquer colonies, and to fight for hegemony over the world market.
>
> (Rubin 1989: 24–5)

In this context, the absolutist state becomes the vehicle for unbridled territorial expansionism, of colonialism by the developed (by the criteria of the times) capitalist powers.

Genoese and Venetian companies achieved their commercial and financial supremacy over the whole Mediterranean region through the strength of their states' navies and armies, which defeated the Byzantine Empire and built castles and other strongholds on major Aegean islands, in the Peloponnese and around the Black Sea, where they also established maritime settlements and cities, for centuries resisting the encroaching Ottomans in a perennial endeavour to obtain a monopoly over naval and trade routes. It was Venice's victories over Genoa in the battle of Chioggia in 1380, over Verona in 1402 and Padua in 1405 along with its military control over the rest of eastern Lombardy in 1406 that brought into existence the expanded Venetian territory, the 'terra ferma', that ensured the Republic's economic supremacy over its rivals. Piracy and slave trading with the Ottoman authorities were part of the process of 'primitive accumulation', that is profit creation, for many Italian privateers, especially from Venice and Genoa, from the eleventh century onwards.

The discovery of the New World and of the Cape of Good Hope similarly paved the way for Spanish and Portuguese expansionism, which in the Americas took the form of establishing colonies (in the early sixteenth century initially mainly Spanish, but also Portuguese in Brazil). Backed by their homelands, the European intruders met with rather weak resistance from the native civilisations. The role of state intervention and military power for the creation of the administrative, legal and infrastructural prerequisites for capitalist rule and capital accumulation is especially evident in the case of Spanish colonies in the Americas.

The Spanish throne negotiated contracts (capitulaciónes) with private 'conquistadors' (conquerors: mostly members of the lower aristocracy or military officials) who travelled to the new world at their own expense but were granted higher administrative authority over the lands to be occupied along with a 20% share of the profits from trade or from the seizure of Indian gold and silver. In 1521 the Spanish conquered and destroyed the Aztec capital Tenochtitlan, establishing the Viceroyalty of New Spain (Virreinato de Nueva España), which besides the North American, Central American and Caribbean territories under Spanish rule also included the Spanish colonial territories in the Asia-Pacific region – the Philippines. Conquest of the Inca capital Cuzco in 1533 led to the establishment of the Viceroyalty of Peru (Virreinato del Perú, inaugurated in 1542) in South America, later to be divided into two more viceroyalties. The Spanish state authorities organised the colonies in accordance with an intensely hierarchical bureaucratic model. The corresponding legal order was designed to prevent the creation of a feudal nobility (relations of servitude and personal dependence between Spanish settlers) in the New World. The Spanish central authority for the Colonies (Consejo de Indias) ruled over the authority responsible for trade activities (Casa de Contratación), the viceroyalties, 30–40 governors, 10 royal courts, military authorities, financial institutions, and

30–40 episcopacies. The city settlements of Spanish colonists as well as those of indigenous people were supervised by royal 'corregidores' (chief magistrates) (Pleticha 1996, Vol. 9).

But in this early period European populations willing to become workers did not settle in the Spanish or Portuguese territories of the New World, at least not in the numbers needed for the formation of a fast-growing internal capitalist market and so of a capitalist economy and society.[6] Having, until the colonial invasion, lived in a pre-capitalist social framework, the indigenous populations were now drafted into forced labour (and Christianization) under slave or semi-slave conditions, above all in the silver and gold mines and on the huge plantations. The dramatic demographic decline of these indigenous populations due to their harsh living conditions and the illnesses imported from Europe was compensated for by the slave trade, with the massive importation of African slaves to the Spanish and Portuguese colonies. This created a large social space of non-capitalist production processes (slavery and forced labour), which however produced for the capitalist market (domestic and international).

Unlike in America, European colonists and state powers in Asia (in the early sixteenth century mainly Portuguese, later Dutch, etc.) were confronted with the military strength of Asiatic states and empires. They therefore succeeded initially only in creating a network of coastal settlements and military strongholds to safeguard each power's maritime transport and trade. This was the situation with the Portuguese. They conquered several strongholds on the East-African coasts and the city of Goa in India (1510), and so attained control over the trade between India and the Mediterranean. They also extended their power further towards the East through the conquest of the Malaysian port of Malacca in 1511, which allowed them to control a large part of the trade from India to Indonesia and China. Portuguese trade was centrally organised and was controlled by the throne, which had created a state company, the 'Casa da India', directed by a governor-general. The company reached China in 1517 and Japan in 1543.

Following the Spanish and Portuguese expansion in the early sixteenth century, other important European powers (Holland, England, France ...) sponsored active colonial policies along similar lines. The direct consequence of this was the formation of new colonial empires and conflict over colonial territories and global hegemony:

The end of the 16th century saw England emerge victorious from her war with Spain [...]. England's main rival in the 17th century was Holland, who possessed the world's strongest merchant fleet and a flourishing commerce and industry. The 17th century for England was the century of its struggle against the Dutch while the 18th was taken up with its struggle against the French. Of the years extending from 1653 to 1797, England spent 66 of them engaged in naval wars. The outcome was that England emerged as the world's mightiest seafaring and colonial commercial power.

(Rubin 1989: 31)

Marx regarded colonialism as a basic aspect of the historical process of 'primitive accumulation of capital' and as one of the historical prerequisites for the transition from pre-industrial (manufactory) to industrial capitalism:

> The colonial system ripened trade and navigation as in a hot-house [...] The colonies provided a market for the budding manufactures, and a vast increase in accumulation which was guaranteed by the mother country's monopoly of the market. The treasures captured outside Europe by undisguised looting, enslavement and murder flowed back to the mother country and were turned into capital there.
>
> (Marx 1990: 918)[7]

Colonialism continued even after the victory of industrial capitalism and the formation of gigantic industrial enterprises. In the new historical period too it functioned as a vehicle for extended reproduction of capital and the social and political processes structurally interconnected with it, as will be discussed in the next chapter.

The antagonisms between the world's major capitalist countries led in the last quarter of the nineteenth century to clashes for control of whatever overseas territories had not yet come under the colonial yoke, and for redistribution of the colonies, in parallel with the development of nationalism in all capitalist countries. In the period between 1876 and 1900 the colonial territories of the eight most important colonial powers expanded from an area of 46.4 million square kilometres with 314 million inhabitants to 72.9 million square kilometres with 530 million inhabitants (Sternberg 1971: 428–9, Mommsen 1977: 31–8).

4.5   Decolonization: The emergence of new capitalist states

Our first provisional conclusion from the above brief presentation is that colonialism played an important role in the process of expanded reproduction of capitalism on a global scale and that the state always constituted a crucial moment in this process. But an opposite trend also makes its appearance during the historical phase of colonialism: *decolonization* through the formation of new, sovereign states in former colonial territories. *The decolonization process also enjoys support from the state.*

Starting from the British colonies in North America in 1775–6 and the War of Independence (1775–81), which resulted in the creation of the United States of America in 1783, a process of decolonisation through creation of new (capitalist) states gathers momentum throughout the nineteenth century, in parallel with further colonization and conflict among capitalist powers over the colonies. This process countering colonization is equally dependent on (capitalist) state power, being, by definition, a *process of state creation*. A crucial historical moment in this process is the formation of the Latin American states. The French occupation of Portugal (1807–14) and of Spain (1808–14) brought about a rapid transformation of political and ideological relations in both countries (a rise of nationalism and constitutionalism), which accelerated the corresponding processes in the colonies, consolidating the political power and ideological hegemony of the local ruling classes, state apparatuses and administrative elites. The establishment of juntas which *de facto* governed the colonies during the occupation of the motherlands led to the development of liberation movements of fighters for independence from the Spanish and Portuguese thrones (libertadores). Chile and Colombia became independent in 1810, Paraguay and Venezuela in 1811, Argentina in 1816, Peru, Costa Rica, Guatemala and Nicaragua in 1821, Brazil and Ecuador in 1822, Mexico in 1824 (1810), and Bolivia and Uruguay in 1825. The independence of Haiti had been proclaimed in 1804 following a revolution of the slaves in Saint-Domingue in 1791, inspired by the French Revolution. This process of decolonisation runs parallel to the national revolutions and breaking up of empires in Europe (Greek Revolution in 1821 against the rule of the Ottoman Empire, Belgian Revolution of 1830 against Dutch rule, etc.).

The process of decolonisation (state creation) continues side by side with the further strengthening of colonial powers in the period 1860–1913. It was however to become the dominant trend in international developments after the Second World War, when the strengthening of the anticolonial movements and local bourgeois classes in the colonies resulted in the formation of independent (capitalist or state-capitalist) states:

At the beginning of the twentieth century there were some fifty acknowledged States. Immediately before World War II there were about seventy-five. By 2005, there were almost 200 [...] The emergence of so many new states represents one of the major political developments of the twentieth century. It has changed the character of international law and the practice of international organizations. It has been one of the more important sources of international conflict.

(Crawford 2006: 4)

Colonialism contributed to capital accumulation on a global scale. But historical development,[8] and above all the tendency towards decolonisation after World War II, indicates that it was not a necessary accompaniment to, or a prerequisite sine qua non for, the expanded reproduction of social-capital.

The same conclusion can be arrived at via Marxist theory, and specifically from Marx's analysis of the 'Reproduction and Circulation of Aggregate Social Capital' in Vol. 2 of *Capital* (Marx 1992: 425–599), where it is demonstrated that under certain conditions the uninterrupted expanded reproduction of capital can take place in a 'pure' capitalist society without there being any need for territories or 'third parties' external to the capitalist social relations: that is either capitalists or wage labourers (also see Tugan-Baranowsky 1969 and 2000; Milios et al. 2002: 162–88).

In any case, the collapse of colonialism and the formation of a large number of capitalist social formations are an important breach in the history of 'world capitalism', which should not be underestimated, as it all too often is by 'dependency theorists' who claim that ex-colonial territories remain under a 'neo-colonial' yoke. It is clear that since the eclipse of colonialism, capitalist social formations to varying degrees, depending on their strength, have developed other (non-colonial) forms of (economic, political or/and ideological) expansionism. But, as we propose to argue in the following chapters, this applies not only with former colonial powers but practically with all capitalist countries.[9] What can be inferred from the above brief analysis is that a theoretical understanding of the (capitalist) state, and of the closely related nation-building enterprise, is absolutely necessary if one is to decipher both the process of colonisation and imperialism (as manifested in the tendency of all capitalist powers to seek to expand economically, politically and ideologically beyond its national territory) and the process of decolonization (with the attendant emergence of rival expansionist, and even colonial or imperial, trends in the emerging new states). This theoretical analysis also facilitates understanding of how colonial rivalries began to intensify at the turn of the nineteenth/twentieth centuries, the period that comprised the political backdrop to the formulation of the classical theories of imperialism and will also enable us better to comprehend the international social and economic order from the aftermath of World War II to the present day.

5
Capitalist Mode of Production and Social Formation: Conclusions Concerning the Organization of Capitalist Power

Following what has been argued in the previous chapters, especially in Chapter 4, we can at this point draw certain conclusions regarding the organization of capitalist power at the level of the (national) social formation and the state, vis-à-vis the 'international capitalist system', that is the imperialist chain.

5.1. On the notion of the capitalist mode of production

5.1.1 Marx's theoretical object in *Capital*

Marx perceives that specific societies consist of a mosaic of social class relations (and of specific historical manifestations of these social relations), not all of which are characterized by the same type of social cohesion (i.e. permeated by the same type of class power). They constitute, rather, the specific historical result of the evolution of society, which, as a rule allows for the 'survival' of elements with roots in previous types of social organization, previous historical systems of class power (e.g. feudalism).[1]

Marx seeks out and isolates those elements of social relations which: *firstly*, comprise the unique character of capitalism, of each capitalist society, of capitalist class domination generally, serving to distinguish it from other types of class domination (and of the corresponding social organization); and, *secondly*, constitute the permanent, 'unaltered' nucleus of the capitalist system of class domination, irrespective of the particular evolution of each specifically studied (capitalist) society. That is, he abstracts those consequences of class struggle ascribable to the particular forms in each case of the historical manifestation of the capitalist system, which do not necessarily constitute elements of the core of the class relations of capitalist power. Thus a new theoretical object emerges: the (capitalist) *mode of production*. On the basis of the theoretical analysis of the mode of production, each particular class society (each particular class social formation) can thus be studied in depth.

5.1.2   Capitalist mode of production

The *CMP* is the causal *nucleus* of the *totality* of capitalist power relations: the fundamental social-class interdependencies that define a system of social power (a society) as a capitalist system. It is the concept that enables the dominant structural characteristics of each and *every* capitalist society to be deciphered.[2]

It is established in the *capital-relation* initially at the level of production: in the separation of the worker from the means of production (the worker thus being transformed into a wage-labourer, possessing only his labour power) and in full ownership of the means of production by the capitalist: The capitalist has both the power to set in operation the means of production (which was not the case in pre- capitalist modes of production) and the power to appropriate the final surplus product. For the labourer to be transformed into a wage-earner, the feudal hegemon must give way to the modern constitutional state and his subjects be transformed, on the judicial-political plane, into free citizens:

> This worker must be free in the double sense that as a free individual he can dispose of his labour-power as his own commodity, and that, on the other hand, he has no other commodity for sale, i.e. he is rid of them, he is free of all the objects needed for the realization of his labour-power.
>
> (Marx 1990: 272–3)

In pre-capitalist modes of production, in contrast, ownership of the means of production by the ruling class was never absolute, and the labourer was never free. The ruling class enjoyed *proprietorship* of the means of production, that is it appropriated the surplus product, but the working-ruled classes still retained de facto possession of the means of production (i.e. the power to set them in operation, see Harnecker 1985, Poulantzas 1973). This is not unrelated to significant corresponding structural characteristics of society at the political and ideological levels also. Economic exploitation, that is to say, the extraction of the surplus product from the labourer, was complemented by *direct political coercion*: the relations of political dependence between the dominant and the dominated, and their ideological (as a rule religious) articulation.

The (capitalist) mode of production is not exclusively an economic relation. It applies at all levels of society (social instances). It also includes the core of (capitalist) political and ideological relations of power, that is the particular structure of the capitalist state. It is thus evident that the capitalist class possesses not only economic, but also *political power*; not because the capitalists man the highest political offices in the state, but because the structure of politics in capitalist societies, and above all the capitalist state (its hierarchical bureaucratic organization, its 'classless' functioning on the basis of the rule of law, etc.) corresponds to capitalist class domination, ensuring its overall preservation and reproduction. It is similarly evident that the dominant bourgeois *ideology* (the ideology of individual rights, of equal rights, of national *unity*, of the common interest, etc.) favours perpetuation and reproduction of the capitalist social order and in general the long-term interests of the capitalist class:

> Certain relations of production presuppose the existence of a legal-political and ideological *superstructure* as a condition of their peculiar existence [...] this superstructure is necessarily *specific* (since it is a function of the specific relations of production that call for it).
>
> (Althusser and Balibar 1997: 177)

It is thus evident that capitalism is not reducible to the (world) economy taken in isolation, ignoring the state and/or the political and ideological relations of power. The state is an important influence on the way economies are organized in the normal course of capitalist development; important economic forces activate the reproduction of nation-states. Capitalist power over the working classes is simultaneously economic, political and ideological. It is mediated by the capitalist state for each national social formation.

5.2. The capitalist state as nation-state

5.2.1 The social formation

The mode of production is accordingly the *differentiating feature* of a system of class domination and class exploitation. In a given society there may be a number of modes (and forms) of production, and therefore a complex class configuration. *The articulation of different modes of production is contradictory and always accomplished under the domination of one particular mode of production.*[3] The domination of one mode of production (and in particular the CMP) is a corollary of the tendency towards dissolution of all the other *competing* modes of production. But there are always countervailing tendencies: the (political, economic, ideological) strength of pre-capitalist oligarchies may prevent the dissolution of pre-capitalist modes of production and block capitalist development. All these issues are crucial for the investigation of capitalist development (as will be more extensively argued in Chapter 7).

(Capitalist) social formations are not simply a distillation of social relations deriving from a variety of modes of production (under the dominance of the CMP). They also comprise *concentrated history*, the history being that of the modification through class struggle of the respective strengths of the contending classes, within one and the same system of class power. In other words it is the history of the forms of domination by capital that establishes the context for the particular historical synthesis. The fact, for example, of being confronted by a capitalist social formation says nothing about whether the working day will be 12, 10 or 7 hours, the welfare state services more or less extensive, workers' trade unions strong or weak, etc.

5.2.2   On the national character of the capitalist state

Capitalist exploitation is rendered possible, and appears as a 'natural order', by virtue of the functioning of the state. The nation in its modern-day sense is an inseparable aspect of the capitalist social order, very tangibly expressing the political and ideological-cultural predominance of capital, which homogenizes every community within a political territory into a 'national community'. In the context of capitalist social relations and the dominant bourgeois ideology, the state appears as the political product, indeed the political consummation of the nation assuming the form of a national state. In reality, the nation is the 'product' or rather an aspect of the state: it expresses the ideological and institutional cohesion of a political territory, that is of a (would-be) capitalist social formation.[4]

At the economic level the state makes a decisive contribution to creating the overall material conditions for reproduction of capitalist relations. These include policy for managing the workforce, interventions for an increase in the profitability of aggregate social capital, state management of money and the national currency, the institutional and legal framework safeguarding the 'freedom' of the market, mechanisms for imposing labour discipline and organizing institutions of social 'pacification'. These material conditions differ from country to country, however much convergence there may be today between advanced capitalist countries.

At the political and ideological-cultural level, the state legitimates the exercise of bourgeois political power as 'national independence'. The nation concentrates within this framework aspects of the ideological dimension of capitalist power, that is to say the material results of subjection – of all that is indeed subjected – to the jurisdiction of a state. The nation is inseparable from the institutions that impose its dominion and confirm their existence, such as universal suffrage for 'nationals', that is adults who belong to the nation and are integrated as citizens into the state, which appears as an embodiment of the national interest and national popular sovereignty.

Through this mechanism *the nation 'transforms', that is to say renders universally binding, the class interests of capital, presenting them, setting them in operation, as national interests.*[5] A capitalist social formation is thus *national* in the dual sense of the term: what lends it coherence is the element of national unity. Capital is constituted as social-national capital. Its long-term interests are formulated and safeguarded as national interests. This homogenisation 'effaces' the boundaries between the classes, that is class power and exploitation (transforming them into demarcation lines between professions) or merely relativizes them (representing them as something secondary in the broader context of national unity and cohesion).

We can draw two basic conclusions from the above argumentation.

Firstly, national unity is not just an 'imagined' construct (or 'community'). It expresses the mode of functioning of the state, of institutions of 'democratic rights'. *It manages in this way to present the world as a world of nations, and to make it function as a world of nations.* Class power and exploitation seem to stay out of the firing line. The class interests of workers are hidden from sight – either in the form of notional *harmony of social interests* or through *relegation of class struggle to a secondary role* subordinated to dominant inter-national or imperialist relations. What appears to exist is 'conflict' or 'emulation' between national interest and foreign national interests.[6] It is thus arguable that a great deal of the literature about imperialism or international political economy is based on this structural misconception. Blatantly so in what is called realist literature. The very same problematic can moreover be found both in the world system approaches (dependency theories) and in the various historicist approaches (for more on this see Part I and Chapters 7 and 10). A more comprehensive understanding of imperialism (or the world order) would from this viewpoint see it as a determining factor that lends coherence to the state and to interstate structures, taking precedence over the class struggle, as is also evident in the centre–periphery approaches.

Secondly, as the nation constitutes the historically shaped and specifically capitalist unity (cohesion) of the antagonistic classes of a
social formation, *it tends to unify the 'internal', that is the national, and
demarcate and distinguish it from the 'external', that is the 'non-national'*.
What is involved is a complex and relatively autonomous process
of nation-building in the age of capitalism (i.e. the age of nations
and nation-states), which often entails the emergence of irredentist
demands: the 'desire of a nation' to 'liberate' populations living in
areas that have not been incorporated into the 'fatherland', and
to make them part of that state; the demand for territorial expansion
of the state so that it may embrace 'the entire nation'. In this sense
there is an immanent *imperialist tendency* for territorial expansion
inside every capitalist state. The degree according to which this political imperialist tendency manifests itself throughout the historic age of
capitalism depends on the class struggle and the form of international
imperialist relations.

5.2.3   The state and the reproduction of dominant bourgeois ideology

A theory of the capitalist state must take into account its decisive role
in the systematization and reproduction of the bourgeois ideology. As
systematization and reproduction of ideology presupposes the functioning of apparatuses especially suitable to it, such a theory would presuppose reference to the *ideological state apparatuses*: 'nationally' oriented
scholarship, media, church, parties, trade unions, etc. constituting and
reproducing bourgeois ideology and power as a whole. This is exactly
what Althusser's theory of ideology does.[7] It is an analysis of the reproduction process of the capitalist power relations on all social levels, with
emphasis on the role of the state and its ideological state apparatuses
in this process.

Marx argues that the structural elements of the ruling ideology
(freedom, equality, justice ...) necessarily emerge as a 'function of the
specific relations of production that call for it' (Althusser in Althusser
and Balibar 1997: 177).

> In wage labour [...] even surplus-labour, or unpaid labour, appears
> as paid [...] *the money-relation* conceals the unrequited labour of the
> wage labourer. [...] *All the notions of justice held by both the worker and
> the capitalist, all the mystifications of the capitalistic mode of produc-
> tion*, all capitalism's illusions about freedom, all the apologetic tricks
> of vulgar economists, have as their basis the form of appearance

discussed above, which makes the actual relation invisible, and indeed presents to the eye the precise opposite of that relation.

(Marx 1990: 680, emphasis added)

Althusser theorised the manner of emergence of *socially necessary misrecognitions* (socially necessary in the sense that they underwrite those practices that reproduce capitalist relations of production) and integrated it into a broader theory of ideology (and so of ideological state apparatuses).[8]

The starting point must be a view of ideology as a totality of *social practices* which are reproduced, taught and implemented in ideological institutions openly or tacitly linked to the state and operating to reproduce the social 'order'. The main element is not that ideology is associated with various forms of indirect coercion but that the ideas in which it is codified are organic, that is they contribute to the reproduction of the relations of production. They thus not only become 'acceptable' to members of society but are experienced by them as expressions of the truth of social life. In this sense they are the foundations of a *necessary relation between subjects and the conditions of their lives*.

The most important element in this approach is the link between ideology and the subject (and his/her subordination), which Marx conceptualises in a way entirely different from anything in previous philosophical tradition. As has been shown,[9] it emerges from Marx's analysis that 'reality' is not only the thing, the entity, the real 'sensible thing' but also the illusions, the 'supersensible thing'.[10] These constitute necessary components of reality, even though they amount to a misapprehension of it and a naturalised projection of historical constructs. Just as real are the non-transparent and ideologically coerced behaviours which emerge from this reality.

In this way Marx's theory transcends the classical distinction between the society and the individual subject, revealing that *there are no subjects outside of society but practices which constitute subjective identities on the basis of historical elements*. The subject does not constitute the world, as asserted by idealism, but the world gives birth to the subjectivity of the individual in bourgeois society as the possessor of himself and his commodities in coexistence with the world of things.[11] This entails an inversion of the philosophy of consciousness and the subject.

5.2.4 The nation manifests itself as a totalitarian tendency

Within a nation-state *the nation manifests itself as a totalitarian tendency*: incorporation of the populations of the state into the main body of the nation, and differentiation through negative discrimination against whoever does not become part of the nation, sometimes to the point of expelling them from the main body of the nation.

Historically, the process of political structuring of a nation through attainment of independence is generally described in terms of the 'tendency towards freedom' at first implied in it: emancipation from an empire or a multinational state entity (embodying – for those seeking 'national independence' – national subjugation and oppression). The 'tendency towards freedom' is frequently manifested through the irrevocable decision of large sectors of the population seeking independence to apply the principle of 'Freedom or Death', sacrificing their lives for the sake of national integration in an independent nation-state.

But alongside the 'tendency towards freedom', no less inherent in the character of every nation, there also exists the 'tendency towards totalitarianism'. This is the tendency towards both expansion and homogenization of the 'internal' dimension of the national polity, that is to say the national-cultural homogenization of the populations who *will* be located within the state, that is this polity. This polity, actually expressing a historically concrete class sovereignty and power (e.g. the German Nation and State), is only distinguishable from kindred systems of class sovereignty and power (e.g. the French Nation and State) through its *particular national* characteristics (Germany vs. France).

The 'tendency towards totalitarianism' becomes evident even in the bourgeois revolutionary movements of the early nineteenth century. The 'tendency towards totalitarianism', towards national homogenisation of all – without exception – of the peoples of the polity, is inherent even in the most democratic and liberal variants of bourgeois domination (when the bourgeoisie are leading the armed struggle for an independent democratic nation-state). We may see, then, that the 'tendency towards totalitarianism' does not operate only 'inwardly', within a particular cultural and linguistic population (evolving into a nation in the present-day sense of the term) along with whatever 'minorities' may happen to be on the territory it inhabits. At the same time it also operates 'outwardly', seeking to expand everywhere it does not meet with effective (national) resistance, incorporating and homogenizing every territory (and every other community), and subsuming it in the prospective national-state structuring of the dominant nationality. To put the matter differently the 'tendency towards totalitarianism' could be said to entail not merely an inward-turning impulse (national homogenisation) but also an outward-looking impulse of national expansion, even when its predominance is no longer particularly likely, given that it is coming up against the homogenization-expansion process of the neighbouring nationality.

The 'tendency towards freedom' and 'tendency towards totalitarianism' coexist in that indivisible ideological-cultural unity that is nationalism. Nationalism proclaims the timeless indivisible unity of the people-nation, and the unquestionable historically and ethically validated propriety of their every position and claim in any international political conjuncture. Of course when the process of constructing the nation-state has been consummated, following attainment of the much-vaunted national independence, the 'tendency towards totalitarianism' will establish itself as the predominant facet in power relations. To cite a formulation of Poulantzas (1980: 114–5):

> National unity [...] becomes *historicity of a territory and territorialization of a history* [...]. The enclosures implicit in the constitution of the modern people-nation are only so awesome because they are also fragments of a history that is totalised and capitalised by the state. Genocide is the elimination of what become 'foreign bodies' of the national history and territory: it expels them beyond space and time [...] Concentration camps are a modern invention in the additional sense that the frontier-gates close on 'anti-nationals' for whom time and national historicity are *in suspense*.

Nationalism does not survive merely as the predominant ideological facet in social relations, national unity and national interest. It also serves at the same time to construct this national unity and these national interests in *contradistinction* and (potentially, and depending on the historical conjuncture) in *conflict* with the national interests of other nation-state constructs, other 'national unities'. This is particularly evident in the era of 'classical imperialism' that led to World War I.

The tendency towards totalitarianism is a tendency towards elimination of 'the alien' or 'the foreigner' from the main body of the nation: whether through incorporation into the national population or, to the extent that this is impossible, through expulsion beyond the borders of the state, or conversion into a 'minority', with limited rights. Only in the event of a specific political relation of forces between national groups (or states) may it favour federal solutions based on political and institutional equality between the different national communities.

6
Capitalist Mode of Production and Monopolies

6.1 The theoretical problem

As stated in the previous chapters, the idea of a 'final stage' of capitalism, shaped by the formation of monopolistic enterprises that eliminate capitalist competition, was first introduced into Marxist literature by Rudolf Hilferding's *Finance Capital* (1909),[1] a book strongly influenced by many of the ideas put forward by J. A. Hobson in his *Imperialism: A Study* (1901). Hilferding has always been regarded as a major Marxist theoretician of his time who further developed Marxist theory by extending consideration to certain socio-economic developments of capitalism that had not made their appearance during Marx's lifetime: the formation of monopolies and the evolution of capitalism into a new, 'ultimate' stage.

In what follows we propose to argue against the above hypothesis. Our main argument will be that, although it was regarded as the 'Marxist orthodoxy' for nearly eight decades, the theory of 'monopoly capitalism', that is the theoretical system first introduced through Hilferding's *Finance Capital*, constitutes an interpretation of Marxist theory that is more in the character of a revision than a further development or actualization of Marx's theoretical analysis.

6.2 Marx's value theory and the early Hilferding

As argued in Chapter 5, Marx's economic theory, and more specifically his value theory, does not have as its object of study any specific capitalist country or 'historical form' ('historical stage') of capitalism, but the CMP, that is the structural elements of the capitalist system as such, irrespective of its specific forms of historical appearance or level of development.

According to our understanding of Marxian value theory (Milios et al 2002; for a converging approach also see Heinrich 1999, Arthur 2002), Marx's theory of value constitutes not a 'modification' or a 'correction' of Classical Political Economy's theory of value, but a new theoretical domain, thus shaping a new theoretical object of analysis. Marx's notion of value does not coincide with Ricardo's concept of value as 'labour expended'; it constitutes a complex notion, a theoretical 'conjunction' which makes possible a deciphering of the capital relation through combining the specifically capitalist features of the labour process with the corresponding forms of appearance of the products of labour. In this way value becomes an expression of the capital relation and of the CMP, independently of any temporal or spatial peculiarities (historical era, geographical region or country).

In Marx's theoretical system, money constitutes the only form of appearance of value. Value is determined, of course, by 'abstract labour', that is by capitalistically expended labour (labour process for-exchange and for-profit). But abstract labour does not constitute an empirical magnitude that could be measured with a stopwatch. It acquires a tangible existence only in the process of exchange, in the price of the commodity. The essential feature of the 'market economy' (of capitalism) is thus not simply commodity exchange (as maintained by mainstream theories) but monetary circulation and money. The Marxian analysis holds that exchange is necessarily mediated by money.

In Marx's theory both value and money are concepts that cannot be defined independently of the notion of capital. In summary, the value of commodities never appears as such, as an immediately perceivable (empirically observable), and thus measurable, entity. It finds expression only through the forms of its appearance, that is commodity prices. The forms record the *relationship of exchange* between each commodity and *all other commodities*. Hence, value and price are not commensurable quantities; they belong to different levels of abstraction. Value is the concept that deciphers prices, shows what prices are, without determining their exact level. Values as such cannot be measured quantitatively, and it is even more impossible to refer to the level of any value at all as such, taken in isolation. In Marx's words: 'Value can only manifest itself in the social relation of commodity to commodity' (Marx 1990: 138–9).

Hilferding in his early writings (1904) adopted a different, 'mainstream' interpretation of value theory, which we have elsewhere defined as 'Ricardian Marxism' or the 'classic version' of the value theory (see Milios et al 2002, Milios 2003).[2] This version incorporates into Marxist theory the viewpoint of the Classical School of Political Economy on value as 'labour expended': from this perspective the value of each commodity is determined independently, and is commensurable (qualitatively identical) with price (i.e. belongs to the category of *empirically* tangible quantities). Consequently, value can be reduced to (production) price by means of mathematical calculation (some kind of MELT, i.e. the 'monetary expression of labour time'). Hilferding (1904) defended the main thesis of 'Ricardian Marxism', namely the commensurability between value and price, as follows: 'we have commensurability, inasmuch as prices and values are both expressions for different quantities of labour [...] they are qualitatively homogeneous' (Hilferding 1949: 161). He initially praised this 'Marxian value theory': 'The law of value is not cancelled by the data of the third volume [of *Capital*], but is merely modified in a definite way' (ibid.: 157).

6.3   Marx's concept of 'Social Capital'

Most important for our analysis is the fact that, despite different interpretations of Marx's economic analysis, most versions of Marxism until the publication of *Finance Capital* accepted an identical point of view concerning the relationship between the capitalist economy as a whole and the individual enterprise. This point of view was based on theses explicitly formulated by Marx outlining a fundamentally 'macroeconomic' approach to the capitalist economy. According to it the immanent causal regularities ('laws') of the capitalist system apply at the level of the capitalist economy and society as a whole, from where they are imposed as 'incentives' on the individual constituent elements of this economy. As Marx clearly noted: 'the immanent laws of capitalist production manifest themselves in the external movement of the individual capitals' and 'assert themselves as the coercive laws of competition, and therefore enter into the consciousness of the individual capitalist as the motives which drive him forward' (Marx 1990: 433).[3]

The notion which corresponds to the overall causal relationships of capitalist production is, according to Marx, *social capital* (Gesamtkapital). In another formulation, the immanent causal relationships governing the capitalist economy transform the totality of enterprises ('individual capitals', in Marx's terminology) into elements of social capital, that is they situate them within an economic system, which then exercises a conditioning influence on them. It is in this way, according to Marx, that capital constitutes a historically specific social relation of exploitation and domination.[4]

Social capital is thus the concept of capital at the level of the capitalist economy as a whole, that is it is the complex concept embracing not only empirically detectable regularities of a capitalist economy but also all the 'laws' – the hidden causal determinants – of the capitalist system (the CMP). Embodied in the structural framework of social capital, the individual 'capitalist is simply personified capital, functioning in the production process merely as the bearer of capital' (Marx 1991: 958). He/she is not the Subject of initiative and change; he/she is subjected to the laws of evolution and change of social capital, imposed as incentives on his/her consciousness through *competition*.

6.4   Free competition as a structural feature of the capitalist mode of production

We now propose to focus on the question of free competition, given that it makes possible a profound insight into matters of causality and into the content of notions such as monopolies and technical change in Marx's and Hilferding's respective theoretical systems.

Free competition, in Marx's conception, ensures the reciprocal engagement, peculiar to the capitalist system, of institutionally independent production units, imposing on the respective capitals the laws of capitalist production. *Competition makes it possible for the separate capitalist enterprises, the individual capitals, to constitute themselves and function as social capital.* Through their structural interdependence, that is to say their organization as social capital, the individual capitals proclaim themselves a *social class*: they function as a uniform social force counterposing itself to, and dominating, labour.

As individual capitals, enterprises are supposed to maximise their profit. This tendency is, however, through free competition, subordinated to the laws inherent in the concept of social capital, and more specifically to the process of equalization of the rate of profit and the formation of a tendentially average profit. The tendency towards equalisation of the rate of profit is thus *a structural characteristic of the capitalist relation as such.*

This tendency is related to two processes:

(a) Competition *within each branch* or sector of production, which in principle ensures for each commodity the 'establishment of a uniform market value and market price' (Marx 1991: 281). Competition within each branch of production therefore tends in every instance to impose on all the individual capitals the more productive manufacturing techniques and in this way to equalize the rate of profit.

(b) Competition *at the level of overall capitalist production*, which ensures such mobility of capital from one branch to another so that a uniform rate of profit tends to emerge for the entire capitalist economy (the general rate of profit). The shaping of the uniform general rate of profit is achieved on the basis of *production prices*. These are precisely those prices for the product of each individual capital that guarantee a rate of profit (= ratio of the total profit for a certain period of production to the total capital advanced) equal to (tending towards equality with) the general rate of profit in the economy.

'Freedom of capital', its concentration and centralization, and its capacity to move from one sphere of production to another – mobility facilitated by the credit system and necessitated by competition, because every individual capital seeks employment where it can achieve the highest rate of profit – are the terms that secure predominance of the tendency towards equalization of the rate of profit. It is in terms of this theoretical reasoning that free competition is to be regarded as an indispensable feature of the CMP. As Marx puts it:

> *Free competition* is the relation of capital to itself as another capital, i.e. the real conduct of capital as capital. The inner laws of capital – which appear merely as tendencies in the preliminary historic stages of its development – are for the first time posited as laws; production founded on capital for the first time posits itself in the forms adequate to it only in so far as and to the extent that free competition develops, for it is the free development of the mode of production founded on capital; [...] Free competition is the real development of capital. By its means, what corresponds to the nature of capital is posited as external necessity for the individual capital; what corresponds to the concept of capital, is posited as external necessity for the mode of production founded on capital.
>
> (Marx 1993: 650–1)

By introducing the idea of 'the elimination of free competition among individual capitalists by the large monopolistic combines' (Hilferding 1981: 301), Hilferding in *Finance Capital* substitutes for Marx's macroeconomic view a 'microeconomic' approach, according to which the characteristics of the 'dominant form' of enterprise (individual capital) shape the whole capitalist system (the social capital), determining its patterns of evolution and change. What we have here is a reversal of the flow of cause and effect in the relationship between social capital and individual capital, constituting a *paradigm shift within Marxian economic theory*. This shift is associated with the general *institutionalist* problematic of that time, hinted at in the works of Weber, Veblen and Schumpeter. Here, enterprises (individual capitals) are perceived as autonomous and dissociated entities.

Unlike Soviet Marxists and other heirs to his theory of 'monopoly capitalism', Hilferding himself was frank enough to admit that his approach was not compatible with his early approach and Marx's value theory: 'It seems that the monopolistic combine, while it confirms Marx's theory of concentration, at the same *time tends to undermine his theory of value*' (ibid.: 228, emphasis added).

6.5   Marx's conception of monopolies as forms of individual capital

The above conclusion concerning the paradigm shift introduced into Marxist economic theory by Hilferding's *Finance Capital* may be further elucidated on the basis of Marx's monopoly theory in Volume III of *Capital*. The theory is explicitly formulated by Marx, contrary to the belief that monopolies can be studied only in the framework of the 'latest phase' of capitalism, which appeared only after Marx's death. Marx's theses can be summarised as follows.

The fact that there is a tendency towards equalization of the rate of profit that causes individual capitals to constitute themselves as social capital does not mean that at any given moment the rates of profit of different individual capitals will automatically be equal. On the contrary, there is an evident possibility that some inequalities will be reproduced in the *actual* rates of profit, albeit within the context of the tendency towards equalization of the rate of profit, and not invalidating such a tendency.[5]

Monopoly is thus defined in Marxist theory as an *individual capital* that systematically earns an above average ('extra') rate of profit (not, as in neoclassical theory a company that monopolizes the market). Monopoly is accordingly not the polar opposite of free competition. It is a *form of individual capital*, generated precisely within the framework of free competition: not outside and/or alongside free competition but through free competition and in accordance with the logic of its functioning.

In *Capital* Marx draws a distinction between two main types of monopoly: *natural* and *artificial monopolies*.

Natural monopolies arise out of monopolistic possession of the natural elements of production, leading to increased productivity (by comparison with the social average) and increased (monopoly) profit:

> Possession of this natural force forms a monopoly in the hands of its owner; a condition of higher productivity for the capital invested, which cannot be produced by capital's own production process; the natural force that can be monopolized in this way is always chained to the earth.
>
> (Marx 1991: 784–5)

Artificial monopolies also secure their monopoly status on the basis of conditions of labour productivity higher than the social average within a certain branch of production. In this case, however, the higher-than-average productivity derives not from monopolization of a natural resource but from the technological superiority of the specific individual capital when compared to average conditions in its own specialized branch of production. This technological superiority is reflected in the above average profit rates.

> The individual value of these articles is now below their social value; in other words, they have cost less labour-time than the great bulk of the same article produced under the average social conditions. [...] The real value of a commodity, however, is not its individual, but its social value; that is to say, its value is not measured by the labour-time that the article costs the producer in each individual case, but by the labour-time socially required for its production. If, therefore, the capitalist who applies the new method sells his commodity at its social value [...], he sells it [...] above its individual value, and thus realizes an extra surplus-value.
>
> (Marx 1990: 434)

The extra profit enjoyed by an artificial monopoly 'acting as a coercive law of competition, forces its competitors to adopt the new method [of production]' (Marx 1990: 436). Artificial monopoly is thus brought into existence through free competition and abides in the midst of it, though at the same time its monopoly position is under continual threat from competition. The same is true of natural monopoly, given that its superior productivity, which derives from monopolization of a natural resource by the specific individual capital, may very well be forfeited as a result of technical innovations introduced by its competitors.[6]

6.6 Social capital and average profit

It follows from the above that monopoly profit cannot be the predominant characteristic of the CMP. The predominance of the tendency towards equalization of the general rate of profit is the social condition that ensures the self-organization of individual capitals into a ruling capitalist class: 'The various different capitals here are in the position of shareholders in a joint-stock company. [...] This is the form in which capital becomes conscious of itself as a *social power*, in which every capitalist participates in proportion to his share in the total social capital' (Marx 1991: 258, 297).

To recapitulate: Marx's theory proceeds on the assumption that free competition is a structural feature of capitalist relations, one not susceptible of abolition. It is only with the evolution of free competition, not with its phasing out, that there can be any association with the development of capitalism. Social capital is not the sum of the individual capitals. It is the social predominance of capitalist relations, adequately secured and elaborated through the equalizing processes of free capitalist competition. On this point Marx is unequivocal:

> Capital arrives at this equalisation [of the general rate of profit] to a greater or lesser extent, according to how advanced capitalist development is in a given national society: i.e. the more the conditions in the country in question are adapted to the capitalist mode of production.
>
> (ibid.: 297)

Contrary to Marx's theory, Hilferding and the other 'classical' Marxist writers on imperialism formulated their approach on the basis of the supposed antithesis between free competition and monopoly, a view which became the central tenet of all theories of 'monopoly capitalism'. Our main argument in this chapter is that this thesis evokes an empirically verifiable phenomenon, the tendency towards concentration and centralization of capital and the establishment of very large corporations, but gives no sign of being able to comprehend this phenomenon in accordance with Marx's theoretical system as developed in *Capital*. It does not take into account that while monopoly pertains, according to Marx's theoretical system, to the category of individual capital – denoting an enterprise which on account of its peculiar position in the capitalist production process earns higher-than-average profit – free competition relates exclusively to the category of social capital and is the pre-eminent condition for integration of *all* individual capitals into social capital.

6.7   Individual vs. collective capitalist

We shall close this chapter by putting forward some basic conclusions to serve as an introduction to the arguments to be presented in the next chapters.[7]

(1)   We have seen that alongside the *individual capitalist*, sometimes in an antagonistic relationship with him, stands the *collective capitalist*, the idealized personification of *social capital*. Capitalist competition and the consequent tendency towards a uniform rate of profit is not just a formal prerequisite to the movement of individual capitals, as occurs, for example, in the analyses of Classical Political Economy. On the contrary, it corresponds to a structural process that imposes the terms the existence and functioning of individual capitals. Capitalist competition in the final analysis reflects the totality of laws regulating the coexistence of individual capitals and their merger in social capital.

(2)   The concept of the collective capitalist points to the unity of the bourgeois class and so to the *capitalist state*, whose ultimate purpose is to secure the long-term strategic interest of the bourgeoisie. This form of political unity can only be the final result of a complex interplay of contradictions, always structurally determined. As we already argued, the state is subsequently permeated through and through by the class struggle.

Within the framework of a social formation there can be no conception of individual capital without it being an element of social capital. This means that irrespective of the formal 'legal' owner (shareholder), every individual capital is necessarily stamped with strategies of exploitation corresponding to the class-struggle and history of a specific social formation. The functions of the individual capitalist, the decisions that he/she is required to 'take', are in the final analysis derivable from the dynamics of capital as a social relation and not from some psychological or institutional characteristics which a particular 'group' of people is supposed to possess.

7
Is Imperialism the *Latest* Stage of Capitalism? Reflections on the Question of Periodization of Capitalism and Stages of Capitalist Development

7.1 Introduction

The title of the present chapter includes a question we are obliged to answer more tentatively than Lenin attempted to answer it, almost a century ago, in his similarly titled book. But it is a question that conceals another, much more basic to Marxist thought: *is imperialism a specific 'stage' of capitalism*? This inevitably diverts our discussion to issues of 'history', of 'transformations', of 'phases' or 'stages' of capitalism.

On the basis of what has been said previously, it also becomes evident that the concept of periodization cannot involve the structure of capitalist power relations per se. But if the structural characteristics of the capitalist organization of societies cannot be divided into periods or phases, how is it possible to imagine the historical evolution of a social formation, or even more so of the history of the contradictory international formations of the 'imperialist chain'?

This chapter will be concerned with providing an answer to the preceding question. The central argument of the present analysis is that, as already argued in Chapter 4, imperialism has from the outset been a basic characteristic of historically existing capitalism. It is not the product of a specific historical stage of capitalism. This assumption makes it possible to trace many seemingly different historical events or periods to the same structural cause. The battles for the expansion of borders; the clashes over the acquisition of international markets during the mercantilist era; colonialism, world wars, regional warfare, periods of imperialist tension and calm, the era of the Cold War: all these are simply different historical forms of the relations between links in the imperialist chain, that is to say contradictory and unequal interlinking of different social formations on the international plane.

This argumentation represents a breach with various forms of historicism that are to be encountered with increasing frequency in today's heterodox economic and social thought.

7.2 On the periodization of capitalist social formations

Theories of monopoly (or state monopoly) capitalism hold that transformations of structural characteristics of the capitalist system, linked as they supposedly are to domination by monopolies, lead to the shaping of a new stage of the CMP (see our critique in Chapter 6). Those who structure their argumentation on the more general problematic of historicism come to similar conclusions. The common characteristic in all these approaches is insistence on the historic variability of the structural relationships of exploitation that are the essence of the CMP.[1]

It is characteristic that even theoreticians who have been critical of the conception of state monopoly capitalism or have attempted to distance themselves from the logic of historicism have often accepted the view that the *CMP* can be divided into historical stages. A characteristic example is Poulantzas (1975: 43–4), who seems ultimately to regard monopoly capitalism as a stage of the CMP. He even thinks that within this imperialist stage of the CMP certain separate phases are to be distinguished, which do not however correspond to further transformations of the CMP but are the historical outcome of class struggle (ibid.).

We argue that the CMP, as the 'inner core which is essential but concealed' (Marx 1991: 311, or MEW, vol. 25: 219: 'innerer, wesentlicher, aber verhüllter Kerngestalt') of capitalist relations at all levels of society, *is not subject* to structural transformations or divisible into stages. But the development of a particular capitalist social formation can readily be broken down into stages and/or phases. What is then involved is not transformation of the immanent 'laws' that pervade the CMP (that is to say every type of capitalist domination) but rather the consolidation of some specific social relations and correlations of power, within the historic process of class struggle. It is a question of the results of class struggle within (developed) capitalist social formations, involving such matters as the length of the working day, the forms of concentration and centralization of capital, the specific procedure for shaping state and reproductive mechanisms, the form of the power bloc (that is to say the specific bourgeois fractions and their reciprocal relations) and the participation or non-participation of other classes apart from the bourgeoisie (e.g. landlords) in the power bloc. In other words *the overall social correlations of power.*

The reference here is to the relatively differentiated historical modes of constitution of a capitalist *social formation* that emerge from the different historical stages of the class struggle and not, indeed, from transformation of the structural characteristics and functioning of the CMP. In this sense we are justified in speaking of stages of capitalist evolution and development: *as stages in the historical development of capitalist social formations.*

7.2.1   Capitalism of absolute surplus-value

As discussed in Chapter 4, the first historical era of capitalism is characterized not only by the coexistence of pre-capitalist modes of production but also by pre-industrial forms of capital and forms of indirect subordination of labour to capital (or hybrid forms of piece-wage labour).

In other words, in its initial stages of development, capitalism may have acquired predominance within a social formation even though the proportion of the total working population engaged in wage labour may have remained relatively small. In such cases capitalist exploitation also takes other forms besides those typical of developed capitalism. Behind the facade of commodity relations capitalist domination can be detected, despite the fact that wage labour and the capitalist enterprise in their fully fledged form remain a marginal, or at least relatively limited, phenomenon. *The picture conveyed is thus one of an economy to a large extent commodified, given that the relations of indirect subordination of labour to capital assume many different forms.*

Networks of merchants, buyers-up and 'middlemen' link together the (farmer or artisan) producer with the big merchant (and financial) enterprise through a variety of intermediary relationships involving the flows of money and commodities: what this shows is that the personal relationships and kinship links, the locality factor, linguistic affinities and, lastly, ethnicity function 'nodally' for the propagation and development of the moneyed commodity economy, that is to say for pre-industrial (merchant) capitalism. The networks of monetized communication and business dealings which end up fostering long-distance trade are merely the external aspect of the disintegration of pre-capitalist relations of social organization – of closed 'autonomous' communitarian structures and the non-monetized 'natural' economy – to the advantage of the pre-industrial-merchant capitalism of the era.

An analysis concerning the indirect subordination or formal subsumption of labour to merchant capital and to the middleman can be found in the third volume of *Capital*, Chapter 20, (especially pp. 452–5) and also in the first volume of *Capital*, Chapters 13 and 14, and in the

Results of the Direct Production Process. Marx conceptualizes the direct producers who are subject to the merchant's command as a hybrid form of piece-wage-labour, paving the way for fully fledged capitalist relations of production:

> The transition from the feudal mode of production takes place in two different ways. The producer may become merchant and capitalist [...] Alternatively, however, the merchant may take direct control of production himself [...] This method [...] without revolutionising the mode of production, [...] simply worsens the conditions of the direct producers, transforms them into *mere wage-labourers and proletarians* [...] appropriating their surplus labour on the basis of the old mode of production [...] The merchant is the *real capitalist and pockets the greater part of the surplus-value.*
>
> (Marx 1991: 452–3, emphasis added)

It his 1893–1900 writings on the *Development of Capitalism in Russia* Lenin also clearly comprehended, and drew attention to, the capitalist character of an economy based on buying-up and the big commercial enterprise. He described production for the buyer-up as a form of capitalist manufacture:

> Nothing could be more absurd than the opinion that working for the buyers-up is merely the result of some abuse, of some accident [...] This form of industry, then, already implies the deep-going rule of capitalism, being the direct predecessor of its last and highest form – large scale machine industry. *Work for the buyer-up is consequently a backward form of capitalism*, and in contemporary society this backwardness has the effect of seriously worsening the conditions of the working people, who are exploited by a host of middlemen (the sweating system), are disunited, are compelled to content themselves with the lowest wages and to work under the most insanitary conditions and for extremely long hours, and – what is most important – under conditions which render public control of production extremely difficult.
>
> (*LCW*, Vol. 2: 434–5, emphasis added)

By taking control of the craftsmen's production process, in other words, merchant capital takes control of their means of production, albeit in an informal or indirect way. Consequently, one may conceive of industrialization as a process of transition from one (the 'underdeveloped') capitalist form to another (the 'developed').

We define this historically first era of capitalist rule, in which, besides the large commercial and financial corporation or manufacturer, indirect subordination or formal subsumption[2] of labour to capital based on buying-up remained prevalent, as *Capitalism of Absolute Surplus-Value*, following Marx's analysis in Chapters 16–18 of Volume 1 of *Capital* and in the *Results of the Direct Production Process*.

As emphasized by Marx, production of both absolute surplus-value (e.g. through the prolongation of the working day or increase in the intensity of labour) and relative surplus-value (i.e. through increases in labour productivity due to technological progress) are tendencies that are permanently inherent in capitalism, having been present from the first moment of the birth of capital, with the shaping of processes of direct subordination of labour to capital (the great commercial and financial enterprise; later the great industrial enterprise). Nevertheless, each tendency is predominant in different historical eras at the level of society as a whole. The era of mercantilism and commercial capital may be defined as the era of predominance of the production of absolute surplus-value in the advanced capitalist social formations of the time.

This era of Capitalism of Absolute Surplus-value reaches its end when the economic and social results of the industrial revolution become apparent. The industrial revolution is not a 'moment' in England's or any other nation's economic history, but a transitional process (and a historic period) during which real subsumption of labour to capital prevails, precisely through the spread of industrial production into all major branches of capitalist production.[3] As Hobsbawm (1993: 42, 207) aptly argued:

> Let us begin with the Industrial Revolution [...] This is at first sight a capricious starting-point, for the repercussions of this revolution did not make themselves felt in an obvious an unmistakable way – at any rate outside England – until quite late in our period; certainly not before 1830, probably not before 1840 or thereabouts [...] Only one economy was effectively industrialized by 1848, the British, and consequently dominated the world.

The above argument, about the transitory character of the industrial revolution towards Capitalism of Relative Surplus-value in the developed capitalist social formations of the time means that our analysis puts emphasis on the social rather than the technological aspects of historical evolution.

In a similar vein, that is approaching Russian society from the starting point of Marx's categories, Lenin reaches the conclusion that

the   transition from the historically 'undeveloped' form of merchant capitalism to industrial capitalism is a result of the development
of class struggle (*CW*, Vol. 3: 541–2). The transition from manufacture
to large-scale industrial capitalism signifies a change in the relation of
forces between merchant and industrial capital. Large-scale industry
itself embodies the typically capitalist centralization and regulation of
the productive process (division of labour in the factory, establishment
of a productive hierarchy and mechanization, authoritarian factory
discipline) and so abolishes the mediating intervention of merchant
capital which characterized its preceding phase.

It could be argued, following Lenin's train of thought of the
period 1893–1900, that the transition to industrial capitalism from
pre-industrial capitalist forms characterized by indirect subordination
of labour to merchant capital merely consummates the generalization
of direct subordination of labour to capital. It does not emerge from
any ineluctable technological imperative or from linear growth of the
'productive forces', but (exactly as in the case of the dissolution of pre-
capitalist modes of production) is a consequence of the overturn of pre-
industrial social and political relations in favour of industrial capital.

7.2.2   Capitalism of relative surplus-value

From the beginning of the nineteenth century a number of transformations in fact took place in England and later in almost all of the
countries of advanced capitalism into which the industrial revolution
had been introduced. In the early periods of capitalist development a
correlation of forces particularly favourable to capital had been created
by virtue of the class struggle. This correlation enabled capital, despite
the rapid increase in the productivity of labour through the use of
machinery, continually to lengthen the working day while at the same
intensifying the work process, with simultaneous mass deployment of a
humiliatingly badly paid labour force of children and women.

The industrial revolution at first involved only certain industrial
sectors and was accompanied by traditional forms of production of
absolute surplus-value. Pauperism and mass poverty were a component of the industrial revolution up until the 1860s, affecting a
great part of the population, the workers on the land and textile
workers after 1820, and unskilled workers, such as women and
children (Schweers 1980: 254–5).[4] 'Despite a 6–7% annual increase
in production, the cotton industry [in England] accounted for only
7–8% of gross domestic production, with only limited consequences
for domestic cloth manufacturing and minimal effects in terms of

covering ultimate demand: 77% of textile workers in 1838 were women and children, who were selected on account of their great adaptability to labour discipline in industry, and worked a 16-hour-day and eight-day week for exceptionally low wages (women 1/3, children 1/6 of the adult male wage)' (Hurtienne 1981: 115).

The particular negative balance of forces for the working class was obvious at the political level. Thus in England in 1867 the first workers (skilled workers) obtained the right to vote. A further extension of the franchise was seen in 1884. But significant layers of the population, the rural proletariat, the urban poor, all women, remained without voting rights even after the Third Reform Act.[5]

By contrast, in the next historical phase, roughly 1870 and afterwards, an opposite movement takes place. The so-called Great Depression of the period 1873–96 accelerated the spread of the industrial revolution outside Britain (and France), in other leading capitalist countries such as Germany, the USA, the Scandinavian countries, etc. At the same time, the combativity and the degree of trade union and political pre-paredness of the working class undergoes rapid development, shifting the balance of forces to the benefit of the working class. In England, France and the USA, from 1870 to the First World War, the working day is reduced at a rate of five hours per week every five years. At the same time there is a significant reduction in wage flexibility. Workers' wages increase from a fixed-price basis of 100 in 1850 to 128 in 1873 and 176 in 1896. Wage reductions in periods of crisis remain by contrast rela-tively small: from 137 in 1867 to 132 in 1871, from 137 in 1879 to 134 in 1880, from 136 in 1881 to 135 in 1882, etc. (Stone 1999).

These changes bring about a number of decisive transformations in all the countries of developed capitalism. It was in reality the end of a whole historical period during which capitalist accumulation was based decisively on an increase in absolute surplus-value: lengthening of the working day, employment of women and children for extremely low wages, etc. This Capitalism of Absolute Surplus-value reaches its limits, then, with the end of the century. At the same time, the politi-cal and trade-unionist strengthening of the working class now leaves capital with only one route for increasing the production of surplus-value and thus accelerating the accumulation process: production of relative surplus-value, through an increase in the productivity of labour which means 'to cheapen the worker himself' (Marx 1990: 437), despite increasing popular consumption.[6]

We might at this point put forward the thesis that from the last three decades of the nineteenth century until the First World War (and in certain countries a little later), *the countries of developed capitalism pass from the historical stage of Capitalism of Absolute Surplus-value to the historical stage of Capitalism of Relative Surplus-value.* These are transformations that pertain not only to the production process or the labour process but also to the process of social reproduction as a whole, including at the political and ideological level. This is a point that deserves further emphasis.

The transition to *Capitalism of Relative Surplus-value* is linked to the following transformations within the advanced capitalist social formations:

(i)   Transformation of the labour process through increasingly widespread application of scientific knowledge in production.

(ii) Transformation of the production process at every level of society, through concentration and centralization of capital, reduction of the specific weight of non-capitalist sectors of the economy, especially in the production of consumer goods,[7] expansion thus of the domestic market, growth of big cities (which are precisely the site of the ideological and reproductive apparatuses of the capitalist state), numerical expansion of the new lower-middle class, etc. Concentration and centralization of production means at the same time creation in most industrial sectors of a small number of gigantic industrial enterprises bringing together a large part of the production and in this way acquiring the capacity to function for a greater or a smaller period of time as monopolies, chiefly artificial monopolies. But what is most important here is that these big capitalist concerns function, through their special position in the expanded reproduction of social capital, as the hegemonic fraction of the ruling class.

(iii) The expansion of capitalist production to all the countries of developed capitalism leads to a corresponding expansion of foreign trade, a phenomenon causally linked, as we shall discuss in the next chapter, to the growth of capital exports.

(iv) The changes in the labour and production processes are linked to corresponding transformations at the political and ideological level. For a start what is involved is the rapid reinforcement of the significance and the field of application of the economic policy of the state, as a result of the problems that emerge from the expanded process of accumulation of capital, increased international competition, the slowing down of the growth rates after the mid-1870s and the sharpening of intra-bourgeois contradictions. On the other hand, there are a number of state functions that emerge as a result of the transformation in the labour and productive process which we described, and which aim at controlling the process of extended reproduction of the labour force, in correspondence with the new facts of capitalist relations of domination and exploitation.

Here, to be schematic, the following transformations are to be included. (a) The extension of the education system, which now embraces the offspring of the working class and finally shapes a uniform national apparatus, whose functions and whose hierarchical gradations issue from the principles of meritocracy and equality. (b) The restabilization of the family (as a unit of consumption and mechanism for reproducing the labour force), after its temporary collapse, at least in relation to the working class, during the transitional period from the Capitalism of Absolute to the Capitalism of Relative Surplus-value. (c) The shaping of the social welfare system, which gradually incorporates institutions of the 'social state', through intermeshing of state social welfare with labour legislation and the functioning of the trade unions.[8]

The transformations we have described, which apply for all social levels in advanced capitalist formations, distinguish the form of capitalist domination even in the first period after the industrial revolution in the nineteenth century (capitalism of absolute surplus-value) from the later form of this domination (capitalism of relative surplus-value). That which was transformed is not the 'laws' of capital accumulation corresponding to the CMP, or in other words the structural characteristics of capitalist relations at all social levels, but the conditions and forms of appearance of capitalist relations in the historical perspective. In other words it is a question of historical transformation of the power balance and accordingly of the organizational forms of power in developed capitalist social formations.

In this modified social, political, institutional and international framework the preconditions were shaped which led to the rise of nationalism in all countries of developed capitalism and to the intensification of the antagonisms among them on the international arena, over markets, colonies and political influence. *The era of classic imperialism is thus the specific historical outcome of the antagonisms and contradictions which prevailed during the transition of developed capitalist social formation to Capitalism of Relative Surplus-value and not the expression of a transformation of the CMP (from the stage of 'competitive' to the stage of 'monopoly capitalism').*

In this sense the analyses of Poulantzas in *Political Power and Social Classes* on the configuration of the power bloc are of exceptional significance. Unlike in his later writings, Poulantzas here maintains that the category of the *stage* can be determined only in relation to the concept of the social formation, not in relation to the mode of production:

> The power block is related to the periodization of the capitalist formation in typical stages [...] The power block constitutes a contradictory unity of *politically dominant* classes *under the protection of the hegemonic fraction* [...] It is clear that the *typical configuration* of a determinate power block depends on the conjuncture [...]: in any case it offers us a framework for deciphering the class relations typical of a *stage* of a determinate formation, by setting the *limits* of its typical form.
>
> (Poulantzas 1973: 234, 239 and 242)

This analysis by Poulantzas corresponds to the positions we have developed here on periodization of the developed capitalist social formations.

For the moment the requirement is for us to retain the following conclusion. The Capitalism of Relative Surplus-value is that stage in the development of capitalist social formations that in the relevant literature (as we saw in detail in the first section of this book) historically came to be perceived as, and named, the imperialist stage of capitalism or monopoly capitalism. What is involved is the reorganization, through the historic process of class struggle, of the (economic, political and ideological) capitalist relations of production, which are interwoven with the simultaneous expansion of capital. As we shall in any case examine in detail below, it was above all the proliferation of developed capitalist formations after the Second World War that increased the needs for internationalization of trade and capital. In contrast to what is asserted by numerous scholars, this occurs precisely because *it is through international relations that the process of capital accumulation within developed capitalist formations is promoted and reinforced.*

The mistake that is made by classical (but also by most contemporary) theories of imperialism consists chiefly in interpreting this historical process of transformation not as a result of the class struggle but as a consequence of the formation, and the predominance, of monopolies. Further than that, they consider that this predominance of monopolies is a stage in the development of the 'productive forces' shaping a new stage of the CMP. It is an economistic-evolutionary interpretation of a specific type of historical evolution.

7.3 The structure of social totality and the historical forms of the state in the Marxian framework

It is useful to recall certain positions touching on the character of the state which we formulated earlier in Chapter 5. There are different forms of criticism of the instrumentalist conception of the state, which as we have seen is the key prerequisite in classical analyses of imperialism (and not only them). Interesting from the viewpoint of Marxism is a certain differentiation from economism which at the same time manages to avoid being equated with the problematic of historicism that is powerfully present in a number of contemporary economic and social analyses.[9]

Before proceeding, however, to the question of the state we must supplement some of the previously developed theses (see Chapter 5) with a few comments on the structure of capitalist production relations and their effectivity in the context of the CMP. We need this digression because it is rather clear that a *general* critique of theoretical humanism does not suffice to demarcate the field of Marxian analysis. The Marxian problematic represents *concrete* social 'subjects' as the *material embodiment* within capitalism of the existing power relations, which however *are not undifferentiated* as between themselves. They coexist within a social totality, *decentred* and properly *structured*. The *specific difference* of Marxism must be sought in the particular definition of the *social whole* or the particular determination of the *connection* between different *power relations (economic, political, ideological) that reproduce capitalist exploitation*. Within this perspective Althusser's work is indeed valuable.[10]

The *principal contradiction* in the CMP is the contradiction of the relations of production, which *in principle* divides society into two fundamental (and unequal) classes: the *capitalist* and *working* classes. The specific structure of the relations of production reflects the *social preconditions* of the production process. *These social relations are on no account reducible to mere relations between human beings, to relations that only involve men*. This means that they are irreducible to any *anthropological* inter-subjectivity. In contrast to the historicist approaches, the relations of production are in their essence a *double relation*: a relation between the agents of production ('groups' of people), which of course signifies the relations between these agents, and the means of production. But it is not a question simply of combining elements, because the relations between these agents and the means of production *determine their very nature*, which remains unaltered until some new historical configuration emerges. As a result, a specific structure of capitalist relations of exploitation corresponds to capitalism, but as we have seen in detail in the above section, it cannot be periodized.

The agents of production of course embody other *secondary* power relations (contradictions). Certain relations of production presuppose the existence of specific *legal-political* and *ideological* relations: the so-called *superstructure*. The secondary contradictions are not the pure expressions or phenomena of the principal contradiction (relations of production) but on the contrary are essential even to its very existence. They actually constitute its condition of existence, just as the principal contradiction constitutes their condition of existence.

The relations of production not only constitute the basic contradiction of the social whole but also *in the last instance* determine the *general form* of superstructure, that is all the secondary contradictions and social forms. This means that the modes in which they react upon the primary contradiction – the indices of their own effectivity – are already determined by it. However, the *index of effectivity* of the secondary contradictions presupposes *first* that there is a *relative autonomy* to their existence with respect to the primary contradiction, and *second* that there is a *reciprocal action*, an overdetermination,[11] of these secondary contradictions on the primary contradiction.

In plain terms, this is the logic of Marx's elaborations, aptly commented on by Engels in his famous letter to Bloch:

> According to the materialist conception of history, the *ultimately* determining element in history is the production and reproduction of real life. Other than this neither Marx nor I have ever asserted. Hence if somebody twists this into saying that the economic element is the *only* determining one, he transforms that proposition into a meaningless, abstract, senseless phrase.
>
> (MEW, Vol. 37: 463)

The multiplicity of the forms that the secondary contradictions may take in capitalism, the political and ideological relations and forms of the superstructure, in no way negate their specifically capitalist 'nature': that is the specific way in which they exist within the complex social whole. The message in Marx's analysis is most definitely not that 'everything' is mechanically determined by the economy. The well-known Marxist topographical metaphor of infrastructure and superstructure reasserts the 'act' of *determination in the last instance* by the economic element (the specific structure of the production relations), underlining the essential difference between the social elements, the specific unevenness in the relations of social power relations and the *decentred* character of the complex social whole.

If these are the realities then there can be many different forms of institutional organization of capitalism (at the national and international level), without this meaning that there are shifts in the structural characteristics of capitalist relations of power. The original and unique evolution of capitalist social formations does not in any circumstance imply a shift of the structural relations of power as conveyed in the analysis of the CMP. In the case of the state something like this means that its *structural* role can be represented in many different historical forms depending on the correlations of power at the level of the social formation. Capitalist power relations nevertheless remain unchanged, as does the basic role of the state in organizing the political hegemony of the bourgeoisie. Change in the relations of production can come only after a revolutionary seizure of state power and imposition of the hegemony of the working class with the prospect of the fading away of the state.[12]

Social classes do not exist except insofar as there is a struggle between them. They do not exist independently of it. The concept of *relations of production* involves a *distributive process* dividing 'people' into classes while simultaneously constituting them as social *subjects*. Classes *are born out of the antagonism inherent in this distributive process*. This *relational* conception of *power* has significant consequences for the manner in which social institutions, and specifically the *state*, are defined within the rubric of Marxian analysis.

On the one hand, the power of the capitalist state must be approached in terms of the objective (political) interests of capital. Within this framework the state plays a *central organizational role*, representing and organizing the long-term political interest of the bourgeois class, politically unifying its various class fractions, all of which occupy positions – albeit *unequally* – on the terrain of political domination (Poulantzas 2000: 127–9).

On the other hand, the capitalist state is not merely an instrument in the hands of the power bloc. It has its own specific autonomy. The state always retains *relative autonomy* vis-à-vis one or the other fraction of the power bloc for the sake of securing the general interest of the bourgeois class under the hegemony of one of its fractions (Poulantzas, ibid.). Nevertheless, the state does not organize the political unity of the power bloc from without. The contradiction within the ruling classes and fractions, the balance of forces within the power bloc, all exist as *contradictory relations that are enmeshed within the state* (ibid.: 133), with the result that the state always appears in a specific form that is the outcome of the *material condensation of the social relationship of forces* (ibid.: 128). Thus, the state's autonomy in no way negates its status as a centre for the exercise of political power on the part of capital. It rather becomes the result of what takes place within the state (ibid.: 135).

Understanding the state as the material condensation of a relationship of forces (always 'inside' capitalist domination) means that we must also understand it as a *strategic field* and a point of intersection of various power strategies (ibid.: 136). Thus, unlike in the instrumentalist conception, class contradictions are not taken as something external to the state. And unlike in the conception of the state-as-a-subject, the contradictions within the state cease to be external to the class struggle.

The state concentrates in itself not only the relationship of forces between fractions of the power bloc but also the relationship between that bloc and the dominated classes (ibid.: 140). The form of any given 'social state policy' is intertwined with the complexities of the developing class struggle. For as long as it entails real economic concessions imposed on the dominant classes by the struggles of the dominated classes – characteristic examples are the Keynesian-type policies that were implemented in the Western world in the 1950s and 1960s – this 'social' policy can in no way draw into question capitalist power structures and certainly cannot be understood as representing some limitation on the political power of the dominant class. The basic motive behind the guarantee of certain economic interest to 'the lower orders' (dominated classes) is one of their *political disorganization*. It is indeed often the most effective way of securing the hegemony of the dominant classes (if the direction taken by the class struggle is not one favourable to capital).

7.4   On the analytical similarities between economism and historicism

As Althusser (Althusser and Balibar 1997: 119–20) very pertinently argued, the historicist interpretation of Marx 'was born out of a vital reaction against the mechanism and economism of the Second International, in the period just preceding and, above all, in the years just following the 1917 Revolution'. In this connection we should be in no doubt of the radical characteristics of Luxemburg's and Mehring's historicism, which was developed initially by the German Left, to be subsequently revived in the works of numerous theorists such as Korsch, Lukacs and naturally Gramsci. Even Lenin himself, who was so genially judgemental of this movement of 'leftish' reaction against the mechanistic conventionality of the Second International, recognized that it did then at that time contain authentically revolutionary elements, especially in Luxemburg and Gramsci.

The above remarks remain relevant to the conjuncture within which they were formulated. They are very far from characterizing the theoretical conjuncture of the present day, in which the various currents of historicism appear to have gained ground (without becoming predominant) in the field of social and economic theory, and the attempts to generalize the logic of historicism to investigation of imperialism are not without interest. For example, the interventions of Cox (1987, 1999), Gill (2003), Pijl (1998) and Overbeek (2000) who persist in evoking the work of Gramsci[13] are significant in this respect (for more details on these approaches see Chapter 10).

One of the basic elements in historicist thought (and here the reference is to the standard mainstream work in the relevant literature) is a certain return to the *problematic of the subject*. Usually human beings are represented as *a malleable product of history*. While such a conception stands in contrast to 'abstract' structuralisms or to non-humanist historicism, in fact it retains a strong humanist aspect, in the philosophical sense of the word. This is so because there is a feature of human nature that is not historically mutable in any way, insofar as *human 'nature' always has the power to alter and control historical structures and institutions*.[14] The key expression for the theoretical strategy of historicism is thus given to us, by Gill (2003: 16), who, following Vico reasserts that: 'human beings make society and thus the social world is a human creation.'

Central to this train of thought is the concept of *agent*, which of course is not entirely reducible to the (historical) institutions and continues to play a major theoretical role. Agents might be individuals or groups of people but the difference in any case is not so great. The relations between social groups can be reduced in the final analysis to *interpersonal relationships* among the subjects that comprise them, in this way defining the social behaviour of subjects. While social institutions exercise an influence on individuals, individuals themselves exercise a reciprocal influence on institutions. In this way, *institutions* and *agents, although distinct*, are interlinked in a circle of mutual interaction and interdependence.[15] This perception is the authentic product of the conjunction of *humanism* and *historicism*. In terms of this logic, the human nature of agents is constantly undergoing transformations through the historical development of institutions. Nevertheless, agents continue to play the major role, remaining the *constitutive subject* of institutional development. Concrete men are, in history, the actors of roles of which they are also the authors (Althusser 1997: 139–40).

It is not our intention here to embark upon an exhaustive discussion on the preconditions for the historicist problematic. Suffice it to say for the moment that while the theoretical viewpoint in question endeavours to overcome the economistic and mechanistic weaknesses both of classical Marxist approaches and of the theory of world systems, it fails ignominiously to achieve its objective. The reason for this is that, endeavouring to reverse the economistic problematic, in reality it *re*discovers its own basic principles.

To the logic of economism everything seems to be determined mechanistically by the economy. Take, for example, the analysis of Hobson. Capitalist production necessarily leads to crises of underconsumption. These crises have as an irrevocable outcome, on the one hand, concentration of surplus production which seeks purchasing outlets abroad and, on the other, concentration of surplus capital which likewise seeks out terrain for utilization abroad. This process (on the economic plane) *determines* the (imperialist) policy of the state, shaping accordingly its institutions (on the political plane).

If there is something that characterizes the above problematic, it is a certain conception of the social whole that diverges significantly from the corresponding conception we encounter in the work of Marx (presenting similarities with the conception of the social whole to be found in Hegel). In the logic of economism the historical existence of the social totality is such that all of its elements (economic, political, ideological) always *coexist* at one and the same time, and are therefore contemporaneous with one another in one and the same present. There are no distances or even differentiations in the manner in which the social moments evolve and develop (Althusser 1997: 94–7). For example, in Hobson's system, the moment of underconsumptionist crisis is inexorably marked by the moment of imperialism, and vice versa. Whichever plane we isolate, it *expresses* all the others and is also *contemporaneous* with all the others. The only difference in the problematic of economism is that the contemporaneous coexistence of the social planes *is mechanistically determined* by developments at the level of the economy.

A corresponding problematic for society as a whole, rejecting mechanistic determination by the economy in order to embrace the *radical supremacy* of politics, in fact is nothing more than a variation of the same (basically Hegelian) argument. It is precisely the 'trap' into which historicism has fallen. In fact historicism opposes economism by adopting exactly the same logic: conferring on the political and ideological superstructure the most active qualities of the infrastructure (economic basis). This transfer of qualities can be understood in terms of a decision to entrust to political 'consciousness' the determinate role as regards the economic level (voluntarism as opposed to economism). Or to put it differently: 'if there really are two distinct ways of identifying the superstructure with the infrastructure, or consciousness with the economy – one which sees in consciousness and politics only the economy, while the other imbues the economy with politics and consciousness, there is never more than one *structure* of identification at work – the structure of the problematic which, by reducing one to the other, *theoretically* identifies the levels present' (Althusser 1997: 138–9).

A citation of formulations from the same historicist approaches may help to make the above remarks more comprehensible. We could briefly mention the analyses of the neo-Gramscian current which has been linked notably – as already mentioned – with the name of Cox. The basic idea is that the state (the political plane) – depending on the characteristics of the *historic bloc*, that is to say the configurations of social forces upon which state power ultimately rests – shapes both the structure of the production relations and the form of the mode of production (and by extension the social formations). Obviously, the actions of the state are conditioned by the manner in which 'the world order impinges upon the state':

> [T]he formative phases of production relations are determined by transformations in forms of state that are by definition accompanied by the displacement of one historic bloc by another and of one *raison d' état* by another. [...] New modes of social relations of production become established through the exercise of state power. States also make the choice for societies in regard to their modes of development. The actions of a state in these matters are, in turn, conditioned by the manner in which the world order impinges upon the state. *Thus any attempt to explain the transformations of production relations must refer to states and world orders.*
>
> (Cox 1987: 106, 105, 108 emphasis added)

The extract just quoted provides admirable confirmation of the preceding remarks. Historical structures, and particularly relations of production, are under continual transformation, whose parameters are set by the state (contemporaneous with the political plane). 'The state is the *agency* that can activate and channel the potentialities of a social formation either toward maintaining the existing social order or toward bringing about a new order' (Cox ibid.: 106).

What is constructed, then, is the image of a social whole, each plane of which is *synchronic* with the others and also *expressive* of the others. Each state form corresponds to a specific historic bloc of forces, particular relations of production, particular ideological and moral representations, a specific international conjuncture. The avoidance of economic reductionism is possible precisely because the moment of the political, and specifically the functioning of the state determines and redetermines the structure of social relations as a whole (for similar positions see Gill 2003).

We thus come back to the familiar position of Gramsci (1971: 366) on the 'reciprocity between structure and superstructure', which is nothing more than a reformulation of the contemporaneity of the social planes. The observed *reciprocity* between the infrastructure and the superstructure means that – given the effectivity of the political sphere – one expresses the other in a relationship of *reciprocal correspondence and reflection*. Society comprises a solid structure susceptible to continual transformation in accordance with the succession of different historic blocs.[16]

The foregoing remarks pose two basic theoretical questions, with which we shall now, sequentially, concern ourselves. The first refers to the question of capitalist development, which is closely related to the already discussed problem of periodization/transformation of capitalist social formation. The second question, which will concern us in Chapter 10, refers to transformations of the imperialist chain which, as we saw in detail in the first part of this book, correspond to the structure of the international sphere.

7.5   On the question of capitalist development

On the basis of the above analysis we may now tackle the development/underdevelopment question, which, as we have seen, occupies a very significant position in the literature on imperialism. Why has economic growth been blocked in certain countries or regions, which either remain 'underdeveloped' or allow a development spatially confined in 'enclaves'? Why, on the other hand, do certain formerly underdeveloped countries or regions at certain conjunctures achieve an economic take-off, with high growth rates which ensure a process of catching-up, that is diminishing their growth gap between themselves and the developed countries?

From the above discussion it evidently follows that the predominance of the CMP and its expanded reproduction is both synonymous with and a prerequisite for economic development. The questions to ask in relation to development are thus following: What conditions lead to pre-capitalist social structures being replaced by the CMP? To what extent do such structures constitute an impediment to capitalist development?

7.5.1 Prerequisites for capitalist development

A preliminary caveat, inferable from the above analysis, is in order here: *All 'prognoses' as regards the development–underdevelopment question are to be rejected prior to the completion of a concrete analysis of the economic, social and class structure of a given society.* In other words, one should avoid dogmatism, both in its positive variant ('all countries will inevitably follow the same historical stages of development') and its negative variant ('Less Developed Countries' (LDCs), or 'peripheral' countries will remain underdeveloped).[17]

Marxist analysis recognizes first and foremost the possibility of capitalism (and capitalist development) emerging as a consequence of class struggle. It outlines the necessary preconditions for such a historical development. The final ascendancy, or the deflection, of this tendency is not a given *a priori*, for example, derivable from some a-historical, permanently present essence (e.g. the propensity for technical progress or 'dependence'); its outcome is always determined by existing social relations of power. Marx wrote in a famous 1881 letter to the Russian socialist Vera Zasulich:

I have shown in *Capital* that the transformation of feudal production into capitalist production has as a starting point the expropriation of producers, which mainly means that the expropriation of the peasants is the basis of this whole process [...] I restricted, therefore, this 'historical inevitability' to the 'countries of western Europe' [...] Surely, if capitalist production is to establish its domination in Russia, then the great majority of the peasants, that is of the Russian people, must be transformed into wage-earners and consequently expropriated, through the previous abolition of their common property. But in any way the precedent of the West will prove here absolutely nothing [...] What threatens the life of the Russian community is neither a historical inevitability nor a theory; it is the oppression by the side of the state and the exploitation by the intruding capitalists, who are becoming powerful with the support of this same state and to the disadvantage of the peasants.

(MEW, vol. 19: 396–400)

Lenin's methodology followed the same path, avoiding dogmatism in its positive variants. In 1894 he wrote:

No Marxist has ever argued anywhere that there 'must be' capitalism in Russia 'because' there was capitalism in the West, and so on [...]. No Marxist has ever regarded Marx's theory as some universally compulsory philosophical scheme of history, as anything more than an explanation of a particular social-economic formation.

(Lenin, *CW*, Vol. 1: 192)

According to this classic Marxist approach, concrete analysis and not some general theoretical premises will determine whether an underdeveloped country is or is not moving towards capitalist development. Only in the event of the CMP and the real subsumption of labour under capital becoming through class struggle fully dominant in a social formation is capitalist development (and the concomitant technical progress) established as an inherent tendency of social evolution (albeit temporarily interrupted by cyclical crises):

But this inherent tendency to capitalist production does not become adequately realized – it does not become indispensable, and that also means technologically indispensable – until [...] the real subsumption of labour under capital has become a reality.

(Marx 1990: 1037)

Capitalist development is therefore a matter of the possibility – and the extent – of domination by the CMP in a specific social formation (society); it can be postulated only at the level of the (capitalist) social formation, where the rates and the direction of capitalist development are determined not only by the existence of antagonistic (non-capitalist) modes of production, or of early forms of formal subsumption of labour under capital, but also by the ensemble of all historically shaped social forms which 'overdetermine' the 'laws' of capital accumulation pertaining to the CMP. The variable patterns of capitalist development can thus be considered a corollary of class struggle. Particular forms of the class struggle determine the historical ability of capital, of the bourgeoisie, within an existing social formation, to impose its power and hegemony at all social levels (economic, political, ideological). 'The decisive socio-economic characteristic of the underdeveloped countries is, conversely, a social relation of forces, in other words, an ensemble of determinations, that hinders the expanded reproduction of capitalist power relations, which are, thus, "confined", socially and spatially, to the interior of the so-called capitalist-enclosures' (Hurtienne 1981).

7.5.2 Capitalist development and the 'Agrarian Question'

We argued above that the ability of the bourgeoisie in the LDCs to extend its influence over the antagonistic (pre-capitalist) modes of production and bring about the latter's disintegration is the most important prerequisite for capitalist development.

In social formations where pre-capitalist modes of production continue to reproduce themselves on an expanded scale, the social and spatial territory of capitalist relations and of capital accumulation suffers restriction (what has been described as 'dualism', etc., see Chapter 2), even if at the level of the society and of the state overall the CMP is dominant. This is the most typical situation for a (capitalist) LDC: *Capitalist development cannot conquer the strongholds of pre-capitalism.* Capital accumulation therefore proceeds at a relatively slow rate. To the extent that pre-capitalist social relations do eventually dissolve, however gradually, they give rise to a marginalized population that cannot immediately be assimilated into capitalist social relations.

In the social formations that are defined as 'developed capitalist countries' there exists by contrast only one mode of production, the CMP. Capitalist relations are articulated only in the form of simple commodity production, in the agrarian and non-agrarian sectors of the economy. The extensiveness of the form of simple commodity production, its maintenance in the different sectors of a capitalist society, or on the contrary, the rate of its dissolution or the extent of its reproduction, depend first and foremost on an increase in labour productivity in the dominant, capitalist sector of the society.

In the process of transition from (capitalist) underdevelopment to capitalist development, *agrarian reform* is typically cited as one of the major turning points, given that agrarian property constitutes the basis of all pre-capitalist modes of production (Senghaas 1982). In most cases the tendency is for agrarian reform not to generate capitalist relations of production in the agrarian sector of the economy, but merely to encourage the development of relations of simple commodity production based on land ownership by direct producers. There is no inherent antagonism between agrarian production of this type and industrial capitalism. On the contrary, it may under certain circumstances serve as an economic precondition for accelerated development of the latter. The subordination of the peasants to state economic policy (price regulation for agrarian products) and the credit system (purchase of the means of production with the assistance of bank loans) guarantees low prices for agrarian products and a lowering, therefore, of the costs of reproduction of the labour force. The case of agrarian reform makes clear once more the decisive role of the state in capitalist development.

7.5.3 Early (pre-industrial) forms of capital

We have defined a less developed country as a country in which pre-capitalist modes of production are still strong, playing an important role in the reproduction of the overall structure of the society. Nevertheless, in an LDC an important role is played not only by pre-capitalist modes of production, but also by pre-industrial forms of capital, forms which have also dominated developed capitalist societies throughout the historical era of Capitalism of Absolute Surplus-value, as argued above.

The political economy of development has much to gain from giving serious consideration to this theoretical interpretation of class relations. If one focuses on class relations of production and exploitation, then the very extensive diffusion of cottage industries and sub-contracting relations throughout most LDCs (but also the rise in façon-production and sub-contracting in the developed capitalist countries, with 'labour flexibility' rising on the one hand while on the other more and more enterprises concentrate on marketing commodities produced for them by sub-contractors) can be perceived correctly as an alternative to formal wage-labour relation types of capitalist exploitation.

7.5.4 The question of innovation and technical change: Abstract and concrete analysis

As may be inferred from the above analysis, technical change and innovation should be viewed as emerging from the regularities determining the capitalist system as a whole, that is, from the trends regulating the expanded reproduction of social capital. Innovation and technical change are the main instruments for increasing labour productivity and, 'no less than other socio-economic activities, were best analysed as social processes [...]; the focus of Marx's discussion of technology and innovation is [...] upon a collective, social process' (Rosenberg 1982: 35). Marx himself wrote that: 'A critical history of technology would show how little any of the inventions of eighteenth century are the work of a single individual' (Marx 1990: 493). It is thus production relations per se that impose on individual capitals the drive towards innovation and technical change (ibid.: 433).

In contrast to this approach, most theories of imperialism (especially the centre–periphery theories) share a different point of view for the question of 'who is the vehicle of technological progress.' Following Hilferding's (and Schumpeter's) ideas, these approaches allow for only one answer: the multinational corporation or the monopolistic enterprise is 'the most powerful engine of that progress and in particular of the long-run expansion of total output' (Schumpeter 1950: 106). This monopolistic enterprise is considered to be the causal factor of evolution in the 'latest phase' of capitalism, which 'decides' to develop an 'auto-centred' capitalism in the metropolis, while only generating 'the development of underdevelopment' in the periphery.[18]

Matters are much more complicated in Marx's approach. From the abstract plane of Marxian analysis – outlined above – of the structural interconnections of capitalism in general, that is, from the plane of social capital and the CMP, it is possible subsequently to move to lower levels of abstraction, that is to say, to more concrete objects of investigation, pertaining to specific capitalist societies, in certain economic (or political) conjunctures, and so on. It is at this lower level of abstraction that the question may be posed of which sector of capital in a given concrete situation takes the lead in innovation and technical progress. According to Marx's approach, in other words, concrete analysis will show how (and to what extent) the general tendency towards technical change emanating from the domination of the capitalist social relations of production and exploitation is being tangibly elaborated in the case under investigation.

Part III National Territory and International Space: Internationalization of Capital, Financialization and Imperialist Chain

8
Internationalization of Capital

8.1 Two provocative questions on the apologetic character of the Dependency Problematic

8.1.1 Critique of capitalism or of underdevelopment?

The theses presented on social capital and the state as centre of capitalist political domination are at the same time *a critique of dependency theory in all its variants*. In most approaches to the subject, dependency implies that international relations, that is relations external to the (non-imperialist and thus 'dependent') social formation, *attain priority* in the process of mediation and condensation of class struggle by the state, and so in the relations of class exploitation and domination within each separate state formation. Eric Hobsbawm (1977: 8) has provided a particularly succinct formulation of this conception:

> Their first observation will be that the multiplication of independent sovereign states substantially changed the sense of the term 'independence' for most of them into a synonym for 'dependence' [...] They are economically dependent in two ways: generally, on an international economy they cannot normally hope to influence as individuals; and specifically – in inverse proportion to their size – on the greater powers and transnational corporations.

But dependency approaches do not only devalue the role of the state[1] in class struggle, while simultaneously overvaluing the role of the 'international system;' they necessarily end up positing two distinct models of capitalist society, which supposedly emerge from the differential functioning of the capitalist mode of production in each type of society.

While the periphery develops in a heterogeneous and asymmetrical fashion, the centre is homogeneous, 'autocentric' (the capitalist mode of production tends to be exclusive) and symmetrical (different levels of productivity converge and there is close interlinkage between the different economic sectors). While the periphery is outwards-oriented and de-integrated, with a limited and more or less non-extended internal market, the metropolis flourishes on the strength of a continuously expanding internal market.

This contraposition of the model of the periphery to the model of the centre effectively whitewashes the capitalism of the centre. The exploitative and 'irrational' character of the system may be duly condemned, but the basic political conclusion that emerges as far as the centre is concerned is the same as that of the dominant ideology. The interests of the working class and the popular masses of the centre converge with those of 'their' ruling classes, as workers benefit from the exploitation of the periphery and the social system develops and progresses in such a way that the conflicts within it are blunted.

The capitalism of the centre is of course perceived as being responsible for the plight of the peoples of the periphery. As we have seen, the picture is here reversed. The popular classes of the periphery have every reason to be revolutionary. But as already indicated in the first part of this study, these popular classes of the periphery cannot directly strike at their 'number one enemy', the capitalism of the centre. They cannot overthrow it. They can strike at it only indirectly, through a 'national course' that can effect delinkage from the bonds of dependence, as the methodology *par excellence* for the securing of 'national independence'.

Precisely because distorted development and underdevelopment are regarded as being the inevitable concomitant of imperialist dependence, the course towards symmetrical and dynamic development can be identified with the struggle for national independence. *Centre–periphery theories favour not a radical politics of seizing power by the workers but intervention with a view to securing all-round development for the place in question.* Development is disconnected from its social content: expanded reproduction of capital, capitalist accumulation. They thus tend to present an overly rosy picture of the capitalist political and social power towards which the countries of the Third World are enjoined to strive. Or to put it another way, dependency theories conceal the fact that capitalist accumulation is primarily a process for consolidating capitalist relations of domination and exploitation.

8.1.2 Dependency or low levels of capitalist development and international marginalisation?

The basic hypothesis of the theories under examination here is that underdevelopment is the result of dependency. But to approach matters concretely we must again ask: What are the specific processes that link the periphery to the options of dependency? What are the relations that confine a country to a peripheral role in the context of the 'international division of labour'?

Leaving aside for the moment the theory of unequal exchange (with which we shall concern ourselves later on in this chapter) we may recall that all approaches perceive as basic factors in underdevelopment: (a) 'Plundering' of the periphery, with continuing transfer of resources to the centre. (b) The 'action' of foreign capital, which distorts the social structure and develops only certain selected industrial sectors.

These factors, in principle, set the parameters for the content of the dependence, while by contrast the outer-directedness, the social and economic distortion, the disintegrative pressures, the narrowness of the market, etc. appear primarily as the side-effects of dependence, which indeed function reflexively, reproducing underdevelopment and dependence.

Both the converging interpretations representing underdevelopment as the direct result of dependence, and also the variety of more or less diverging approaches such as that of Córdova – placing particular emphasis on the thesis that dependence is generated by the alliance of the ruling classes of the periphery with imperialism which hinders the expansion-development of capitalism in the regions where pre-capitalist relations predominate – evidently cause more problems than they are called upon to solve. Even if we accept that the transfer of profits from the peripheral countries to the countries of the centre contributes to the development of the latter and the underdevelopment of the former, we may nevertheless note the following. Empirically, this 'plunder' is neither the basic outcome nor the basic motivation for capital exports and internationalization of production. On the contrary, this 'plunder' is less significant for developed countries than cross-investment of capital among developed capitalist countries.

How is one then to explain that the proportional share of international capital movements and international trade being channelled to the Third World always remains small compared to the respective shares of developed capitalist countries? Moreover the so-called Third World countries that attract Foreign Direct Investment (FDI) and other forms of foreign capital are those characterised by processes of rapid economic development (China in the present historical phase, countries of South-East Asia such as Taiwan and South Korea in the 1980s and 1990s),that is countries that succeed in diminishing, or even in some cases completely closing, the development gap between themselves and the more advanced countries. Such was also the case with many European countries during the nineteenth and twentieth centuries – until the 1970s (Hurtienne 1981, Senghaas 1982, Harris 1986, Milios 1989).[2]

As shown in the two tables 8.1 and 8.2 that follow, inward FDI[3] flows in the developing countries hardly reach the 36% margin of global inward FDI in the period 1998–2000 (28.7% in 2006–7, see the respective columns). This empirical evidence does not only falsify what may be codified as the 'colonial extra-profits' approach, but also the 'surplus of capital approach' of classical theories of imperialism, which remained intact in modern approaches. Finally it also challenges the main hypothesis of the 'unequal exchange' approach, that there is a tendency towards a uniform rate of profit in the global economy.

It is worth remembering at this point that (a) in industrial countries, according to the *surplus-of-capital approach*, while the volume of capital intended for accumulation increases rapidly, investment opportunities contract, making it necessary for capital to be exported, while (b) according to the colonial extra-profits approach colonial or low-developed, low-wage countries become a source of extra-profits by reducing the cost price of industrial products, so that these territories seem more likely to attract international capital movements. *But the reality is that most FDI takes place among developed countries and investment opportunities have not contracted in the industrial countries. It is simply that the comparatively low productivity of labour in the Third World makes for a low profit-rate in these countries, notwithstanding the low labour or raw materials costs.*

In any case, the comparatively small participation of developing countries in the global flows of direct investments belies the main thesis of the centre–periphery theories that the development of industrial capitalist countries has its source in the countries of the Third World. Similarly groundless is Córdova's supposition that dependence favours pre-capitalist economic forms and relations, in this way obstructing development. Let us assume for a moment that imperialism forms alliances with the ruling classes of the dependent countries. If the dynamic of the internal balance of forces in a country leads to a contraction of pre-capitalist relations, why should imperialism oppose this dynamic? For example why are the *latifundistas*

Table 8.1 Distribution of FDI by region and selected countries 1980–2005 (per cent)

Region	Inward stock				Outward stock			
	1980	1990	2000	2005	1980	1990	2000	2005
Developed economies	75.6	79.3	68.5	70.3	87.3	91.7	86.2	86.9
European Union	42.5	42.9	37.6	44.4	37.2	45.2	47.1	51.3
Japan	0.6	0.6	0.9	1.0	3.4	11.2	4.3	3.6
USA	14.8	22.1	21.7	16.0	37.7	24.0	20.3	19.2
Developing economies	24.4	20.7	30.3	27.20	12.7	8.3	13.5	11.9
Africa	6.9	3.3	2.6	2.6	1.3	1.1	0.7	0.5
Latin America and the Caribbean	7.1	6.6	9.3	9.3	8.5	3.4	3.3	3.2
South, East and South-East Asia	8.8	8.5	17.2	13.8	2.5	3.4	9.3	7.8
South-East Europe and CIS	–	0.01	1.2	2.5	–	0.01	0.3	1.2
World	100.0	100.0	100.0	100.0	100.0	100.0	100.0	100.0

Region	Inflow				Outflow			
	'78–80	'88–90	'98–00	'03–05	'78–80	'88–90	'98–00	'03–05
Developed economies	79.7	82.5	77.3	59.4	97.0	93.1	90.4	85.8
European Union	39.1	40.3	46.0	40.7	44.8	50.6	64.4	54.6
Japan	0.4	0.04	0.8	0.8	4.9	19.7	2.6	4.9
USA	23.8	31.5	24.0	12.6	39.7	13.6	15.9	15.7
Developing economies	20.3	17.5	21.7	35.9	3.0	6.9	9.4	12.3
Africa	2.0	1.9	1.0	3.0	1.0	0.4	0.2	0.2
Latin America and the Caribbean	13.0	5.0	9.7	11.5	1.1	1.0	4.1	3.5
South, East and South-East Asia	6.7	10.0	10.7	18.4	0.6	5.1	5.0	7.7
South-East Europe and CIS	0.02	0.02	0.9	4,7	–	0.01	0.2	1,8
World	100.0	100.0	100.0	100.0	100.0	100.0	100.0	100.0

Source: UNCTAD, FDI/TNC database (www.unctad.org/fdistatistics).

Table 8.2   FDI inflows, by host region and major host economy, 2006–2007 (Billions of dollars)

Host region/economy	2006	2007[a]	Growth rate (%)
World	1 305.9	1 537.9	*17.8*
Developed economies	857.5	1 001.9	*16.8*
Europe	566.4	651.0	*14.9*
European Union	531.0	610.0	*14.9*
EU 15, 1995	*492.1*	*572.0*	*16.2*
France	81.1	123.3	*52.1*
Germany	42.9	44.8	*4.4*
Italy	39.2	28.1	*– 28.1*
Netherlands	4.4	104.2	*2 285.1*
United Kingdom	139.5	171.1	*22.6*
New European Union members (10)	*38.9*	*38.0*	*–2.3*
United States	175.4	192.9	*10.0*
Japan	–6.5	28.8	
Developing economies	379.1	438.4	*15.7*
Africa	35.5	35.6	*0.1*
Latin America and the Caribbean	83.8	125.8	*50.2*
Asia and Oceania	259.8	277.0	*6.6*
West Asia	59.9	52.8	*– 11.9*
South, East and South-East Asia	199.5	224.0	*12.3*
China	69.5	67.3	*– 3.1*
Hong Kong (China)	42.9	54.4	*26.9*
India	16.9	15.3	*–9.4*
Singapore	24.2	36.9	*52.6*
Transition economies	69.3	97.6	*40.8*
Russian Federation	28.7	48.9	*70.3*

Source: UNCTAD, *Investment Brief No 1, 2008a.*
[a] *Preliminary estimates.*

of north-eastern Brazil more useful to imperialism than the coffee barons of Sao Paolo?

It follows from the preceding that at the periphery there is not some kind of special underdeveloped capitalism or even a peculiar variety of capitalist development as a result of dependence. There are certain limitations on development of the capitalist mode of production for reasons that go back to the internal class and political relation of forces, the class struggle and social relations of power within peripheral social formations. What we reject is the thesis that all industrialization in the countries of the periphery occurs in response to the external factor, the global market, creating enclaves of outer-directed structures disconnected from the rest of society. This hypothesis of outer-directed industrialization is altogether mistaken. Not only does it betray ignorance of the conditions for expanded reproduction of capital but it is also contradicted by empirical data on industrialization of the countries of the periphery, which show that industrialization has been linked first and foremost to the internal market.

It is of course evident that the reference here is to post-WWII nation-states of the periphery. The situation was different in the case of the colonies, when the imperialist countries subjugated the colonized regions through raw military and political violence. Imperialism then exerted a decisive influence on the development of these regions, precisely because it functioned there as political power favouring 'modernization'. But in any case the colonial past is not sufficient basis for an interpretation of a society's subsequent development. The Latin American countries began to organize themselves as nation-states in the 1820s. Canada acquired its independence, always as part of England's Commonwealth, in 1867. Cyprus and India were decolonized by the same imperialist power in the same historical period, but nevertheless are very different from each other in terms of developmental levels.

Many examples could be cited but there is always only one conclusion. The general schema of the 'global capitalist economy' and the 'global class struggle' proposed by the centre–periphery theories not only cannot replace specific (class) analysis of each separate social formation but also, moreover, misconceives historical development and conceals the real social-class conflicts.

We are thus faced, again, with a type of argumentation similar to that which projects the myth of the 'narrowness of the market': one element of the social structure that is linked to, and determined by, the overall level of development of the capitalist relation is ceded autonomy from the social structure and designated as *the* cause of non-development. Just as there is no question of an internal market as a separate and self-contained issue that does not depend on the degree of development of capitalism (as Lenin argued in *The Development of Capitalism in Russia*), so certain secondary aspects of underdevelopment are elevated into direct manifestations or results of dependence, and consequently into 'causes' of underdevelopment.

Capital – we have stressed this many times – is a social relationship. Capital accumulation, capitalist development, is a social process upheld by a specific type of domination and exploitation of labour power. Capitalist development is identified with the emergence of some specific class relations and structures. Dependence is not something pre-existing; it does not determine class relations. On the contrary, the character of international relations that 'bind' a social formation with what may be schematically described as the 'international system' is determined by these relations of class power.

Contrary, then, to the assumptions of theories of the periphery, industrialization of the Third World proceeds mainly in relation to the internal market as an endogenous process of capitalist accumulation. The dynamism and the breadth of this process depends on, and is determined by, each social formation primarily on the basis of the internal correlation of class forces, social relations of domination, etc.[4]

Improvement in the competitive position of certain countries in the international market is linked to the development of the class struggle within them, that is to say to the degree of penetration of the capital relation, increase in the proportion of surplus value, etc. Only under such conditions is it possible for the level of wages to become a factor in competition at the international level.[5] But what is involved here is not a 'new' phenomenon, as asserted by the writers previously mentioned. Since the end of the nineteenth century, a number of 'agricultural' countries (mainly European) joined the ranks of the advanced capitalist countries through radical reorganization of their social and productive structures. At the same time there was a thoroughgoing transformation of the balance of power, internationally, both economic and political, among the imperialist countries.[6]

Closing this section, we are now in a position to make a response to the question we touched upon in the first part of this chapter. If the proportion of foreign investments in the less developed countries remains constantly at low levels, this occurs because the productivity of labour and, above all, from the viewpoint of capital, the rate of profit remains significantly lower in these countries than at the 'centre'.

8.2   International trade and capital exports

8.2.1   Exchange rates and the modification of competition on the world market

The internationalization of capital is predicated on international competition between national social-capitals. The formation of the global market in conjunction with this international competition makes it evident that although it does not comprise a uniform capitalist economic structure, *the 'international capitalist system' nevertheless does not amount merely to the aggregation of certain self-contained social formations but to a much more complex structure, a chain of international relationships and causal connections that emerge precisely from the intermeshing of the different (capitalist) social formations, the various systems of capitalist power, between themselves.*

The global market is not just the area for international transactions, but the economic and social framework for international capitalist competition, by means of which international market prices are formed. The global market and the formation of international prices do not, however, lead to the formation of a general rate of profit for the 'global economy' (that is to say, in Marxian terms, the creation of international production prices), precisely because the national composition of capitals (as national-social capitals) *modifies* the functioning of capital competition in the global market and so preserves and reproduces international differences in the productivity of labour and national rates of profit.

Capital movements and, especially FDI, among industrial countries and its correlation with international trade have been penetratingly investigated in Germany by several authors[7] who, using the terminology 'modification of the law of value on the world market', have claimed that FDI is undertaken by enterprises in a national economic sector that initially enjoys a leading competitive edge in the world market. This sector acquires extra-profits by exporting commodities to foreign markets, where the labour productivity of local producers is lower. These extra-profits obtained by the country with the higher labour productivity are however soon eroded, through an overvaluation of its national currency due to its trade balance surpluses. Correspondingly, trade deficits lead to a devaluation of the currency of the less developed country. The advanced country's position in the foreign market is now threatened by local producers, as changing currency parities transform relative costs into absolute differences in costs – unless there is a shifting of production (i.e. FDI) in this foreign market.

Real-term currency devaluation therefore operates protectively for the less developed industrial country, triggering an internal FDI within it. But sectors in this less advanced country where labour productivity exceeds the country's average can through this exchange rate mechanism derive an advantage (extra-profits) in international trade even with higher developed countries. The erosion of this advantage in international competition (e.g. through unfavourable exchange rate adjustments) may lead to flows of FDI from less developed to more highly developed countries. *FDI then ceases to be mainly one-directional and becomes cross-directional, as productivity gaps between industrial countries diminish.*

In what follows we will present this approach in more detail, albeit in a simplified manner, leaving out of account 'other factors', such as the financial system and its crises, differences in the rates of inflation, business cycles, etc. Just as the domestic market is the arena for determining the value of commodities that compete with each other and are realized within it – *so the global market too is the area for determining the value of the commodities competing with each other at the international level.* The market, both the internal market and the international market, makes visible the social interrelationship and cohesion that prevails between the separate individual labour and production processes. The global market is thus the quintessential expression of the economic and social linkage and interdependence of individual capitalist productive processes (or, to put it differently, individual commodity producers) associated with different (national) social capitals.

It is true that parallels may be drawn between the domestic and international markets, but the former is not merely a sub-category of the latter. At the international level, national constitution of social capital reflects specific lines of division between the different (national) spheres of circulation, which are expressed primarily through the existence of different national currencies, that is the absence of a common international currency. Thus, while at the national level commodity prices are automatically expressed in units of the national currency, at the international level a transformation takes place. The commodity that is exported and circulates on the international market must 'change its name' in currency terms, that is to say express its price in an international or foreign currency.

The absence of a general equivalent (money) at the international level accordingly necessitates the creation of an exchange relationship between the monetary units of the different countries. This exchange relationship ideally expresses the real position of the different national capitals in the international competition. The disequilibria (deficits or surpluses) in the balance of trade and by extension the balance of payments of one country set in motion corrective mechanisms of adjustment of currency exchange rates (devaluation or revaluation of the national currency owing to trade deficits or correspondingly surpluses), which restore the correspondence between the position of the country on the international scale of labour productivity and the international position (exchange parity) of its currency. We will linger for a little on these matters, because they provide the means for better comprehending the mechanism whereby extra-profits are generated through international trade and correspondingly the relationship between these extra-profits and capital exports.

Let us commence with the international hierarchy of labour productivity. The national capital that operates with a labour productivity above the international average for the production of a specific commodity receives an additional profit, which of course is not the case of the national capital operating with socially average labour productivity by international standards. Commodities of the same kind have one and the same value on the global market but they have nevertheless been produced by capital with different national labour productivities. Thus following Marx's presentation in Vol. 1 of *Capital* it can be argued that the internationally uniform value corresponds to different 'national values' of the commodity in question, in exactly the same way that the value of a commodity on the domestic market corresponds to different 'individual values' of the different individual capitals.[8] The commodity we are examining thus represents a 'national value' that is lower than the international for the capital at a higher-than-average level of development by international standards. Given that in the international market this commodity's value exists only as its international value, a higher-than-average international profit accrues to the national capital at a level of development higher than the international average and a lower than average profit to the national capital whose level of development is lower than the international average.

The question here then is one of international competition that is similar to competition within a national industrial sector. Capitals of unequal labour productivity compete in the production of similar commodities. In the domestic market, this intra-sectoral competition leads to inter-sectoral competition, with capital moving from one productive sector to another, and the establishment finally of production prices. One prerequisite for such a development is however the creation at the outset of a uniform rate of profit *in each sector* of production, a tendency, that is, towards abolition of additional profits and more general intra-sectoral inequalities in the rate of profit by: (a) dissemination and generalisation of more productive manufacturing techniques within each sector, (b) elimination (through closure or absorption by other capitals) of individual capitals that are unable to modernize their productive techniques sufficiently to achieve average levels of labour productivity.

At the level of the international market there are nevertheless certain *decisive obstacles*, which cancel out the tendency towards entrenchment of these two processes. Constitution of capital at the national level as social capital brings about a decisive transformation in the terms of international competition and tends to abolish the extra-profits of the most developed capitals and so the pressure on the less developed national capitals. There can therefore be a relative stabilization and reproduction on a more permanent basis of the international differences in labour productivity, making less possible the development of international inter-sectoral competition, which in turn does not lead to formation of international production prices and a general rate of profit at the international level.

It is a question in other words of *modifying the law of competition* in the global market. In the ideal case (that is to say if we ignore every state's protectionist measures such as tariffs, export subsidies, favouring of domestic firms in public sector provisioning, 'quality specifications', etc.), the conditions for capitalist competition are modified by the existence of different national currencies and the corresponding monetary exchange rates. The fluctuation in these exchange rates thus has a protectionist effect for the less developed national capitals.

Countries with the internationally highest labour productivity are initially in a position to sell on the international market the commodities they produce at prices lower than those of their less productive competitors, so that they not only reap extra-profits but also steadily expand their market share, to the detriment of their competitors. The result for the most productive countries is that significant trade surpluses are generated, with a parallel continuing increase in the trade deficits of countries of internationally lower labour productivity. Under the pressure of deficits in the trade balance, the less developed country is obliged to devalue its national currency, while correspondingly the surpluses in the trade balances of the more developed countries set in motion a process of revaluation of *their* national currency.

On the global market, readjustment of the price of the national currency has a protective function for the less developed (national) capitals. The international differences in labour productivity can thus be reproduced; the extra-profits reaped by the most developed national capitals are dissipated. Through devaluation of the currency of the less developed country the high national prices of its products are transformed into average (and even low) international market prices. Correspondingly, the low national prices of the products of the more developed country are similarly transformed, through revaluation of the national currency, into prices approximating the international average. As observed by Busch et al. (1984: 49): 'On the one hand it becomes impossible – in contrast to what happens at the national level – for there to be continuing appropriation of extra-profits by national capitals of above average productivity [...]. On the other hand national capitals of below average productivity can also be kept successfully on the international market.'

As we have seen in Chapter 1, the analysis of foreign trade put forward by Bukharin (1972b) detected the potential in principle for extracting extra-profits on the global market, but was not able to perceive how these extra-profits were undermined by modifications in the functioning of the law of competition at the international level. It was not able in other words to comprehend the effects of the national composition of social capital on international competition between capitals. That is why the analysis was not able to penetrate into the causal relationship linking capital exports with commodity exports. Capital export from a country (or a sector of national industry) with a lower rate of profit to a country with a higher rate of profit has as one of its basic prerequisites this abolition of the extra-profit initially reaped, through international trade, by the more developed country. In reality this amounts to an aggressive move on the part of the capital with the higher level of development, aimed at overcoming the obstacles posed by state assistance to its competitors on the international market (exchange mechanisms but also protective state measures) so as to be able once again to appropriate extra-profits or increased profits.

8.2.2   International trade and capital export

The relationship between international trade and the internationalization of capital through foreign direct investments is implicit in the key finding that emerges from modification of competition on the international market. *First phase*: the most developed countries through commodity exports achieve extra-profits and in this way increase their average national rate of profit. *Second phase*: exchange rate adjustments halt the process of destruction of the capital of the less developed countries by the capitals of the more developed capitalist countries. The surpluses and the deficits in the balance of current accounts of the national capitals participating in the global market offset each other. *Third phase*: the capitals on the global market from the most developed countries replace commodity exports by shifting their productive units to what were formerly their export markets. In this way they abolish protection for the less productive national capitals and so benefit from new extra-profits, by transferring to the host country their more competitive techniques of production (incorporating them in the social conditions of the host country). This capital export, which proceeds regionally and in a single direction, reproduces the tendency towards equalization of national rates of profit. However, as exchange rates reflect a country's average level of productivity, the below-average sectors of production are not adequately protected and are in danger of being ruined by international competition. If the capitals of these sectors wish to retain their international competitiveness, they are obliged either to reduce their production costs through an increase in productivity and/or a fall in real wages, or to institute a national sectoral protectionism and/ or subsidies. Another possible way of regaining competitiveness in the international market is by shifting production to economically less developed countries, because in this way the corresponding sectoral capital again enjoys protection from exchange rates and has also the advantage of lower wage costs per item manufactured.[9]

Precisely because the mechanism of fluctuating exchange rates protects the industry of the less developed country as a whole, that is involves all of the nation's commerce, it leaves the less developed industrial sectors relatively unprotected while at the same time relatively overprotecting the more developed industrial sectors of the country in question. If these overprotected sectors of the less developed country possess at least average international productivity of labour, they can secure extra-profits even from trade with the more developed country. Reduction in the extra-profits through implementation by the more developed country, for example, of selective protectionist measures will trigger capital exports from the less developed to the more developed country. The same result will be elicited by a relative devaluation of the currency of the more developed country on account of an increase in its trade deficits in the sectors of relatively lower (than the average national level) productivity of labour.

These positions on capital export, which emerge from the theory of modification of competition on the international market, pertain mainly to the international economic space of developed capitalism and the so-called new industrial countries.[10] These are countries among which international competition between (national) capitals evolved in its developed form. This condition is not secured in the relations between the industrial capitalist countries and many of the countries of the Third World: the low or spatially circumscribed development of capitalist relations in the latter results in a low rate of profit (despite the low organic composition of capital), while at the same time their external trade with industrial countries tends to take the form of a radically differentiated commerce (e.g. industrial products as against raw materials or agricultural products). For analysis of capital export to the LDCs of the Third World a different approach is therefore necessary.[11] As demonstrated by Schweers (1980) the channelling of capital exports to the Third World (not only the LDCs but with the exception of the NICs) is motivated by other types of incentive, such as exploitation of raw materials and cheap manpower in labour-intensive sectors.

The point is frequently made that in order to deal with competition from newly-industrialized countries in which the price of labour power continues to remain particularly low, certain labour-intensive industries in the developed capitalist countries are in the habit of transferring part of their production to such low-labour-cost countries, reimporting the finished products to the endangered markets. We should note in this connection that this is a secondary (if not marginal) form of direct productive investment. Again, these investments have acquired importance primarily in those countries that are in a process of rapid capitalist development (new industrial countries) in which the low wages can accordingly function as a comparative advantage internationally. Here too, however, because of the logic of capitalist development, the types of foreign investment that predominate are those previously mentioned, that is those linked to modification of competition on the international market and/or to state import substitution measures and in which the proletariat is regarded as particularly disciplined, hardworking and relatively well educated.[12]

These findings from the theory of modification are corroborated very precisely by the picture of capital exports and internationalization of capital following the Second World War.

(1) For a start there is a concentration of FDI outflows from the developed capitalist countries of the OECD of more than 85% of direct foreign investments. The dominant position in capital exports from the wartime period and after is occupied initially by the USA, a direct consequence of the fact that American industry and the American economy were initially first in the world in terms of labour productivity. Among the other developed capitalist countries only those enjoying a relatively high level of development, that is to say the German Federal Republic, Japan, Great Britain, Canada, Switzerland, Holland and France, showed significant levels of capital export. Nevertheless, the volume of direct foreign investments carried out by these countries is smaller than the volume of direct investments made in them from abroad (by the other developed countries). Characteristically, it is only after 1974 that the volume of West German capital exports (direct investments abroad) overtakes that of direct foreign investments in West Germany. Significant levels of direct investment by Great Britain, on the other hand, are a historical outcome of Britain's pre-war hegemony on the global market, that is they mostly involve investments in affiliates established abroad before the Second World War.[13]

(2) Displacements and changes in the international hierarchy of productivity of labour in the post-war period to the detriment of the
USA (labour productivity in the United States grew much more
slowly than that of Japan or the European countries) had significant
effects both at the level of international trade and at the level of
international capital movements. Up until the early 70s, when the
Bretton Woods system of stable exchange rates was still in force,
these shifts in labour productivity were bringing about a restructuring of international trade to the advantage of Japan and Western
Europe (an increase in their shares of international trade with
parallel contraction of the American share). Subsequently, after the
collapse of Bretton Woods, there were big exchange-rate readjust-
ments, from which emerged a significant reorganization of the
regional distribution of direct foreign investments abroad: whereas
in the 60s the USA was exporting ten times more capital (net capital
outflows) than Japan and six times more than Western Germany,
there was a sudden drop in these ratios in the second half of the
70s. The USA was now exporting only 1.3 times more capital than
the Federal Republic of Germany.[14] As shown in Table 8.1, the share
of US FDI outflows as percentage of total outflows from developed
countries decreased from 39.7% in the period 1978–80 to 15.7% in
2003–5.

(3) This international development to the disadvantage of American
capital was accompanied by a parallel increase in direct foreign capital investments (chiefly Japanese and European) in the USA. From
the second half of the 1980s direct international investments cease
to be a one-way direction (from the USA to other industrial countries) and acquire a cruciform character, as it were, with differences
in productivity diminishing among the developed capitalist countries. Conjunctural factors also played their part in this change. At
the same time, as certain developing countries reach high levels
of capitalist development and are so transformed into exporters
of goods and services to the developed world and other developing countries, they also develop the tendency to become capital
exporters: 'while only 6 of these economies had outward FDI stocks
of more than $5 billion in 1990, this now applies to as many as
25 of them. [...] the top sources of FDI (in terms of stock data) from
developing and transition economies are Hong Kong (China), the
British Virgin Islands, Russia, Singapore, Taiwan Province of China
and Brazil' (UNCTAD, *Investment Brief*, Number 3, 2006).

In any case it becomes evident from the above data that *the combination of import penetration and improvement in the international competitiveness of local production is the prerequisite for the inflow of foreign investment capital in the form of direct investments.*

The theory of modification allows us also to decipher the riddle of liberalization of international trade throughout the entire ascendant phase of capitalist social formations following the Second World War.

Let us recall, to begin with, that the classical theorists of imperialism generalized the pre-war economic conjuncture and characterized as utopian any thought that international trade might be able some day to dispense with excessive tariffs and other measures of state protectionism. In today's world, by contrast, it is very common for the post-war liberalization of trade to be seen as an expression of American hegemony in the global market, or at any rate as a policy by means of which American economic interests are secured worldwide. Of course the American-hegemony variant is unable to explain either why the USA's position in international trade has weakened (to the advantage of the European countries and Japan), in conditions, precisely, of liberalization of international trade, or why the USA's competitors were promoting this liberalization in every possible way.

The modification theory interprets as follows the enigma of liberalized international trade. As the 'modified competition' in the international market not only protects the less developed national capitals but at the same time promotes institutionalization of an international division of labour that brings relative advantages even to countries occupying a subordinate position on the scale of labour productivity, the more productive sectors in the poorer countries push their national state in the direction of liberalizing the global market. It is only the less developed capitals or productive sectors that press for protective state intervention in correspondence with these cause–effect relationships, and indeed even in the more developed country. The reason for this is that the international competitiveness even of branches at below-average levels of development (in the more developed country) is adversely affected by the inevitable consequences of global trade for the division of labour.

During the ascendant phase of the economic cycle, the high growth rates of national social capital ensure the hegemony of the dynamic sectors of industry and so the opening of the national economy to the global market, with the minimization of every kind of protectionist measure. The crisis of overaccumulation since the first half of the 1970s (Ioakimoglou and Milios 1993) had undermined the capacity for expansion of most capitalist countries on the global market at the rates that were possible in preceding periods. At the same time certain branches of Western European and American industry (iron and steel, the automobile industry, shipyards, textile mills, clothing manufacturers) went into a deep crisis, from which the corresponding export capital of Japan and certain newly industrializing countries were able to derive benefit. This conjuncture led in the 1980s to the institutionalization by the USA and certain European countries of selective protectionist measures, curtailing the freedom of international commercial transactions that had prevailed in the preceding period.[15] *As neoliberal policies and restructuring of capitalist production has again shifted the balance of forces to the benefit of capital and restored high levels of profitability in most capitalist countries since the mid-1990s, protectionist measures have been displaced by the hegemonic trend towards market liberalization and financialization* (see Chapter 9).

8.2.3 The tendency towards equalization of the rate of profit on the global market and 'unequal exchange'

What was said above concerning modification of competition on the global market also implies a necessity for revision of the theoretical schema of 'unequal exchange' as propounded by Emmanuel.

As we have seen, Emmanuel postulated a uniform rate of profit on the global market. But one of the effects of the modified functioning of competition on the global market has been to make possible (among other causes) a reproduction of differences in the rate of profit and the productivity of labour as between the different countries: the elimination of extra-profits through the mechanisms of the exchange rates reduces competitive pressure and makes it possible for the different national rates of profit to be reproduced.

The hypothesis of the uniform global rate of profit would presuppose an even greater flow of capital from one country to another. But the main point is that the hypothesis of the uniform rate of profit on the global market cannot be justified on the basis of the specific direction maintained throughout the entire post-war period by international capital: *'cross-investments' between developed industrial countries, with parallel continuing marginalization of the poor countries of the Third World.* By contrast, the existence, at least tendentially, on the international market of a uniform rate of profit should be linked with a much more intense movement of capital towards the periphery – which would then eliminate underdevelopment. As correctly noted by Busch, this is where the 'paradoxical in Emmanuel' starts to appear: 'Emmanuel cannot assert on the one hand that there is an international average rate of profit and on the other derive the problem of Third World underdevelopment from the existence of precisely this average rage of profit' (Busch 1973: 63).

Capital movements towards the poor countries of the Third World (the Least Developed Countries, see UNCTAD, 2008b) continue to be marginal, because the rate of profit in these countries remains at very low levels internationally, contrary to what is asserted by the theory of unequal exchange.

Moreover, the theory of unequal exchange presupposes an oversimplified schema of international specialization, involving two absolutely distinct groups of countries, each of which produces commodities the other does not produce competitively. In reality the developing countries import and export to and from the industrial countries, albeit on a different scale, commodities of every kind (UNCTAD, ibid.). Thus, overall, the theory of 'unequal exchange' does not only represent a radical deviation from Marxist theory, as Bettelheim had the opportunity to demonstrate, but also presents an entirely distorted picture of the real processes entailed by internationalization of capital. Without the (arbitrary) hypothesis that a uniform rate of profit is generated on the global market, the theory of 'unequal exchange' collapses (see Chapter 2).

But refutation of Emmanuel's theory on the average international rate of profit does not imply total absence of the international processes tending towards equalization of the rate of profit as between the different national social capitals. It is just that these processes involve almost exclusively the developed capitalist countries to which international capital movements are primarily confined. The processes of equalization of the rate of profit are unfolding on account of modification of competition on the international market, through capital transfers.

Capital exports from a country of higher labour productivity to a country of lower labour productivity entail two types of consequence: on the one hand there is an acceleration in the process of accumulation in the capital-importing country, something in general tending to reinforce the tendency towards contraction of the overall rate of profit in the country. On the other hand, the repatriation of a part of the profits to the capital-exporting country serves to raise that country's rate of profit. This does indeed tend to reduce the differences between the overall rate of profit of the more developed capital-exporting country and the rate of profit in the less developed industrial country that is importing capital. We should bear in mind that this is a process exclusively involving developed capitalist countries and the so-called newly industrializing developing countries. By contrast the most least-developed countries of the Third World continue to play a marginal role in international capital movements, and so in the international tendency towards equalizing national rates of profit. We should bear in mind too that this international tendency towards equalization of the rate of profit is in all cases a process much weaker than the corresponding process (elaboration of a general rate of profit) within a uniform social formation.

As is also obvious from the evidence cited on internationalization of capital, it is not the 'low wages' (as Emmanuel claims) but the productivity of labour and the profitability of investment (the rate of profit in a country), as determined by the overall production and social relations, that 'decide' the direction of the international trade and capital flows. Furthermore, the organization of each social national capital at the level of its own national state, expressed, *among other parameters* in the existence of a specific national currency for each country (absence of a single international currency for all countries), as well as the persistence of protectionist economic policies which restrict international trade,[16] precludes the formation of international *production prices* and thus the formation of an international general rate of profit at the level of the world market.

The rate of profit therefore differs from one country to another and is subjected to an equalization process only among developed capitalist countries, on the basis of constantly increasing volumes of international investment. This process is amplified by the rapid growth of the globalized financial sphere, as will be discussed in the following chapter. The underdeveloped countries, by contrast, are positioned at the lower levels of the international hierarchy in rates of profit, due to the weakness of capital's control over both pre-capitalist and pre-industrial social relations on the one hand, and over the working classes on the other, which leads to a consequent low productivity of labour in these countries. The underdeveloped countries are thus only weakly integrated into international trade and marginally involved in capital movements.

9
Financialization: *Market Discipline* or *Capital Discipline?*

9.1 Introduction to recent discussions: Neoliberalism, financialization, crisis

A crucial aspect of nearly all contemporary approaches to imperialism is the idea that the domination of neoliberalism and of the globalized financial sector of the economy produces a predatory version of capitalism, a capitalism that inherently tends towards crisis.

The current financial crisis is without precedent in the post-war period. This is acknowledged by the majority of mainstream economists. There is a growing consensus on the need to *regulate* many parts of the economy. Great debates have been set in motion on the future of regulation, proclaiming the end of the Reagan era.

All these discussions are important, but they do not tell the whole story. Financial *instability* and *income redistribution* are crucial aspects of modern capitalism but they do not capture its *essence*.

Recent heterodox literature is dominated by a single and persistent argument. The argument[1] is that contemporary financial liberalization should be approached as a process in which the financial elites and financial intermediaries, that is contemporary *rentiers* in the Keynesian terminology, have a leading role in working out the details of the neoliberal form of capitalism. Writing in the mid-1930s, Keynes (1973: 377) predicted the eventual extinction ('euthanasia') of the rentiers 'within one or two generations'. Many present-day Keynesians portray the developments of the last decades as the return of the rentiers three generations later to take over the economy. Neoliberalism thus amounts to the 'revenge of the rentiers' (Smithin 1996: 84, coins this phrase), who are said to have shaped the contemporary political and economical agenda in accordance with their own vested interests.

The relevant economic literature, according to Epstein (2001: 1) coined the term *financialization* to denote this phenomenon of 'the increasing importance of financial markets, financial motives, financial institutions, and financial elites in the operation of the economy and its governing institutions, both at the national and international level'. In this quasi-Keynesian discourse the economic and political strengthening of rentiers entails: (i) an increase in the economic importance of the financial sector as opposed to the 'real' industrial sector of the economy, (ii) the transfer of income from the latter to the former, thereby increasing economic inequalities and depressing effective demand, (iii) the exacerbation of financial instability, transforming it into a central aspect of modern capitalism.

It is not our intention here to provide a comprehensive and in-depth account of neoliberal financialization as seen from the Keynesian standpoint. The analysis in question certainly deals quite competently with such crucial aspects of modern capitalism as structured credit products and the related risky financial innovations, lax oversight, deregulation and financial fragility (Wray 2008). Moreover, it also argues that financialization has contributed to *radical restructuring* and equally radical changes in the behaviour of firms (especially large corporations).

According to recent post-Keynesian and institutionalist analyses,[2] industrial corporations have ceased to be the 'steam-engine of the economy' that Keynes and Schumpeter portrayed them as in the past. Their priority is to serve the interests of rentiers (i.e. of major shareholders and the financial institutions representing them): to increase remuneration for major shareholders, enhancing their influence over company decision making at the expense of the interests of other stakeholders' (viz. workers, consumers and managers). It appears that two relevant changes have taken place in enterprises.[3] *Firstly*, joint-stock companies are now conceived of as portfolios of liquid subunits that home-office management must continually restructure to maximize their stock price at every point in time. *Secondly*, and as a consequence of the first change, there is a fundamental (forced) change in the incentives of top managers who now think rather in terms of maximization of short-term stock prices. The end product of the whole process is anti-labour business policies on the one hand and on the other a focus on short-term (speculative) gains rather than on long-term economic development, stability and employment.[4]

Hence, for Keynesian-like argumentation, neoliberalism is an 'unjust' (in terms of income distribution), unstable, anti-developmental variant of capitalism whose direct consequence is contraction of workers' incomes and the proliferation of speculation. It is a regime that *focuses economic activity on the search for profits in the sphere of circulation*. To put matters schematically, the rentier owners of financial securities induce a fall in the 'price' of labour so as to increase the value of their stocks (bonds and shares) at the same time engaging in speculation so as to obtain short-term advantages vis-à-vis rival rentiers.

This general conception seems to be prevalent in the realm of Marxist discussion also. For a number of theoreticians influenced by it, neo-liberal capitalism has not succeeded (at least to date) in restoring the profitability of capital (the rate of profit) to high levels, that is to say to levels satisfactory for dynamic capitalist accumulation (what could such levels be? one wonders).[5] It appears to be entrapped (since the mid-1970s) in a perennial crisis, the end of which is not readily visible. The result of this is that large sums of capital are unable to find outlets for investment. This has two probable consequences. *Firstly*, this 'surplus' capital stagnates in the money markets, creating 'bubbles', or is used to underpin ineffective policies of forced accumulation that depend on lending and debt (Brenner 2001a, 2008; Wolff 2008). *Secondly*, this capital circulates internationally in pursuit of *accumulation by dispossession* (Harvey, see Chapter 3), even profiting, that is to say, not from exploitation of labour but from direct appropriation of income chiefly from those who are not financially privileged or do not occupy an appropriate *position* in the market for credit (Lapavitsas 2008).

We do not propose here to undertake a comprehensive critique of the abovementioned views. They doubtless reflect significant aspects of present-day capitalism, but in our opinion are unable to provide a sufficiently inclusive account of the reasons for the neoliberal reforms. Their basic weakness – and it is at the same time the link that holds them together – is that *they represent the neoliberal formula for securing profitability of capital not as a question of producing surplus-value but as a question of income redistribution pertaining essentially to the sphere of circulation*. It thus appears that the developmental 'ineptitude'[6] and the instability of present-day capitalism are the result of a certain 'insatiability', or at any rate of bad regulation, in the relations governing income. *Are we in the final analysis all Keynesians?*

Before formulating our negative answer to the above question let us make a passing reference to the present financial crisis.

9.2   The relationship between the financial system and other elements comprising the core of neoliberalism

The development of the financial system under neoliberal hegemony is linked to four basic elements comprising the core of the neoliberal model.

(i) One declared objective has been to deregulate the labour market as a means of reducing the power of wage-earners to demand wage increases and better terms of employment. This has been pursued both by repressive methods and through monetaristic policies for fighting inflation, and has led to a significant increase in unemployment. *It has also been pursued through the weapon of disciplining and sanctioning the behaviour of business and states that is made available through neoliberal money markets.* Here it should be noted that monetaristic policies of increasing interest rates at the beginning of the 80s, apart from significantly boosting unemployment, also had the result of generating a significant sphere for investment of international capital: higher levels of state indebtedness.

(ii) Second, and in one aspect a continuation of (i): international trade and outsourcing, that is to say the exposure to international competition for the purpose of devaluing and excluding insufficiently valorized (i.e. 'non-competitive') capital are predicated, among other things, on the freedom of movement of capital along with the rest of the neoliberal complex of financial regulation (non-bank financing, development of differentiated international financial markets). These elements have been mechanisms for 'schooling' labour in the requirements of capitalist restructuring and continuing accumulation. Confining ourselves to the effects that non-bank financing of businesses has had, we detect some significant effects on the mode of operation of these businesses, particularly those that have access to money markets. To name just a very few: *Firstly,* we see an *increase in company debt* in relation to the same capital, insofar as the debt increases the profitability of the capital and so sends signals of profitability to the money markets. *Secondly,* for regular continuation of financing *it is demanded* that every enterprise *has high profit indicators* – every suspicion of insufficient valorization increases the risk of burdensome terms of financing and reduces the companies' competitive potential (e.g. increases the risk of its being taken over). *Thirdly,* shares do not comprise the key measure for financing of enterprises but are raw materials for buyouts and mergers. In other words there is a handling of cash flows and sale and repurchase decisions with shares that increases the share prices (which can play a role in accumulation when what is required is investment that will have a long-term yield). The trade unions, indeed working people in general, experienced these results as loss of bargaining positions. The argument was and is simple: accept what we propose, otherwise the company will lose its potential for financing. Doubts will be generated as to its profitability and there will be danger of it being bought out, with resultant loss of work-places, or of the production chain being restructured and a part of the chain transferred to other countries.

(iii) *Privatization of sectors of state activity and change in the composi-tion of state activities.* Expansion of the space for investment of individual capital is another central element in the neoliberal model. Privatizations are an important factor in bringing about a broadening of the financial sphere. This too has consequences for wage-earners. At a minimum there is a requirement for increased financing, as distribution free of charge is replaced by commodities which have a price or insofar as the method of costing changes when they pass from the public sector into the control of private capital. As a result, a basis is created for *an increase in the debt of households* that have access to the banking system; but the potential is also generated for penetration, when required, by banks into new sectors of the market, such as, for example, student loans. Within the same logic as privatization and greater sanctification of profit is the reduction of tax for businesses that contribute to maintenance of high levels of state debt. Reforms to the insurance system have introduced noteworthy pursuers of risk-free profits into the com-pany of the banks, insurance companies, mutual capital, hedge funds, etc. and so have evidently brought new pressures to bear on wage earners.

(iv) The securing of consent to the neoliberal model was underwritten by the possibility of access to cheap loans to finance consumer spending or housing or other expenditure and by participation in this global hunt for profits (among the most conspicuous examples of such participation being the private insurance funds or mutual funds), so that there would be increased income to substitute in the best way possible for withdrawal of the state from funding universal insurance systems for health, studies, social services, etc. Accordingly, the seeking out of potential borrowers, that is to say the incorporation into the credit system of certain groups in the population is not merely the result of the greed of the banks and all types of investors but an injunction that is part of the scheme of neoliberal regulation. The privately owned home as a dream that could be made to come true by virtue of neoliberal financial regula-tion became a declared goal of all representatives of the model. The privately owned home as an item of property became a means for access to other facilities of the credit system.

From a different viewpoint, the squeeze on wages, a result and objective of the neoliberal model, *also* put a squeeze on consumer expenditure, such that the introduction of appropriate measures to facilitate *consumer credit* became an escape route for the system, a solution to the problem of managing aggregate demand on the part of the collective capitalist. Today's crisis exposes the difficulties involved in this solution for management of aggregate demand and for organization of consent to the neoliberal programme. In the case of subprimes one can very readily imagine problems with securities from credit cards and quite likely tomorrow securities from student loans, etc.

9.3   From financial crisis to overaccumulation crisis

In the third volume of *Capital* Marx observed: 'as long as the *social* character of labour appears as the *monetary existence* of the commodity and hence as a *thing* outside actual production, monetary crises, independent of real crises or as an intensification of them, are unavoidable' (Marx 1991: 649).

As we know, financial crises are sometimes the prelude to, and sometimes the result of, a crisis of overaccumulation of capital. Sometimes, again, the financial crisis manifests itself 'independently' of the broader economic conjuncture, that is to say does not have any significant effect on the level of profitability and the level of employment of the 'factors of production' in the other sectors of the economy above and beyond the financial sphere or some specific parts of it. This, for example, is what happened in the case of the international financial crisis of 1987, when there was a collapse of share prices in the international stock exchanges, enabling the international press to speak of a 'return to 1929 and the Great Depression'.

It is thus evident that each specific financial crisis must be examined both in relation to its particular characteristics and in relation to its interaction with other spheres of economic activity and the wider economic conjuncture, before it becomes possible to draw conclusions as to its causes, its extent and its consequences. The current crisis is the outcome not only of permanent characteristics of capitalist relations of production and reproduction but also of characteristics that are peculiar to the core of the neoliberal organization of this relation, that is to say to the core of the present form of appearance of capitalist relations of production.

The squeeze on wages and flexibilization of labour relations, that is to say reduction in the bargaining power of workers against capital, are a success story of neoliberalism but *at the same time* represent one of the conditions for the nurturing and triggering of the crisis.

It represents success for the model that it enriches the markets with numerous players and mobilizes every sum of capital that cannot be directly invested in the production process so that it participates in the club of demands on future profit. At the same time, however, this 'depth' means ever great pressures for risk-free profit, for issuing of securities, in other words for intense competition, so that unexplored markets can be subordinated to the world of credit, with consequent downplaying of risk and massive withdrawal from participation and funding when secure profit is jeopardized.

It is finally worth noting that the 'wisdom of the markets', an important element in constructing the core of the neoliberal model, prescribes market evaluation of property (market-to-market value). It is this that has caused the lack of trust between the players because the fall in value of the securities has spoilt the balance sheets of the institutions maintaining them and protracted the uncertainty. The solution adopted is a familiar one. But the result is that it has become possible for a number of elements not to be factored into the overall assessment.

In other words *the conditions for increase in class domination of capital appear simultaneously as conditions undermining that domination.* The crisis designates the moment of convergence of all the abovementioned contradictions.

It is a crisis that has appeared in the financial sphere and is *systemic.* Systemic in the sense that it has been engendered by the elements and the relations that are at the core of the neoliberal model. It is systemic also because it has struck at important nodal points of the system and through them at the terms of operation of the internationalization of capital. It is systemic also because it has hit the most powerful organizational centre of the model: the markets and the financial institutions of the United States, which were the key control points for the overall system of organizing markets, intervening in them, and promoting financial innovations and financial tools. If we take it into account that Britain, the world's second financial centre, has also been affected, and very seriously, we obtain a picture of how the system has been centrally affected. Finally, it is also systemic in that the capacity of the collective capitalist to guarantee the functioning of neoliberal regulation has been crippled.

While the financial crisis is still unfolding, it is now taking on the characteristics of *a crisis of overaccumulation,* which, starting from a ruthless squeeze on the financial sector also drags in other sectors and introduces the economic system as a whole to the operations of liquidation of inadequately valorized capital (obviously at an unequal rate in the different countries and with an intermeshing of the developments in each country both with the developments in other countries and with the financial system).

The interconnectedness of events is thus the reverse of what is often maintained (e.g. Brenner 2008). What is involved is not a continuing crisis of overaccumulation dating from the 70s, which has fed superfluous capital into the sphere of finance, in this way leading to speculation, the 'bubble' and the crisis. The preceding crisis of overaccumulation of capital had already been blunted through the contribution of the neoliberal settlement (in which a decisive nodal point was the functioning of the financial sphere). There had been a return of profits to levels approaching those of the early seventies, production had been restructured, labour made more flexible and wage levels frozen (Ioakimoglou and Milios 2005). The share accruing to wages was continually contracting.

But the blocking of the sphere of finance and credit funding on which expanded reproduction of capital was based was inevitably interpreted as 'involvement' of this expanded reproduction. It was initially expressed in overproduction of (unsold) goods, given that a credit squeeze implies restrictions on productive and individual consumption (perpetuated by credit). This in turn meant an abrupt fall in profitability and the necessity for cutbacks in production, in other words overcapacity of the means of production, overaccumulation of productive capital and the need for a new cycle of restructuring.

The latest decision framework for participation of the state in capital or temporary nationalization of banks and other enterprises (variations on the Brown proposal), is not an answer for the elements that nurtured and triggered the crisis. There has accordingly been a mobilization of the international bureaucracy via various institutions suitably inoculated against the 'virus' of democracy, and it is now promising to discuss the crisis and take measures to prevent its recurrence.

A crisis at the heart of the system puts on the agenda the question of rearrangement and natural registration of the international correlations of power. Systemic crisis does not necessarily spell destruction for the system. It means exposure of its contradictions. And the representatives of the collective capitalist perceive the situation more or less as follows, on the basis of the current dynamic of unfolding and proliferation of the crisis: that it is a disease from which recovery can be assured not just by popping some pill. An operation will be required that will enable the *same* organism to continue to function, albeit in a different way (for example, without excessive leverage, to abandon the preceding meta-phor). But each attempt at regulation means a redistribution of power and most probably cancellation of functions. From the new arrange-ments that are anticipated there will be no interference with the inter-national character of the financial system, securitization, the deepening of the market, the squeeze on working people. These are inviolable terms of each new set of arrangements, on the basis of today's strategy of capital. They are strategic options with no fall-back position. Thus, as perceived by a plethora of organizations and shapers of policy, state intervention must be chronologically limited, must aim exclusively at the generally recognized problem and must leave no trace behind it when the time comes for it to withdraw (particularly traces that would hinder the 'free' functioning of markets).

If, then, the core of the neoliberal dogma must remain intact (with mere readjustment of the relations and the pace of the functioning of its constituent elements), with the overwhelming correlation of power in favour of capital simply taken as a given, the workforce will continue to be treated as the 'flexible' variable, destined to absorb all the shocks, currents and future.

Nevertheless, crisis at the heart of the system also entails breaches in the terms of its ideological hegemony. Citizens understand quite sim-ply: if the state intervenes to save the banks why can it not do the same for the insurance funds, for the health system, for ..., etc.

The traces left behind by the current conjuncture of the crisis do not require any particular skill to detect. *Firstly*, discredit is brought to bear on a basic ideology that the state is 'bad because it is incompetent' and the markets 'good because they are both competent and effective'. States are being called upon to act as guarantors of stability, in other words to implement interventionist policies. This is not something eas-ily to be erased from the collective memory. *Secondly*, the crisis is having adverse effects on the capacity for ensuring consensus because of the effects it is having on the working population and 'underdogs' gener-ally. The limitations of demand management, not through strengthen-ing of wages and the terms of employment but through encouraging excessive household indebtedness, have become evident to all. Both these phenomena strengthen the political forces that seek a different way of managing the capitalist system. From this viewpoint it should not pass unnoticed that Krugman (Nobel prize 2008) in his book *The Conscience of a Liberal* (2007) is in effect calling for state intervention for the creation of trade unions in branches where there is an uninsured workforce, defending the idea of a public and universal health system, demands which make manifest the tension that has been accumulated on account of the polarization imposed by the class struggle of capital against labour. *Thirdly*, there is a readjustment in the international correlation of power. A reform of the international financial system always harbours an inherent potential that there will be a rewriting of international rules and obligations, thus affording an opportunity for recording the correlations of power that have emerged.[7]

9.4   Marx's problematic: *Towards* a different interpretation of neoliberalism

Keynesianism undoubtedly offers a helpful perspective on the neoliberal form of capitalism,[8] mounting a case that is a powerful alternative to the Marxist analysis. It displays the neoliberal formula for profitability of capital not as a question of production of surplus-value but as a question of income redistribution pertaining basically to the sphere of circulation. If it should prove to have the stronger arguments we would have no choice but to admit *firstly* that Marx is nothing more than a forerunner to Keynes – or, even more so, a theorist who offers a useful complement to the Keynesian approach. *Secondly*, that a political bloc between the 'productive' classes (capitalists and workers) is both feasible and necessary for overthrowing the hegemony of the rentiers.

Some time ago, 2008 Nobel prize winner Krugman (1997: 155) asked the following relevant question: *why has the world of finance become so frenetic?* We shall attempt to answer the question in what follows, rejecting Keynesian arguments that the hegemony of the rentier lies behind neoliberalism. Returning to Marx's analysis in *Capital* we will put forward the view that present-day capitalism is a form of capitalism *particularly favourable for valorization of capital*, that is to say particularly well suited, for the bourgeoisie as a whole, for enforcing capital's aggressive exploitation strategies of labour.

9.4.1   The structure of financial sector in Marx's analysis

As we have already mentioned (see Part II), capital could be comprehended as a historically... a historically specific social relation that expresses itself in the form of 'money as an end in itself' or 'money that creates more money'. At this level of generality, the capitalist occupies a specific *position* and plays a specific *role*. He is, and behaves as, the incarnation of autonomous movement of value, *embodying the 'self-movement' of capital M-C-M´*. The theory of capital is not an analysis of the actions of the capitalist. It is not a response to the actions of a *subject*. On the contrary, it is the movement of capital that imparts 'consciousness' to the capitalist. The power of capital is impersonal. In reality it is the power of money as such (Marx 1990: 165–6; Balibar 1984).

Proceeding to a more concrete level of analysis, Marx acknowledges that *the place of capital* may be occupied by more than one subject. There may be both a *money capitalist* and a *functioning capitalist*. This means that a detailed description of capitalism cannot ignore the *circulation of interest-bearing capital*, which depicts the structure of the financial system. Marx's argumentation might be represented in the following schema.

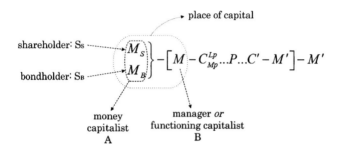

In the course of the lending process, the money capitalist A becomes the recipient and proprietor of a *security S*, that is to say a written *promise* of payment (contingent in character) from the functioning capitalist B. This promise certifies that A remains owner of the money capital *M*. He does not transfer his capital to B, but cedes to him the right to make use of it for a specified period. We will recognize two general types of securities: *bonds* S_B and *shares* S_S. In the case of the former the enterprise undertakes to return fixed and prearranged sums of money irrespective of the profitability of its own operations. In the latter case it secures loan capital by selling a part of its property, thereby committing itself to paying dividends proportional to its profits. If the company has entered the stock exchange and what is involved is share issue, then capitalist B corresponds to the managers and capitalist A to the legal owner.

In any case, in the hands of B the sum *M* functions as capital. Money taken as the independent expression of the value of commodities enables the active capitalist B to purchase the necessary *means of production Mp* and *labour power Lp* for organizing the productive process. The latter takes place under a regime of specific relations of production (comprising a specific historical form of relations of exploitation) and in this way is transformed into a process for producing surplus-value. The money reserve that B now has at his disposal is the *material expression of his social power to set in motion* the productive process *and to control it* (see Chapter 5).

Four very basic consequences are implied by this analysis and are, briefly, as follows.

Firstly, the place of capital (the incarnation of the powers stemming from the structure of the relations of production) *is occupied both by the money capitalist and by the functioning capitalist*. In other words, the place of capital is occupied by agents that are both 'internal' to the enterprise (managers) and 'external' to it (security holders). Marx's general conception abolishes the basic distinction drawn by Keynes between the productive classes 'within' the enterprise and the parasitical class of 'external' rentiers. In his own words: 'in the production process, the functioning capitalist represents capital against the wage-labourers as the property of others, and the money capitalist participates in the exploitation of labour as represented by the functioning capitalist' (Marx 1991: 504). The secondary contradictions developed between the managers and the big investors certainly do exist but they evidently pertain to a more concrete level of analysis.

Secondly, the pure form of ownership over capital (whether it is a question of money or productive capital) is the *financial security*, corresponding, that is, to 'imaginary money wealth' (ibid.: 609). The ownership title is a 'paper duplicate', either of the money capital ceded in the case of the bond S_B, or of the 'material' capital in the case of the share S_S. Nevertheless the *price* of security does not emerge either from the value of the money made available or from the value of the 'real' capital. The ownership titles are priced on the basis of the (future) income they will yield for the person owning them (capitalization in accordance with the current interest rate that embodies the risk), which of course is part of the surplus-value produced. In this sense they are *sui generis commodities* plotting a course that is their very own (ibid.: 607–9, 597–8).

Thirdly, the financial 'mode of existence' of capitalist property – as a *promise* and at the same time a *claim* for appropriation of the surplus-value that will be produced in future – brings into existence a broader terrain within which each flow of income can be seen as revenue corresponding to a 'fictitious capital' with the potential to find an outlet on secondary markets (ibid.: 597–9). Hence, we observe that in accordance with Marx's argumentation, the potential for securitization is inherent in the movement of capital. In any case, as Minsky (1987) aptly put it, 'any attempt to place securitization in context needs to start with early-19th-century commercial bill banking in Britain and the recognition that accepting contingent liabilities is a fundamental banking act. The modern contribution is the development of techniques to "enhance credits" without accepting contingent liabilities or the investment of pure equity funds'.

Fourthly, one of the basic characteristics of the neoliberal model is the increase in non-bank funding of credit, both by states and by enterprises. Above and beyond the other consequences, this places at the centre of the financial markets *risk management*, that is to say the factoring in of the contingency of non-achievement of the expected yield (particularly in an international market where a number of diverging forces are affecting profitability). Because the very character of production of surplus-value as well as the overall claims being placed on the latter is *contingent*, risk management is organically linked to capital movement as such. Since, as we shall see in what follows, the inner workings of an enterprise constitute a political terrain, the production of surplus-value, as a battlefield situation where resistance is being encountered, is never something that can be taken for granted. Techniques of risk management, organized within the very mode of functioning of the 'deregulated' money market, *are a critical point in the management of resistance from labour*.

9.4.2   Market discipline or capital discipline? The essence of neoliberal exploitation strategy

The above general framework has a number of less visible but more crucial implications for the analysis of present-day capitalism. Financial markets are for the most part secondary (liquid) markets. This has two basic consequences. *Firstly*, they contribute to the competition and mobility of individual capitals (strengthening the tendency towards establishment of a uniform rate of profit). *Secondly*, apart from dispensing loans, they comprise sites for renegotiation of debt requirements against future production of surplus-value and so *sites for evaluation (though with evident deficiencies) and monitoring of the effectiveness of individual capitals*. We will elaborate upon this line of thought, citing in this connection the following three points:

(1) The capitalist firm is totally immersed in class struggle. The functioning capitalist (whether she is a small capitalist or one of the top managers of a large enterprise) is the point of articulation between the two distinct fields of capital movement.[9] On the one hand, she is called upon to achieve efficient organization of surplus-value

production inside the factory. This process generally entails a persistent endeavour to modernize the means of production, economize on constant capital and reduce labour's share of the net product.[10] But none of these procedures are mere technical decisions to be taken. They are the mutable outcome of class struggle. Therefore, on the other hand, the capitalist enterprise is the location for the organized confrontation of social forces and in this sense comprises, on a continuing basis, a political field *par excellence*. It bears the inherent imprint of class struggle, a reality sharply in conflict with the orientation of neoclassical or most heterodox approaches.

(2)   Organized financial markets facilitate movement of capital, intensifying capitalist competition. In this way they contribute to the trend towards establishment of a uniform rate of profit in the developed capitalist world and those countries that are tending to enter it (see Chapter 8), at the same time securing more favourable conditions for valorization (exploitation) of individual capitals.[11] Keynes believed that completely illiquid markets would be efficient in the mainstream sense, because 'once investment was committed, the owners would have an incentive to use the existing facilities in the best possible way no matter what unforeseen circumstances might arise over the life of plant and equipment' (Davidson 2002: 188). But such a view is very far from the truth. Illiquid financial markets (or highly regulated markets) mean that capital, not being able easily to move to different employment, remains tied up in specific 'plant and equipment' for reasons that are not necessarily connected with its effectiveness in producing surplus-value (profitability). Or, to put it differently, capital's inability to move generates more favourable terms for conducting the struggle for the forces of labour, given that less productive investments are enabled to survive longer.

Capital does not necessarily have to be committed to a particular employment for a long period of time. Given the liquidity of financial markets, it is always in a position to reacquire its money form without difficulty and seek new more effective areas for its valorization. Capital is always on the lookout for opportunities to make a profit, which cannot come from maintaining effective demand but must come from intensifying class exploitation. What capital is 'afraid of' is not dearth of demand but dearth of surplus-value (Mattick 1980: 78–9). Capital is not obliged to provide for labour employment. On the contrary, a reserve army of unemployed labour is always welcomed by employers. It keeps real wages down and paves the way for compliance with the capitalist's strategies of exploitation (Marx 1990: 781–802). Moreover, flexibility of labour is not only a prerequisite for mobility of capital. It is also the method capital finds most suitable for adjusting to fluctuations in the capitalist economic cycle.

(3) Financial markets generate a structure for overseeing the effectiveness of individual capitals, that is to say a type of supervision of capital movement. Businesses that fail to create a set of conditions favourable for exploitation of labour will soon find 'market confidence', that is *the confidence of capital*, evaporating. These businesses will either conform to the demands of capital or before long find themselves on a downhill path. *In this manner capital markets 'endeavour' (not always reliably) to convert into quantitative signs 'political' events within the enterprise.* Forecasts and predictions embodied in securities do not need to be right. What really matters is this quantification process of political events *per se.* This process should be seen as a *strategy:* operating within a market 'panopticon,' individual capitals are disciplined and forced in permanent reorganization (thus facilitating the imposition on them of the 'laws' of capital).

In order to understand the remark above we have to recall that the place of capital is not occupied by one and only one subject. On the one hand, the manager assumes a critical *intermediary function*, becoming the point of articulation between the *'despotism of the factory'*, which he himself must ceaselessly impose, and the *market discipline*, to which he himself is permanently subject (Balibar 1984). On the other hand, outside of the precincts of the firm, money capitalists come up against a 'performance chart' that is shaped by the financial markets and to a significant extent 'monitors' the conditions of accumulation and valorization that prevail at every moment in production (in relation to different parts of the world). In this way the *organized* financial markets exercise a critical function: *they reward profitable and competitive companies and at the same moment punish those that are insufficiently profitable.*

The decisive criterion is that the *value* of the company's securities (shares and bonds) as they are assessed by the international markets, should be *maximized.*[12] Thus, equity holders' and bondholders' interests are basically aligned with respect to enterprise profitability.[13] The demand for high financial value puts pressure on individual capitals (enterprises) for more intensive and more effective exploitation of labour, for greater profitability. This pressure is transmitted through a variety of different channels. To give one example, when a big company is dependent on financial markets for its funding, every suspicion of inadequate valorization increases the cost of funding, reduces the capability that funding will be available and depresses share and bond prices. Confronted with such a climate, the forces of labour within the politicized environment of the enterprise face the dilemma of deciding whether to accept the employers' unfavourable terms, implying loss of their own bargaining position, or whether to contribute through their 'inflexible' stance to the likelihood of the enterprise being required to close (transfer of capital to other spheres of production and/or other countries). Evidently the dilemma is not only hypothetical but is formulated pre-emptively: *accept the 'laws of capital' or live with insecurity and unemployment.*

This pressure affects the whole organization of the production process, the specific form of the *collective worker*, and the income correlation between capital and labour. It ultimately necessitates total reconstruction of capitalist production, more layoffs and weaker wage demands on part of the workers. Restructuring of enterprise, above all, means restructuring of a set of social relations with a view to increasing the rate of exploitation. It is thus a process that presupposes on the one hand an increasing power of the capitalist class over the production process itself, and on the other a devalorization of all inadequately valorized capital (downsizing and liquidating enterprises) and thus economizing on the utilization of constant capital (which is assured by takeovers). It therefore presupposes not only increasing 'despotism' of manager over workers but also flexibility in the labour market and high unemployment.[14]

Economic restructuring of the firm is synonymous with the capitalist offensive against labour. Hence, to us, *'market discipline' must be conceived as synonymous with 'capital discipline'*. In developed capitalism the key role of financial markets does not have only to do with supplying credit to companies. For example, most trades of shares in listed companies consist of movements from one shareholder to another, with no new capital being supplied.[15] The complementary function of financial markets is to 'monitor' the effectiveness of individual capitals, facilitating within enterprises exploitation strategies favourable for capital. Financial markets commodify the claims on future surplus-value. The striking growth of financial derivatives since the early 1980s assists in the consummation of this monitoring process of scrutinizing corporate asset portfolios (i.e. scrutinizing firms' capacity for profit making) by commodifying the risk exposure.[16]

In conclusion, and in contrast to what the Keynesians assume, neoliberalism is an exceptionally effective strategy for capitalist (and not rentier) hegemony. Moreover, the class content of the effectiveness criterion is incontestable. Effectiveness connotes capital's ability to impose the 'laws' of capitalist accumulation, overriding labour resistance without significant difficulty. Apart from theoretical consequences, this finding has important political implications: *the community of interest of those 'inside' the enterprise (labourers and managers) as against the 'outsiders' of the financial markets is a construction of fantasy.* The fantasy is erected upon the no less fantastic distinction between the 'productive' and 'non-productive' classes, a notion derived from the problematic of Keynes. Such an outlook narrows the strategic horizon of the workers' movement to defence of a 'better' capitalism, that is to say a 'better' system of class domination and exploitation. The Keynesian critique of neoliberalism places the boundaries of the practice of the social movements inside the framework of the society of bourgeois exploitation.

10
The 'Global' Level and the Concept of *Imperialist Chain*

10.1 The two extremes of historicism in the recent literature on the global level and the world order

10.1.1 Once more on the neo-Gramscian historicist problematic of capitalism

We mentioned in Chapter 1 that in their stress on the concept of a 'global capitalism', classical imperialist theories foreshadowed the recent discussions on globalization. The national/international dichotomy was seen as subordinate to the global dynamics of 'imperial' capital. One extreme consequence of this train of thought is the notion that national state formation is but a fragile moment in a wider autonomous global dynamics of capital accumulation. Prior to any attempt to engage with the form of today's imperialist order and with its evolution, it would therefore be appropriate to come back to a question that is of direct relevance to the present conjuncture and has been posed above all (but not exclusively) by exponents of the historicist neo-Gramscian approach. This is what Cox has to say in his synopsis of the basic argument:

> The *global economy* has become something distinct from international economic relations, i.e., from transborder economic flows assumed to be subject to state control and regulation. *Global production* and *global finance* now constitute *distinct spheres of power relations* which constrain the state system at least as much as they are influenced by it. They are bringing about a *new social structure of production relations* superseding the nation-centered labor-capital relations of the past [Cox 1999: 515]. Through this process the nation state becomes part

of a larger and more complex political structure that is the counter-part to international production.

(Cox 1987: 253)

It is a line of thought which in its sundry variants still has numer-ous supporters in the contemporary debate.[1] The general idea could be formulated briefly as follows: There has been a cumulative rise in the structural power of internationally mobile capital. The national–inter-national dichotomy is subordinate to the dynamics of social relations enmeshed in this global capital. The process of class formation might always have been a transnational phenomenon (Pijl 1998) or it could have been present-day capitalism that succeeded in establishing mutual interest and common ideological perspectives between social classes in different countries (Cox 1987, Gill 2003), but in either case what takes place is the rise of a transnational historic bloc and emergence of a tran-snational managerial class ensconced in global governance structures and in command of the global economy (Overbeek 2000: 177). In other words, this globalization process has created a hierarchically stratified *global society* in which *global (or globalizing) elites* set the pace in shap-ing the social order. These global elites merge into a common structural force, even when they are competing amongst themselves for primacy within the overall movement. In reality the celebrated historicist prob-lematic is already under implementation in the international sphere. A new global or transnational historic bloc has *brought into existence a glo-bal economic and political space* with *its own specific* production relations and its own special mode of political organization:

> *Globalizing elites* can be defined as a grouping of organic intellectuals and political leaders within what can be called the transnational frac-tion of the capitalist classes of the world. [...] Such elites are in part constituted by their positions in key strategic locations in transna-tional companies, banks, universities, think tanks, media companies, governments and international organizations such as the IMF, World Bank and OECD, and by the discourse of neoliberal globalization. *Their activities seek to make transnational capital a class 'for itself' by theorizing the world order and by synthesizing strategy.* Key members are located in organizations at the apex of global knowledge, production and financial structures, as well as in key political parties and govern-ment agencies in the major capitalist states, notably in the members of the G7.

(Gill 2003: emphasis added)[2]

Before proceeding with a brief critique of the abovementioned problematic it may be worth pausing for a moment to reflect on how little radically new all this represents in the realm of ideas. As analysed in detail in Chapter 1, what is involved is a reversion (in a perhaps similar historical conjuncture) to positions that were once at the centre of Marxist debate. Both Luxemburg and Bukharin claimed that in the era of imperialism expanded reproduction of the CMP takes place on a world scale, not just at the level of each capitalist social formation. Bukharin's analysis is doubtless the more characteristic, foreshadowing the *potential horizon* of the abovementioned historicist problematic. He introduces the concept of the *global economy*, portraying it as 'a system of production relations and corresponding exchange relations on the global plane' (Bukharin 1972a: 27). On this basis, Bukharin maintained that different national economies constitute *individual moments* of the global economy, articulating a global capitalist division of labour, on the basis of which the conflict between the global bourgeoisie and the global proletariat is enacted (for more details see Chapter 1).

This is not such a different picture from that given to us by Cox for the present-day organization of capitalism, where *besides* the national there is a global economic-political plane, a global 'mode of production'. The only difference is that the concept of imperialism has been replaced in the lexicon of Cox (1987: 137) by the concept of *hegemony* and more recently by that of Empire (Cox 2004): 'hegemony at the international level is thus not merely an order among states. It is an order within a world economy with a dominant mode of production which penetrates into all countries and links into other subordinate modes of production. It is also a complex of international social relationships which connect the social classes of the different countries. World hegemony can be described as a social structure, an economic structure, and a political structure; and it cannot be simply one of these things but must be all three.'

10.1.2 Post-modern empire and the 'labour theory' of society

Manifestly influenced by the wider debate on globalization, the argumentation of the neo-Gramscian analyses permeates a key set of ideas and conclusions that can readily be distinguished in recent analyses of *empire* by Hardt and Negri. The writings of these two scholars reproduce the image of a globalized capitalism, basic aspects of which are the emergence of a global market, the retreat of national states (as modern forms of sovereignty and also as territories that place limits on the expansion of capital) and the proliferation throughout the world of new decentralized forms of governance. In what follows we shall attempt briefly (fully cognizant, of course, of the risks involved) to summarize the *essence* of these writers' project, attempting not to stray too far from matters relevant to imperialism.

It should be noted to begin with that Hardt and Negri (2000: 221–39) are in agreement with many of the arguments in the classical theories of imperialism. This is particularly true of the ideas reproduced in interventions by Luxemburg, Hillferding and Kautsky (ibid.: 221–39). They perceive underconsumption as having been a structural 'dysfunction' within the body of capitalism. *It was a contradiction that manifests itself as a problem of realization.* Insofar as there is not sufficient purchasing power to absorb the goods produced, surplus value cannot be realized. Thus it is not class struggle that poses a danger for capitalism in its initial stages but improper regulation of the channels of circulation. As the familiar argumentation goes, capital has no other prospect than that of 'emigration': *'capital is an organism that cannot sustain itself without constantly looking beyond its boundaries,* feeding off its external environment. Its outside is essential' (ibid.: 224, emphasis added). This formulation already has the potential to prejudice us in terms of 'what is likely to happen' according to these authors. Having accepted the theoretical problematic of Luxemburg, they are unable to evade its consequences, which are none other than acceptance of the trend towards a *globalized economy*: 'capital from its inception tends towards being a world power, or really *the* world power' (ibid.: 225).

But this is not where it ends. The authors understand only too well that capital export is not the definitive solution to the problem of underconsumption because of its simultaneous triggering of a capitalization process. The capital exported to non-capitalist zones 'transforms them into capitalist societies themselves': a 'process of capitalization' comes into operation that *interiorizes the exterior* (ibid.: 226–7). Nondefinitive resolution of the contradiction of underconsumption leads to the 'fundamental contradiction of capitalist expansion': 'once a segment of the environment has been "civilized," once it has been organically incorporated into the newly expanded boundaries of the domain of capitalist production, it can no longer be the outside necessary to realize capital's surplus value' (ibid.).

There are two possible ways by means of which the new contradiction might be resolved: revolution or empire (ibid.:240). In either case *the entity whose existence is at stake is the national state*, with the result that the role of the latter is from the outset manifestly 'ephemeral' and transitional. From the moment that the 'processes of capitalist development determine valorization and exploitation as functions of a global system of production', the national state, constituting an obstacle, 'tends to be surpassed in the long run' (ibid.: 236). *In other words, because capital is global in its range, only a correspondingly 'global state', an empire, could keep track of it in all its movements* (ibid.).

We have already established the basic framework of assumptions that underlies the empire argumentation. But the abovementioned train of thought is predicated on a further essential presupposition: that of *non-correspondence between capital and (national) state*. The state and capital are once again seen as *autonomous entities* (as Harvey, Wood, Callinicos and Arrighi have argued, for details see Chapter 3), and are moreover to all appearances 'a contradictory coupling' (ibid.: 325). The entire history of capitalism can thus be divided up into phases, each of which corresponds to a specific configuration assumed by 'the dialectic between the state and capital' (ibid.: 305). To be concrete:

> Each of the modern paradigms of sovereignty indeed supports capital's operation for a specific historical period, but at the same time they pose obstacles to capital's development that eventually have to be overcome. *This evolving relationship is perhaps the central problematic to be confronted by any theory of the capitalist state.*
>
> (ibid.: 328)

Nevertheless, one basic question remains: when capital has exhausted the non-capitalist 'outside', how can it secure the conditions for its survival? In other words, what can serve to nourish the new capitalism when it has finally ingested its non-capitalist reserves?

The answer given by the writers has little in common with the *catastrophism* that characterizes the classical theories. To a significant extent the internationalization of capital has succeeded in organizing the world on a capitalist basis, bringing to accomplishment the process of *formal subsumption* of labour to capital. This is the writers' term for the gradual exhaustion of non-capitalist reserves, that is to say 'extension of the domain of capitalist production and capitalist markets' (ibid.: 255). In a sense the world is homogenized and thus draws ever closer to a *limit*: 'for more than one hundred years the practices of imperialism had worked to subsume all forms of production throughout the world under the command of capital [...] At a certain point, as capitalist expansion reaches its limit, the processes of formal subsumption can no longer play the central role' (ibid.: 262, 255).

As it approaches this limit, capital enters the phase of *real subsumption of labour to capital*, something which does not involve 'the same processes of expansion' because 'the integration of labour into capital becomes more intensive than extensive and society is ever more completely fashioned by capital' (ibid.: 155). The development of the global market, the outcome primarily of autonomous activity of the multinationals (ibid.: 304, 310; 2004: 169–72), 'cannot be the result simply of financial or monetary factors but must come about through a *transformation of social and productive relations*' (ibid., emphasis added). To convey these transformations the writers resorted to, and continued, the argumentation to be found in the analyses of the Italian *Operaismo* ('workerism') movement, which in 1973 dissolved into 'autonomia', focusing on the theoretical scheme of the *social worker*.[3]

The basic idea of workerism derives from a *particular* reading of Marx's *Grundrisse*, above all the notorious chapter titled 'Fragment on Machines'. The working class is constructed as a *social subjectivity* perpetually resisting capital's endeavours to reduce it to subjection. Particularly with the passage to real subsumption, the logic of capitalist production comes to permeate society, incorporating every moment of social life. Capital appears subaltern and alienated alongside the vital creativity of social labour subjectivity.[4] The latter organizes its resistance both through rejection of exploitation and through activation of a variety of mechanisms of individual and collective self-improvement and self-realization. Labour subjectivity possesses an *autonomous productive and creative force* which capital attempts continually to control and subjugate.

Thus, in the writers' representation, the history of capitalism must not be approached as the unfolding of structural imperatives of capital. The transition from formal to real subsumption *has been marked* by the creative militancy of proletarians throughout the world, and it is precisely this struggle that 'obliged' capital to effect transformations in production relations towards a further intensification of globalization. It is within the 'social worker' that 'conditions of liberation and struggle' were constructed that only capital could control. As a result 'the globalization of markets, far from being simply the horrible fruit of capitalist entrepreneurship, was actually the result of the desires and demands of Taylorist, Fordist, and disciplined labour power across the world' (ibid.: 256).

We see, then, that imperialism with the continuing expansion of capital for more than a century was conducive to the establishment of a stably *uniform* international economic structure:

There was thus a tendency toward the unity of the international or multinational proletariat in one common attack against the capitalist disciplinary regime. [...] The tendency created necessarily a potential or virtual unity of the international proletariat. This *virtual unity* was never fully actualized as a *global political unity*, but it nonetheless had substantial effects.

(ibid.: 262–3)

Workers' struggles throughout the world led to the great crisis in capitalist production at the end of the 1960s, once again forcing capital 'to modify its own structures and undergo a paradigm shift' (ibid.: 261). The transition to the post-industrial informational society was similarly made necessary for capital by the creative resistance of labour. Capital was 'obliged' to modify its paradigm for the work force so as to be in a position to bring under its control a new post-modern form of working class subjectivity that was beginning to emerge: *the world multitude*. Specifically:

The power of the proletariat imposes limits on capital and not only determines the crisis but also dictates the terms and nature of the transformation. *The proletariat actually invents the social and productive forms that capital will be forced to adopt in the future.* [...] The restructuring of production, from Fordism to post-Fordism, from modernization to postmodernization, was anticipated by the rise of a new subjectivity. [...] Capital did not need to invent a new paradigm (even if it were capable of doing so) because *the truly creative moment had already taken place.* Capital's problem was rather to dominate a new composition that had already been produced autonomously and defined within a new relationship to nature and labor, a relationship of autonomous production.

(ibid.: 268, 274, 276)

Here we come to the most widely commented upon part of Hardt and Negri's argumentation, which has to do with the emergence of the multitude. Essentially what we are dealing with here is a variant of the familiar theoretical schema called 'post-industrial society', which in reality is the information society. Post-modern forms of production today 'produce not only commodities but also rich and powerful social relationships' (ibid.: 210). This is so because all of the forms of production 'exist within the networks of the world market and under the domination of the informational production of services' (ibid.: 288). Moreover, the immaterial production of social perceptions, attitudes, knowledge, lends a particularly communicational and linguistic character to production. In reality what is involved is the production of social and political relationships. 'The lines of production and those of representation cross and mix in the same linguistic and productive realm. [...] *Production becomes indistinguishable from reproduction* [...]. *Social subjects are at the same time producers and products of this unitary machine'* (ibid.: 385, emphasis added).

It follows from the above that in one sense the post-modern era has provided a 'historical' solution to the key difficulty in Ricardo's speculation, because now capitalist production itself has de facto homogenized all qualitatively different concrete labour: 'with the computerization of production today [...] the heterogeneity of concrete labor has tended to be reduced, [...] the labour of computerized tailoring and the labour of computerized weaving may involve exactly the same concrete practices – that is, manipulation of symbols and information' (ibid.: 292). In their system Smith and Ricardo reduced all wealth to human labour alone, reducing in this way the whole of political economy to the subjectivity of labour (Althusser 1997: 171–2). In the post-modern outlook of Hardt and Negri, by contrast, it is chiefly social relationships that are 'produced' by homogenized immaterial labour, so that their own transformation in turn becomes possible. These writers are in the final analysis developing a 'labour theory of society'. On this basis, their flirtation with American pragmatist philosophy is in no way surprising (Hardt and Negri 2004: 196–202).[5]

One basic question remains in the end after all this argumentation. On the one hand we have seen that post-modern immaterial production is the outcome of capital's subordinating the spontaneous creative dynamic of the multitude. But on the other hand in many of their formulations the writers accept that (1) 'there cannot be a fully realized world market without the processes of real subsumption' (Hardt and Negri 2000: 255), (2) the post-modern paradigm shift of production 'toward the network model has fostered the growing power of transnational corporations beyond and above the traditional boundaries of nation-states' (ibid.: 304). Consequently, (3) 'large transnational corporations have effectively moved out of the jurisdiction and authority of nation-states' so that this centuries-long dialectic between state and capital has come to an end: '*the state has been defeated and corporations now rule the earth!*' (ibid.: 306). Finally, (4) a new method of world government suitable for capital has emerged (ibid.: 326–36). It thus seems that the spontaneous dynamic of the collective working-class subject has brought capitalism to its consummation in the globalized and homogenized supremacy of capital, with the result that the writers' undertaking becomes quasi-teleological. The proletariat was left with only two options: either to succeed in imposing its revolutionary rule or to 'activate' a totalizing evolution of capital into a global power. This conclusion emerges because the way in which the writers approach the national state is more or less independent of the class struggle in the final analysis. We are back at a standard point of reference for writings on the relationship between capital and the state.

10.2   Rethinking the 'non-correspondence' between State and Capital: Back to the concept of social capital

From the argumentation developed so far the following general conclusion suggests itself: many different narratives of imperialism or international capitalism converge at one, and only one, point: *rejection of the concept of social capital*. Of course the rejection implies a corresponding questioning of the entirety of the analysis that represents the state as a collective capitalist, that is to say as a centre of capitalist political domination (see the argumentation in Part II). This is a reality with, at the theoretical level, one overriding analytical consequence: *capital takes on the appearance of an 'autonomous entity' with a perennial tendency to expand into a geographical field much broader than the political range of an individual state.* In other words the various standpoints on the 'new imperialism', the neo-Gramscian analyses of the 'world plane', the postmodern variants on empire and the traditional World System(s) theories represent alternative attempts at conceptualizing the purported 'lack of correspondence' between the territory of the national state (national borders) on the one hand and the sphere of operations and/or domination of capital (whether or not it retains a 'national identity'). They thus comprise alternative theoretical routes with a common point of departure, a shared theoretical (and not empirical) premise, endeavouring mostly to put forward a more concrete analysis of contemporary forms of internationalization of capital (multinational companies), drawing from them certain conclusions about the state and its relationship with international capital.[6]

If *capital* as an entity overrides the *state* (the non-correspondent effect), then two conflicting outcomes become possible. On the one hand it may be accepted that as capital expands beyond the political boundaries of the state, it does not on that account cease to be the 'possessor' of a national identity. This interpretation brings back to the fore the classical argumentation on imperialism, which both in Hobson's and Kautsky's readings notes the importance of states in 'supporting' the expansion and internationalization of their 'national' capital (see Chapter 3). In the latter, capital no longer retains its national characteristics and its movement creates the prerequisites for entrenchment of global economic-political structures and the subordination of states thereto.

This argumentation fails entirely to perceive the state as what it is in reality: the political condensation of class relations of domination, the factor that underwrites the cohesion *of* capitalist *society*. In consonance with economistic outlooks and with the instrumentalist theory of the state, it sees the state as the aggregate of certain functions that serve (or do not serve) the interests of private capital. In particular, states and capital are represented as distinct social 'agents'. It therefore fails to grasp that capital is a social relationship that is reproduced in a complex way (politically and ideologically overdetermined) in the framework of a specific (national) social formation. Two basic observations become pertinent at this point:

Firstly, isolated individual capitals, or fractions of capital, within a social formation, are transformed through competition (and not through the political influence of the state exercised from outside, as Hardt and Negri (2000: 304–5) mistakenly maintain), into elements of *aggregate social capital*. Through this mutual dependence, that is to say their constitution as social capital, the individual capitals or fractions of capital together acquire the status of a social class and function as an integrated social force that opposes, and dominates, labour (see Chapter 6). In contrast, then to what is resolutely asserted in historicist analyses (for example see Gill (2003: 168), Cox (1999: 137), Hardt and Negri (2000: 305–24), Pijl (1998: 49–64), see also Panitch and Gindin (2003)) there is most definitely a concrete general class interest of social-national-capital, despite the potential for significant intra-capitalist struggles. In this light it is in no way possible for sections or fractions of a collective national capital to *break away* from the aforementioned unity to form a transnational capitalist class or transnational historic bloc or even to be metamorphosed into entities non-correspondent with some specific collective capitalist. Because quite simply, as we saw in detail in Chapter 6, the unity of collective capital is secured by virtue of the mode of composition of the class struggle itself. To put it somewhat differently: international capitalist space acquires its characteristics from the aggregate effects of class domination in the context of each social formation. The particular economic, political and ideological prerequisites for reproduction of the capitalist relation are perpetuated with each of them in a manner that is *nationally specific*.

Secondly, a comprehensive critique of the 'non-correspondence' problematic must include the observation that the creation of *national-social-capital* out of all the individual capitals that accumulate within a social formation *is* a process unrelated to the legal forms of existence (state property, foreign property) of each individual capital. For the overwhelming majority of writers on this subject, the decisive material factors behind the emergence of a global mode of production are transnational corporations and the internationalization of financial markets. The conception of territorial non-correspondence of the state and capital tacitly assumes either that an individual capital never loses the nationality that is ascribed to it by legal property forms or that it can retain a legal form quite independently of any national criterion. Thus, even if it is exported abroad it continues to belong to the country from which it originated, or it acquires a status that transcends national state jurisdictions. Only on the basis of this supposition can the question of territorial non-correspondence be posed.

In contrast to this hypothesis of bourgeois legal ideology, Marxist theory suggests that the legal property forms of the means of production do not necessarily correspond to the real property relations of the means of production. This is the situation above all in the case of stock companies, which supposedly belong to their shareholders as a whole, and/or to state enterprises, which supposedly belong to society as a whole. Something similar applies in the case that interests us here, that of enterprises legally belonging to a foreign or international trust but functioning productively inside a specific social formation, as part of the overall (national) social capital. Marx himself took an interest in this:

> But the circumstance that some means of labour are fixed in location, with the roots in the soil, gives this part of the fixed capital a particular role in the nation's economy. They cannot be sent abroad or circulate as commodities in the world market. It is quite possible for the property titles to this fixed capital to change; they can be bought and sold, and in this respect circulate ideally. These property titles can even circulate on foreign markets, in the form of shares, for example. But a change of the persons who are the owners of this kind of fixed capital does not change the relationship between the static and materially fixed part of the wealth of a country and the movable part of it.
>
> (Marx 1992: 242)

As formulated here by Marx, the key aspect of the question of owner-ship of 'foreign' capital is as follows. Although foreign legal ownership is retained, *this capital is incorporated into the process of capitalist accumu-lation inside the host country, becoming integrated into that country's overall social capital.* The means of production belong to the country's social capital, utilizing the domestic workforce (exactly like every other indi-vidual capital inside the country); the value of the commodities pro-duced is expressed in the local currency. As aptly observed by Neusüss (1972: 150) 'what is involved are capital exports that are obliged to behave as national capital abroad because the capital functions as productive capital in its host country.'

From this viewpoint, reflecting the theoretical system of the *Critique of Political Economy*, the question of non-correspondence between state and capital is a pseudo-problem. Distorting as it does the situation's key aspect, that is the correspondence between state and overall social capital, irrespective of the legal forms of ownership of individual capi-tals, this conception precludes even the most elementary awareness of the secondary side of things. Usually it is argued that what is involved is the 'formal' entitlement of the mother company to decide what will be produced by its foreign subsidiaries. But here again we have to do with movement in the virtual world. Capital exports do not result from the autonomous 'will' or the 'decision' of certain capitalists. The theory of capital is not an analysis of the actions of the capitalist. It is not a response to the actions of a *subject*. The power of capital is imper-sonal. The 'decisions' in question are 'taken' by the social conditions themselves, by the modification of competition on the world market and the differences in the rate of accumulation in different countries, irrespective of who ratifies them.

10.3   Recapitulation: The making of the imperialist chain

Our analysis of the capitalist mode of production in Part II leads us to the conclusion that the reproduction of capitalist relations of domina-tion within a social formation has a twofold repercussion, whose two aspects unfold simultaneously, influencing both the domestic and the international conjuncture.[7] To put it another way, no social formation exists in isolation but only in its relations with other social formations, occupying a specific position (necessarily one of inequality) in the global imperialist chain. The aggregate of these international relations (naturally involving all the basic levels of a social totality: economic, political and ideological), which often find expression in international organizations, is what we might designate the *international terrain* or the *international sphere*. This is a theoretical point of departure directly contradictory (in its existence) to the views previously presented in this chapter. Here is a brief explanation of why this is so.

We saw in Chapter 1 that the concept of the *imperialist chain* was formulated by Lenin in a specific political conjuncture, opening up a fertile theoretical terrain in an endeavour to extend the Marxian problematic. Lenin introduced the idea of the imperialist chain to counter the analyses of 'global capitalism' that were then predominant on the Left. It is the theoretical and not the political consequences of such a standpoint that we wish to dwell upon here. It is arguable, to be schematic, that the whole conception of the imperialist chain *presupposes the correspondence between capital and the state.*

In contrast to what is accepted by the majority of relevant writers, *the relation between capital and the national state is not an 'external' one.* In other words neither the state nor capital are constituted as discrete or autonomous 'entities' the dialectical relations between which are to be the object of investigation. As we argued in Chapters 5 and 7, the state undertakes a dual organizational role: *organizing the political unity of the bourgeoisie while at the same time organizing the bourgeoisie as ruling class.* In this sense the state, along with the totality of its institutions, its mediating and managing functions, *is always 'present' in the composition of social classes and the movement of capital.*[8] The state does not provide extraneous support to the movement of capital but is always to be found 'within it'. Unity of capitalists, reconciliation between their conflicting vested interests, their organization into a single coherent social force and the carrying out of the functions critical for the organization of exploitation would be impossible in the absence of the permanent mediating role of the state. Moreover no strategy of exploitation could be implemented without assistance from the state, drawing our attention to the fact that the state is also 'inside' the working class. (Balibar 1988, ch. 10) *This formative function of the state constitutes a standing negation of every 'formal' or 'external' differentiation between 'state' and 'capital', with the result that the terrain par excellence for class struggle and the composition of class is necessarily that of the nation.* Or, to put it differently, the concept of social capital provides the broadest of all possible hints of the material existence of the state as collective capitalist. The state expresses in this way the 'common interest' of a *capitalist* society.

Between the national state and the individual capital that is deployed on its territory, there is thus formed *a relationship of interiority and correspondence.* In Marx's conception 'politics' is inherent in the 'economy' through a complex dialectic that is both determined and overdetermined. The state is neither a neutral tool nor an autonomous entity into which a parasitical bureaucracy supposedly undertakes to inject uniformity. Capital does not come up against an external state power that is threatening to it, nor does it confront a state power that simply seeks to protect it. The relationship of 'interiority' between state and capital represents a *twofold condition*. On the one hand it precludes the self-diffusion of statist linkages into a global 'empire' that purportedly supervises homogeneously global economic structures. On the other hand it prevents capital that moves beyond the national borders from retaining the 'certificate of origin'.

We see, then, that the true essence of the Leninist concept of the imperialist chain represents a break both with the 'new imperialism' standpoints and with the various globalization theories. It posits an interlinkage at the international level of the different (national-state) economic and social structures, each of which evolves at a different and unequal rate as a result chiefly of the different class and political correlations that have crystallized within it.

This international terrain does not imply any supersession of the autonomy of the states that are the links in the chain. It merely, in a way, *relativizes* it. If imperialism is a permanent possibility emerging out of the structures of the capitalist mode of production, the historical form it will ultimately acquire for a particular social formation depends on the way in which the 'external' situation (that is to say the international correlation of forces) not only *overdetermines* but also *constrains* the practices that emerge out of the evolution of the internal class correlations.[9] If we generalize this observation to the totality of the links in the imperialist chain, we arrive at the manner in which on each occasion the *international conjuncture* is constructed. The latter is incorporated – and exerts its influence – as a *secondary contradiction (in the sense that it does not have priority over class struggle)* within the social formations, meaning that the position (in terms of power) of every state that is a link in the chain and the margins of opportunity for its imperialist action are determined by the overall internal class correlations, which are in turn already overdetermined by the international conjuncture. As we shall see in detail below, we are able in this way to find an interpretation for a whole range of developments in the international conjuncture, and above all those that evidently involve actors other than the 'Great Powers': the Iran–Iraq war, the wars in the former Soviet Union and in Yugoslavia and the creation of new nation-states, the Syrian military presence in Lebanon from May 2000 to April 2005, the Vietnamese military presence in Cambodia from 1978 to 1989, the India–Pakistan conflict, the Cyprus problem, etc.

From this perspective, international organizations neither embody global political authority nor constitute vehicles for the vested interests of a single superpower. The specific historical form of the international or global organizations is a material condensation of the international correlation of forces between the social formations. It follows the same correlations and reproduces them. Its transformations and evolutions take place (albeit with fluctuations and delays) in accordance with these correlations.

The structure of the imperialist chain *has two arguable consequences.*[10]

On one hand, it is the terrain on which a variety of national strategies, often contradictory and incontestably unequal in power, are constituted. These strategies are linked to the interests of each individual collective capitalist and play a mutually complementary role in the state's 'internal functioning' (often contributing, as correctly noted by Weber, to the organization of bourgeois hegemony). These strategies will never radically draw into question the global flows of commodities and capital, that is to say the capitalist nature of the international economic sphere. They will simply demand different versions of the terms on which the game must be played. In any case the global market is inextricably associated with the capital relation. The contribution it makes to its reproduction is dramatic. The antagonism in question is that between the various *national social capitals*, which certainly has a potent political aspect. Indeed to the extent that military power is a distillation, and a guarantor, of all political power, this competition is also metamorphosed into military competition (of various forms). States play an important role, without that meaning that they are autonomous bearers of sovereignty whose sphere of influence also extends beyond their borders. In this sense the interpretation of imperialism that we propose here embraces the dynamic of geopolitical antagonisms, defining the terms within which it manifests itself, which are ultimately subordinated to the evolution of class antagonisms.

On the other hand, the complex game within the parameters of the imperialist chain also operates reflexively when it comes to its effect on the links. Here we are dealing with the other side of the same coin. A concept borrowed from Smith's analysis may well help us arrive at a better description of this process: the concept of the *invisible hand*. The unequal links in the imperialist chain have in common a certain shared strategic interest: *reproduction of the capitalist system of domination*. However great the sharpening of the geopolitical or economic conflicts, they will never *on their own* go so far as to reverse this constant.

The chain must be reproduced as capitalist.[11] Every state as it delineates its strategy in the international area, that is to say on a terrain where all correlations are in flux, contributes in the final analysis to the reproduction of capitalism. *Striving to promote its 'national' interest, in other words, it helps to reproduce capitalism as a stable relationship of power.* Just as society and economy is not the mere 'sum of individual actions',[12] the imperialist chain is not the 'sum' or the resultant outcome of the 'actions' of individual states, but the terrain of expanded reproduction of capitalist rule, which is, however, in the last instance determined by class struggle in each capitalist social formation.

All this will become more comprehensible with the remarks to be made in the following paragraphs. Because the character of the chain is complex and unequal, *often the national interest of capitalist superpowers entails 'duties' that are crucial for the reproduction of global capitalist order.* For example, it is nowadays commonplace for the role of the United States to be described as imperial precisely because of this fact. We are therefore obliged to distance ourselves from two distinct theoretical excesses. There is no global empire that is 'in control' of every state structure. Not even the United States is anything like that. Of course for a variety of reasons the USA embodies a global hegemony that is also expressed through the capacities of its military machine and is necessary for the extended reproduction of the long-term interests of all the bourgeoisies of developed capitalism. The Western alliance, with the USA in the leading role, defending the specific national interests of its social capitals, is *at the same* pursuing a *hegemonic project* for all capitalist states. *The only authentic 'empire' is the imperialist chain in its entirety.*

The notion of imperialist chain supplements Marx's theory of the CMP and social capital, without negating it, as do the approaches of underconsumption, monopoly capitalism, world capitalism, empire...

10.4 Developed and undeveloped social formations

In what follows we shall attempt to describe the specific structural characteristics of the global imperialist chain, at the same time including certain basic historical references that are useful for understanding the line of argument.

Let us be permitted one general observation which will facilitate understanding of the comments in the previous paragraph. Two general categories of social formation are generated in the context of the imperialist chain. *Developed* capitalist social formations, in which dissolution of pre-capitalist modes of production has been consummated and the

Capitalism of Relative Surplus Value has prevailed (the CPM is here articulated exclusively in the form of simply commodity production) and *non-developed* and/or *underdeveloped* capitalist formations, which are characterized by expanded reproduction of pre-capitalist modes of production or early forms of pre-industrial capitalism (see Chapter 7), internally.

10.4.1   The developed social formations

The developed capitalist social formations are the most fully integrated into the network of international (and not only economic) relations. Between them they account for the greater part of international trade and direct foreign investment capital. The dynamic of the export branches of all the developed capitalist formations and the laws of movement of capital in the global market led to the dramatic liberalization of foreign trade after the Second World War. The developed capitalist social formations are the exclusive site of operations for modified capitalist competition on the global market (see Chapter 8).

Expanded reproduction of the aggregate social capital of each developed capitalist formation is thus based to a significant extent on the relations engendered by the internationalization of capital. Or to put it differently: *through international relations there is promotion and reinforcement of the process of capital accumulation within the developed capitalist social formations.*[13] In that sense the liberalization strategies in the international commodities and capital markets (with some variations in the details) embrace all the links occupied by this group. The organization of strategies may weigh more heavily on the stronger links but their acceptance in its most general sense is something *common to all*. There may be disputes over the terms of implementation of the international competition but there will be none over the core of the strategy. It would thus be a mistake to conclude (as many relevant writers do) that liberalization in international transactions has to do only with the vested interests of the superpowers, with their broad acceptance signifying dependence and subordination. On the contrary, as has become evident from the preceding chapters in this section, *the pressure of competition on the national social capital of the less developed countries comprises the necessary prerequisite for vigorous capitalist development.* Of course the efficient condition of this process concerns the ability of the collective capitalist to obtain consent to the class precondition for such a strategy (something which is not always available).

The tight incorporation of the developed capitalist social formations into the network of international relations, and the associated close mutual involvement and inter-dependence among those formations, led to the establishment of a number of institutions of international co-operation or integration (OECD, EEC, European Free Trade Zone, NAFTA, WTO, etc.). The most significant among the processes of this kind, the integration project through the European Common Market, which finally took the form of the 27-member European Union, emerged primarily out of the desire of the leading industrial countries of Europe to limit the supremacy of the USA in the international market (in the field of production, of labour productivity and also of currency).[14] Among the developed capitalist countries there are some that play a leading role as global producers and exporters of commodities and capital. These countries are today for the most part the countries that comprise the G7. Most of these countries are the leading powers of Western imperialism, the vehicles *par excellence* of imperialist policies. Nevertheless, not all these countries are equals in terms of their role in the imperialist chain. Among them, since the time of the Second World War, the undisputed hegemon, both in economic and in political and military terms, has been the USA. These developed capitalist countries 'lead the world' together with other 'alternative imperialist poles' like Russia and arguably China (or, prospectively, even India).

Of course above and beyond the leading imperialist powers mentioned above, it is easy to recognize the existence of an international hierarchy shaped out of the differences in position and strength of every developed capitalist social formation in the imperialist chain. Arrayed in the lower ranks of this international hierarchy are small, or relatively less developed, countries such as Denmark, Finland, New Zealand, Ireland, Greece and Portugal.

The historical development of inter-imperialist conflicts, and the correlations that crystallized among the imperialist countries in the immediate post-World War II period led to a parallel strengthening, through the War, of the international position of the Soviet Union. The corresponding creation of the Eastern bloc led to the formation of the Atlantic political and military coalition between the USA and the most developed capitalist countries of Europe.

The collapse of the state-capitalist regimes of the USSR and Eastern Europe[15] and the economic decline which accompanied the first phase of their 'transition' to Western capitalism, was attended by a revival of nationalism and the formation of new national states, through the dissolution of multinational states such as Yugoslavia or Czechoslovakia and secession from the USSR of nations such as the Lithuanians, the Latvians, the Estonians, the Azeris and other Mohammedan peoples in the wider region of the Caucasus, the Armenians, etc. What was true in the period of the First World War of the Poles, the Hungarians, the Finns, applied again after the collapse of the Eastern regimes for the nations and peoples in question, indicating yet again that the nation is a constituent element in today's Western-capitalist power or that, as argued above, nation, state and capital are manifestations of one and the same system of capitalist class power.

The tight interlinkage between the developed capitalist countries (countries comprising a model towards which most former state capitalist countries of Europe converged) under the hegemony of the United States, is also expressed through their political and military collaboration. The more rapid growth of Japanese and European capitalism, particularly from the 1960s onwards, resulted in a weakening of American economic hegemony within the Western imperialist camp. Despite this, American economic hegemony persists: the USA still occupies the leading position among the developed capitalist formations, both economically and on the political and military plane.

American hegemony on the military-strategic level has never been drawn into question, from the Second World War onwards, within the framework of the imperialist West. Japanese neutrality and the eastern policies of certain European states, however much they modify the inter-imperialist correlations of power at the level of international politics, have not been enough, and have not sought to threaten American political-strategic and military hegemony, which they have moreover helped to stabilize and elaborate further in the new landscape that unfolded during the 1990s, with the military interventions against Iraq (twice), Serbia and Afghanistan.

10.4.2 The less developed or underdeveloped social formations

The underdeveloped or capitalistically undeveloped social formations are comparatively less integrated into the network of international economic and politico-military relations. The differences which nevertheless exist between the economic and social structures of these countries and thus their different mode of integration into the global imperialist chain obliges us to regard them as two separate subcategories of country in the imperialist chain.

The social formations whose economic and social structures stagnate under the stifling influence of non-capitalist modes of production (this is the case, for example, with many sub-Saharan African formations) occupy a marginal position in the global imperialist chain. Colonialism had in the past promoted capitalist relations in these formations but primarily to the extent of imposing a uniform state structure of the capitalist type. Attempts have been made since decolonization to build national unity, that is to construct a nation in the contemporary bourgeois sense of the term. This process sometimes faces as its primary obstacle the extremely sharp conflicts between tribes and clans that even today comprise the basic units of social organization. This is a typical example of non-contemporaneity[16] between the social levels of a formation. A modern state, that is to say a state of the capitalist type, is articulated through economic and cultural structures dominated by pre-capitalist or transitional social relations.

This particular mode of organization of the social levels explains the fact that all attempts to promote the capitalist mode of production have the machinery of state as their point of departure. They thus very often take the form of coups d'état by means of which purportedly revolutionary regimes come to power. The revolutionary mantle donned by the coup d'état makes possible, or at least facilitates, a radical isolation of the underdeveloped country from the global market and the network of international economic relations generally, a prerequisite for potential capitalist or state-capitalist development.[17] Because of the exceptionally low productivity of labour, it is not profitable, if there is subsequent incorporation into the global market, for industrial products to be manufactured on a large scale in the county in question. For the domestic economy there, therefore, remains only the production of traditional agricultural products or raw materials.[18]

A significantly different picture of class relations and the correlations of class power emerges in undeveloped capitalist societies in which there has been some progress of capitalist structures and the capitalist sector of the economy has already created a specific social base (see also Bairoch 2006). This is the situation, for example, with social formations of Latin America, South-East Asia and the 'emerging superpowers' China and India. In these countries capitalist supremacy is secured finally, at the various levels of society (the economy, the state, ideology), despite the expanded reproduction of class relations deriving from pre-industrial or non-capitalist social structures or, above all, of a marginalized population on the outer fringes of the expanded reproduction of the dominant CPM (favelas, etc.), while at the same time there also emerges a corresponding, much more significant, incorporation of these countries into the network of international economic relations (international trade, capital movements, etc.).

Capitalist development in the countries in this category and the corresponding improvement of their position in the global imperialist chain, a process which can lead to their being included in the category of developed capitalist countries (something which occurred in the past, albeit many decades after the industrial revolution in England, with Japan, the Scandinavian countries, the countries of Southern Europe and more recently the countries of South-East Asia), is associated with the potential for removal or dissolution of the pre-capitalist modes of production or of the forms of pre-industrial capitalism and the indirect subordination of labour to capital (see Chapter 7) and development of the productive capacity of the collective worker. It is a process, in other words, whose outcome is determined exclusively by class struggle. For each special case, therefore, for each separate non-developed capitalist social formation, we can investigate both the potential and the limitations of capitalist development only on the basis of a specific analysis of the concrete class relations and their dynamic.[19]

The relatively low productivity of labour in countries in this category led them in the 1960s and 1970s to limiting their degree of integration into the global market through a protectionist state economic policy that was called a policy of import substitution.[20] In the event that its objective of reducing the gap between the national and the average international levels of labour productivity is actually accomplished, or because of 'shortage of capital' with the consequent necessity of taking out international loans for infrastructural works, etc., this policy tends to give way to a policy or industrialization oriented to the global market.[21]

Concluding our discussion of underdeveloped and developing capitalist countries, it is worth making certain observations on those countries incorporated into the global market as particularly significant suppliers of raw materials or primary products. This type of linkage to the global market serves for a start to stabilize the position of that fraction of the ruling classes that controls this export sector of the economy. It consequently has an exceptionally fortifying effect on the position of this grouping within the internal correlation of class forces, both as against other fractions of the bourgeoisie and in relation to preservation of historically inherited forms of organization of the polity (monarchic-type structures in countries of the Persian Gulf, etc.).

In any case the specific function and position in the global imperialist chain of countries that are significant suppliers of raw materials, and particularly the oil-exporting countries, demands special analysis. Here it is worth remembering simply that even in the event that we have to do with a nationalized export sector (e.g. oil), even in the event that the state or state enterprises derive considerable sums from foreign trade, the problem of capitalist development can very well continue to remain unsolved. *Money can function as capital (that is to say be a means for capitalist investment) only if the overall social structures and the corresponding correlation of class forces, permit it to be so employed.* Otherwise it merely provides funding for the international finance circuit.

The preceding analysis may help to facilitate understanding of issues which for dependence theories are merely riddles, and to assist in finding solutions to the problems that arise from them. If underdeveloped and developing capitalist countries have the opportunity to adopt a non-aligned position on the international political scene and, if moreover, they sometimes change their political and military orientation from one day to the next (we need merely recall the expulsion of Soviet advisors in July 1972 from the then pro-Soviet, and immediately afterward pro-Western, Egypt) this is not because the countries in question are dominated by, and dependent on, one or more of the ruling social formations but, on the contrary, because they are countries that are marginal to, and/or only loosely integrated into, the network of international capitalist relations (the imperialist chain).

Closing this section, it is important to address the view that 'globalization', favouring 'deregulation' of markets and openness of economic borders, that is the direct exposure of domestic production to international competition, decelerates economic development and the dissolution of pre-capitalist and pre-industrial production forms in many LDCs. It is well known even to mainstream thinking that most domestic enterprises in these countries need the state umbrella of economic protection to cope with their more developed foreign competitors not only on the international but also on the domestic market. Neoliberalism therefore favours the intrusion of imports, retards domestic capitalist accumulation and so stabilizes the power position of pre-capitalist oligarchies or pre-industrial capitalist forms (the buyer-up and the whole domestic putting-out system). The question then arises, *why, despite the above, the ruling capitalist classes in most LDCs favour the neoliberal agenda of globalization, supporting in this way the imperialist plans of the developed capitalism?* It is not difficult to answer this question on the basis of what has been argued up to this point. These classes are willing to 'sacrifice' domestic capital accumulation *in the less developed sectors of the national economy* for the sake not only of *promoting its more developed sectors* (see Chapter 8 on the modification of competition on the world market) but also of *stabilizing and reproducing their political power*. It thus becomes evident that the liberalization of the world market and the military 'presence' of capitalist superpowers are not unwillingly accepted by these LDCs because, generally speaking, 'imperialism' secures the reproduction of domestic power structures.

10.5   Imperialism after the collapse of the Eastern bloc

The international 'New World Order' emerged out of the collapse of the regimes of 'really-existing socialism' in 1989–91 and the isolation of Russia achieved through the secession of Ukraine, Belarus, Armenia, the Muslim republics and the Baltic republics, and the reorientation of the former allies of Russia (the Czech Republic, Hungary, Poland, Bulgaria, etc.) towards the West (USA and EU). Before proceeding with an examination of the realities of the new period, we should bear in mind that the collapse of real existing socialism was a process whose causes lie within the USSR and the Eastern European countries and whose dynamic was shaped and evolved internally. What was involved, in other words, was *in the first instance* the outcome of class struggle in those countries (and not of 'imperialist pressures and interventions' as is often asserted in Leftist literature).

The Soviet Union (like the other societies of 'really-existing socialism') was a class society, whose ruling class comprised two fractions: the layer of higher state and party officials on the one hand (who staffed both the political apparatuses and the apparatuses of administration and control of the 'planned' economy that secured the collective/state-capitalist appropriation of surplus labour), and on the other the managers of the state enterprises. The hegemonic fraction of the ruling class was the layer of state and party officials, who personified the economic and social system of state-capitalist exploitation and single-party political dictatorship over all the other classes of Soviet society. The conflicts between the two fractions of the ruling class were frequently sharp, chiefly under pressure from the poor performance of the Soviet economy: *the higher levels of the state administration sought more effective control of the enterprises, while the directors struggled to increase the independence of their enterprises from central control by the state, often pushing the demand as far as abolition of state-capitalist regulation, that is to say towards 'transition' to private capitalism.* The economic crisis and the sharpening of the internal contradictions of the Soviet regime at the end of the 1980s finally enabled the subordinate fraction of the ruling class, the managers and the higher-level cadres in the enterprises, to secure the support of the working classes in their effort to overturn and abolish 'central state planning', appropriating as their private property the companies which until then they themselves had managed (under state-capitalist control). One section of the old state-capitalist apparatus (of the 'Communist' party) took over the role of political representation in the newborn 'democracy'.

If then the collapse of 'real socialism' cannot be traced back to 'imperialist intervention' *the question remains* of whether the vacuum left by the disintegration of the Eastern coalition, above and beyond the shift in the correlation of power to the advantage of the West (and particularly the USA), has led to a new quality of imperialist politics that could justify the rhetoric of the international 'New Order'.

So as to be able to answer this question we should first mention two related issues. One of them is the new contradictions that are arising out of the class struggle in the individual social formations and registering at the level of international politics following the collapse of the state-capitalist regimes. The other is the manner in which international politics is being practised by the USA and the Western coalition.

It is understandable that amid these internal developments on the territory of the former Soviet Union and the countries of Eastern Europe, the Western politico-military coalition should emerge as the undisputed hegemonic force in international politics. Notwithstanding its steadily growing power, the influence of Russian imperialism has not succeeded in moving beyond the fringes of Eastern Europe, retaining the capacity to intervene militarily only in regions and among peoples and nationalities such as, for example, the Chechens that are situated inside Russian territory or in its immediate proximity, as occurred with the intervention in Georgia.

How, then, does the Western coalition propose to handle the emerging state entities and the nationalistic tensions? In our view along the same strategic political axes and applying the same ideological schemata as those that were imposed at the end of World War II, with some differentiation reflecting on each occasion the shifts in the international conjuncture.

'Human rights' and 'democracy', the ideological motif for the exercising of international politics in the era of the 'new order' are precisely the same 'universally human values' as those by means of which the attempt was made to legitimate the anti-communist 'deterrence' policies of the epoch of the Cold War. The international standing of human rights was codified by the United Nations in the Universal Declaration of Human Rights in 1948.[22] Did not the interventions in Korea and Vietnam, places so far from American territory or from Europe, take place in the name of these same 'free world' values (that is to say of 'democracy' and of 'rights')? Moreover, does not the two-year longoccupation and administration of Germany by the Allied victors and the international Nuremberg trials (instead of having Nazi criminals tried by the judicial mechanisms of an anti-Nazi post-war Germany) constitute the international-political precedent for the prosecution by 'international courts' of those committing 'crimes against humanity'? It is of little significance for the purposes of the present analysis to mention the obvious, that the transgression of 'universally human values' is identified selectively, in conjunctures of crisis involving weak 'anti-Western' links in the chain, and that issues are blown up out of proportion by the controlled mass media, etc. What we seek to emphasize is that the mechanism for legitimating international initiatives and interventions by the West remains in its general features the same as that which was imposed at the end of the Second World War. In other words, there is little to justify the 'new order' appellation.

Obviously with the end of the Cold War and the entry into the neoliberal phase of capitalism, grounded in a correlation of forces unfavourable for labour, the role of human rights is upgraded within the strategy being organized by the Western coalition. The new correlation of forces in the imperialist chain has ushered in a new consensus, in accordance with which 'human rights' sometimes gain priority over 'national sovereignty'. This consensus reflects the narrower margins for initiative that are now at the disposal of states given the new correlation of forces and the emergence of the aggressively pro-capitalist policies of neoliberalism. These policies, of course, as we have seen, do not accord with the interests only of the big capitalist powers but contribute to reproduction of neoliberal capitalist hegemony at every point in the imperialist chain. In other words they encapsulate the new form of capitalist hegemony as expressed in neoliberal regulation, which is reproduced by collective capitalists at the national level, with the most powerful among them taking care of its reproduction internationally. Given that there is no armed international guarantor of human rights and no legal institutional structure, the general ideal implementation of human rights depends on the dominant nation-states and is, in essence, unrealizable: 'one nation might be willing to violate the sovereignty of another in the name of human rights, but it will simultaneously insist on the principle of national sovereignty, especially its own!' (Hardt and Negri 2004: 275). 'The most powerful nation-states constantly maintain the power to negate any legal actions', hence 'we should not have illusions, then, about the effectiveness of these truth commissions, tribunals, and courts or about the justice we can expect from them. Sometimes they just leave us with the bitter taste of the "justice" imposed by the victors; and at other times they function merely to neutralize and pacify conflict rather than create justice. The pretence of justice too often serves merely to mask the machinations of power' (ibid.: 275).

Reference to human rights 'cannot be taken for granted' but must be treated as 'ideological discourse' redefining sovereignty in a manner conducive to securing capitalist relations in the post-Cold War era of neoliberal hegemony.[23] What is most important, however, is to recognize that since the end of the Second World War, the general political framework within which Western international policy is exercised has remained in many ways unchanged. This framework is nothing other than the stability of the borders that emerged from the conditions of the Second World War and its immediate aftermath. *This framework, which after the population movement at the end of the War corresponds to the interests of all of the Western countries, makes irreconcilable with the principle of 'human rights' every attempt at 'historical union of blood and soil' that would affect existing borders.* It is therefore not surprising that the territories annexed by Israel in 1967 retain to this day the status of 'occupied' territories, etc. Western intervention in the destabilization and disintegration process of the former state capitalist multinational states and the nationalistic wars that followed aimed at saving this principle of stable borders, through maintenance of the existing borders of federated units, which henceforth became interstate borders. Irrespective of the 'human borders', for example between Serbian and Croatian populations, the borders of Croatia were required to coincide with the historically determined borders of the former Yugoslav Republic of Croatia within the federation, even if this entailed movements and 'exchanges' of population. The 'Republic of Croatia' thus acquired the international political status of an independent state, exactly as it occurred with the other former Yugoslav and former Soviet republics, and also with the Czech Republic and Slovakia.

Western insistence on the political framework of stable borders does not of course derive from devotion to principles of law or 'universally human' values. It corresponds to the need for maintenance and legitimation of international political stability and so of the planetary hegemony of the West. To conclude, the 'New World Order' emerged primarily as the international political outcome of class war within the Eastern European social formations and the former USSR. The forces of NATO and the West did not produce these results but attempt to manipulate them, pursuing the same type of political/ideological (and military) initiatives as in the past.

The politics of the United States and its allies in the era of the 'New World Order' is constructed with exactly the same materials as those with which the 'antifascist peace' of 1945 and the ensuing Cold War were constructed. It is an expression of the hegemony at the international political level of the Western capitalist countries under the leadership of the United States. This leadership simply means the capacity to control (partially) the contradictions that develop spontaneously by virtue of the class struggle within the individual social formations and are registered on the international scene as interstate, or quasi-interstate, relationships and tensions. It does not imply any ability to effect a final settlement of these relations, let alone any ability to control the class correlations of power and the dynamics of class struggle within the individual social formations out of which international political tensions grow.

Moreover, the Western imperialist coalition is not without contradictions of its own. As a result of them, for example, Western intervention in Cuba cannot go beyond a US unilateral economic embargo. It cannot even prevent the development of Cuban–Canadian economic relations. This example is important, because if one sought to identify a refractory state in the present international conjuncture of liberalization and globalization of markets, it would be much more appropriate to focus on the Cuba of Castro than on the Serbia and Serbo-Bosnia of Milosevic and Karadjic (with the burnt-down villages and the mass graves of those of the 'wrong' nationality). The disputes and ambivalences in respect to North Korea's and Iran's nuclear programmes is another characteristic example of the contradictions among the leading imperialist countries and in international Organizations such as the United Nations and the International Atomic Energy Agency.

Epilogue
Rethinking Imperialism and Capitalist Rule

The basic idea of this book is simple. To study the phenomenon of imperialism we need a theory of capitalist power. The work of Marx is a truly invaluable starting point for such a theory.

Of course Marxism is an *inherently* schismatic theoretical system.[1] It is therefore entirely to be expected that there will be reproduction within it of organic disagreements and dissension on the subject of imperialism (the preceding analysis in Chapters 1, 2, 3, 9 and 10 is indicative in this respect). As was made clear in any case in Chapter 1, the aforementioned schismatic character of Marxism was already visible in the controversies that accompanied the formulation of the classical theories of imperialism.

There is nevertheless one basic point that should not escape our attention. The classical approaches to imperialism, with a few exceptions – basically reflecting the vacillations of Lenin and aspects of Bukharin's intervention – shared a common conviction: capitalism has undergone radical and structural transformations, with the result that Marx's analysis is no longer sufficient for a comprehensive description of it. The 'latest phase of capitalism' of the era of Hilferding was not exactly the capitalism of *Das Kapital*. This view, whether formulated explicitly or merely by implication, permeates most theoretical analyses of the early twentieth century, at the same time comprising the visible symptom of a deeper encounter between Marxism and the broader heterodox thought of the time.

Let us linger for a little on this point. It is an encounter which was certainly not to the advantage of Marxist thought because it presupposed a *drastic shift* in the Marxist discussion. We could say, schematically, that the Marxist discussion has begun partially to be taken over by concepts, reasoning, arguments, that are unrelated to the theoretical system of *A Critique of Political Economy* as initiated by Marx. The analysis in Chapter 6 is a comprehensive example of what is meant by this. The consensus shared with a few exceptions by the classic Marxist writers of this period is thus anchored in a tacit endeavour to reformulate the questions of capitalist power, introducing through the concept of imperialism a new problematic which does not have the mature work of Marx as its point of reference.

It is at the beginning of the twentieth century that (for a number of reasons both theoretical and political) a more generalized critical stance begins to emerge vis-à-vis the ideologically predominant and institutionally entrenched liberal-neoclassical school of economic thought. Without going into significant detail, it is worth noting that two important theoretical traditions come together within this *sui generis* theoretical opposition, both of which continue to have their followers to this day. The reference, of course, is *in the first instance* to the *theoretical tradition of historicism*, which admittedly has never comprised a single school of thought but has always found expression through a number of different theoretical systems, and *in the second* to the *Keynesian tradition* (or alternatively to the 'economics of effective demand'), which, with its central moment the later intervention of Keynes himself, has managed to synthesize and consummate a whole range of underconsumptionist approaches whose origins can be traced back as far as the analyses of Malthus and Sismondi. At exactly the same time Marxism was beginning to make its appearance on the mainstream theoretical scene. Great historical events, and the class movements that were coming to the fore, undoubtedly had their place in the overall picture. But the generalization of this Marxist debate was definitely determined by the abovementioned theoretical climate, which to a greater or lesser extent (and with very few exceptions) influenced the most important Marxist thinkers of the time.

The key idea in the classical theories of imperialism had already been formulated by Hobson on the foundation of the *essentialist problematic of economism*. The 'new' capitalism is a system of *underconsumption* and of *monopolies*. This fact poses an obstacle to unimpeded capital accumulation in the developed states, obliging commodities and individual capital to embark on a course of international 'migration'. The direction of the migration can be none other than towards the colonies or the undeveloped and so 'dependent' states. Development in the metropolitan centres is based more on exploitation of the colonies than on exploitation of the domestic working class. The political organization of imperialism is perforce conditioned by, indeed contemporaneous with, the rhythms of the economy.

The abovementioned line of thought leads us to some very basic conclusions, which have not been sufficiently highlighted in the relevant debate and which concern the heart of bourgeois rule. The international movement of individual capitals shapes an economic space whose geography does not coincide with the political geography of nation-states. *What is implied, in other words, is a dialectical relationship of non-correspondence between the state and individual capital*. There are two alternative ways in which this insight might be expressed.

First variant: The *classical theories of imperialism* and the directly subsequent *dependency analyses* (in their several variants) accepted that when individual capitals cross national borders they retain their national identity. They perform, in other words, a critical mediating function: they constitute an international economic sphere, more or less homogeneous, investing it with a relationship of structural dependence and probably unequal exchange. This process, pushing class struggle into the murky background, implies a certain conception of the capitalist state which, in advanced capitalist countries, is obliged to be *extrovert* in terms of the movement of individual capitals. This state is a sovereign 'entity', envisageable either as an *inert tool* or as a *self-contained sovereign subject*.

We understand, therefore, that the critique of economism that characterizes the classical theories, which rejects the instrumentalist conception of the state so as to embrace the Weberian alternative of a state that is essentially self-sufficient, is in no way incompatible with the general direction of the abovementioned thoughts on the non-correspondence between state and capital. Given the international character of capital movements, the essence of Weber's and Schumpeter's interventions could be seen as a mere adjunct to one of the above parameters of the same – always – problem: the parameter of *autonomous geopolitical competition* that is inherent in the composition of states (the analysis in Chapter 3 is the most characteristic along these lines). Present-day analyses of *the new imperialism* in their sundry variants show signs of a disposition to re-examine the problem of imperialism on the ground of classical theories when that ground has been 'upgraded' through the deployment of one or more of the variants of the autonomous and non-instrumentalist state. On this new terrain the relationship between state and capital continues as before to comply with the dialectic of non-correspondence. But now the 'interests' of the states come up against those of capital in a game of identification and/or opposition (the first contingency being the preponderant one in most relevant analyses). States are frequently inclined in their own interest to provide support for 'their' capital in its international movements. We thus see a resurgence of the controversy, suitably updated, that once pitted Lenin against Kautsky and vice versa, on the question of ultra-imperialism. The international movement of capitals of specific and 'ineffaceable' national provenance in the view of some writers sharpens inter-imperialist conflicts, while for others it paves the way for a collaborative form of imperialism.

Second variant: As very properly argued by Poulantzas (1975) capital is not a 'thing' devised for purposes of export. Through this formulation he highlighted the problem that arises out of overemphasis on the 'national origin' of individual capital. The analysis quoted in Part II of this book pursues a critique along precisely those lines. Nevertheless, although Poulantzas' analysis does seek to emphasize capital's character as a *social relationship*, it has not completely emancipated itself from the problematic of classical theories of imperialism. As a result, he too perpetuates the focus on the national provenance of capital, many times attributing to individual capitals the tendency to function as vehicles for the introduction into other countries of the 'national' social production relations of their country of origin.

This idea could be taken to its logical conclusion and the assumption be made that internationalized capital is constructed as an autonomous 'thing in itself' throughout the world, without any particular links to any powerful state of origin. New political forms transcending states and certainly transcending nations would be required to deal with this moment. This is a logic that has been associated, as we saw in Chapter 10, with the intervention of Gramsci (in particular when it comes to the concept of the historic bloc). It either considers that there are international production relations that are reproduced alongside their national counterpart (and sometimes in contradiction to them) or that the composition of classes was from the outset a global process or that at a certain point it evolved into being one.

Both the abovementioned variants, which (to be schematic) account for the most significant part of today's writing on this subject, amount to different ways of interpreting the *dialectic of non-correspondence* between the state and capital. In this sense they are theoretical strategies sharing a common point of departure (by accepting the same question). One basic presumption of the abovementioned approaches is rejection of a crucial concept in Marxist analysis: the *concept of social capital*. This rejection has significant consequences for the way of understanding how class power is organized within a social formation and so the way in which we should understand the phenomenon of imperialism. That is something we endeavoured to deal with in Parts II and III of the book.

For reasons that have to do, historically, with the establishment of capitalism through the disintegration of feudalism, the class struggle is constructed as such *within* unequally developed social formations and not globally. Through the process of competition individual capitals are transformed into an integrated social force, that is to say into social capital, in opposition to labour. This process presupposes suitable political forms, with the result that the capitalist state can be understood only as a composite site for organization of the political hegemony of the bourgeoisie. In this sense the state does not possess its own power which it can wield either autonomously or under the external tutelage of the bourgeoisie (social capital). The state expresses the institutionally crystallized dynamic of class power and class struggles as they develop inside a social formation.

There is one basic corollary to all the above: the economic development of capitalism does not depend on the 'desire' of the powerful, or of the 'imperialist' national capitals but on the class struggle as reproduced within the various national state links, which through their inter-articulation comprise what we have designated as the *global imperialist chain* (Chapter 10). This latter notion, deriving from Lenin's intervention, is a way of conceptualizing the complex economic, political and ideological interconnections that develop between the different social formations. It moreover conveys the real content of imperialism, which overdetermines the class struggle but never acquires priority over it. The theory of the capitalist mode of production necessarily constitutes an abstract theoretical object – a concept – presupposing *one* social capital and *one* state. But in actually existing capitalism there are many social capitals and capitalist national states (just as there are similarly likely to be noncapitalist modes and forms of production within a social formation). Therefore, *by adopting the concept of the imperialist chain we assign due significance to the only concept that does not abolish social capital and succeeds in taking into account the many-faceted character of the international reality.*

Much remains to be said about the structure of the imperialist chain and the historicity that characterizes the relations between the unequal links. In Part III we seek to outline the basic principles governing the international movement of commodities and capital, and to identify some of their specific characteristics in the period of neoliberalism. The manifold character of the unequally developing aggregate social capitals involves the prerequisites for its reproduction (e.g. modification of international competition), without this meaning that inequality between countries is not dynamic in its character. The inequalities between the links are not static; the correlations between them fluctuate over time, even at the level of the capitalist superpowers. Class struggle is always the decisive factor.

This historicity of the international relations within the imperialist chain is reflected inside the unequally developed social formations. This reflection has twofold repercussions, as we saw in Chapter 10. *On the one hand*, imperialist chain provides the field of constitution of different, often contradictory national strategies, patently unequal in strength (that is to say overdetermined, in a complex manner, by imperialism). But *at the same time* the unequal links in the imperialist chain have a common strategic interest: *reproduction of the capitalist system of power*. It seems that the imperialist chain *as a whole* 'protects' its weak links. Each state as it forges its own strategy in the international arena, that is to say on a terrain of shifting correlations of power, finally contributes to reproduction of capitalism at the global level. Because the character of the chain is complex and anisomeric, this means that frequently the national interest of the capitalist superpowers 'absorbs' tasks that are crucial for reproduction of the global capitalist order (this is the other aspect of the abovementioned reflection). This does not mean that there is a global empire either in the form of a supranational global mechanism or in that of a national link that is imperial in character. In today's world the Western alliance, with the USA as key protagonist, defending in the final analysis the specific national interests of its social capitals, at the same time shapes a *hegemonic project* for all capitalist states. *The only real 'empire' is the imperialist chain in its entirety.*

Notes

1 Classical Theories of Imperialism: A New Interpretation of Capitalist Rule, Expansionism, Capital Export, the Periodization and the 'Decline' of Capitalism

1. See Chapter 23 of Keynes's *General Theory*, which is titled 'Notes on mercantilism, the usury laws, stamped money and theories of underconsumption', where the author praises Hobson's underconsumptionist approach – referring to his early book *The Physiology of Industry*, co-authored with Mummery (first published in 1889) – as follows: 'I will quote from it to show how significant and well-founded were the authors' criticisms and intuitions' Keynes (1973: 366).

2. Underconsumption designates insufficient demand for, as opposed to supply of, a product, at given prices. Underconsumption means, therefore, relative *overproduction* of commodities *due to a lagging capable-to-pay-demand*. The classical underconsumption theories, as they were developed by Sismonde de Sismondi and Robert Malthus, can be reduced to the following propositions: *First*, that within the capitalist economy there is an inherent tendency towards economic crises of generalized overproduction, due to the inability of capable-to-pay-demand to keep pace with production. *Second*, that, when supply exceeds aggregate demand, there is no endogenous dynamic tendency towards full employment equilibrium, because demand has priority over supply; it is demand that triggers and regulates production and not the opposite, as assumed by Say's Law. However, Sismondi and Malthus have different explanations for the causes of the supposed insufficient demand and different ideas on how it might be countered. At the risk of appearing schematic, there are two basic approaches to be identified in the underconsumption theory:

   The first approach, which was formulated by Malthus, attributes crises (and unemployment) first and foremost to *oversaving by capitalists for the purpose of expanding production*. *The second approach*, formulated by Sismondi, includes the views according to which (given the increase in labour productivity and therefore the increase in the aggregate product) the main cause of crises and unemployment is the labourers' inability, due to low wages, to consume the product that they have produced.

   The 'Narodniks' in Russia and, after the death of Marx and Engels, the 'orthodox Marxists' of the German-speaking lands had formulated a Sismondian-type underconsumptionist theory of crisis based on the assumption that under capitalism production *always* increases faster than society's ability to consume. Expansion of the market for commodities with the assistance of *third persons, in places characterized by non-capitalist modes of production*, now remained the sole (albeit temporary) solution to the immanent realization problem. This approach was, however, discredited within Marxism in both Russia and the German-speaking countries after the theoretical intervention of the Russian Marxist Mikhail v. Tugan-Baranowsky (who also published in German) in the years 1894–1900. Tugan-Baranowsky argued that Marxists, adopting the underconsumptionist approach, part company with Marx, who showed, in the reproduction schemes in volume 2 of *Capital*, that expanded reproduction of a 'pure' capitalist economy is possible and the existence of non-capitalist 'third persons' unnecessary. For a detailed analysis of the historic Marxist controversy on economic crises and underconsumption see Milios et al. (2002: 158–89), Milios and Sotiropoulos (2007).

3. In the course of this he will be led to reiterate one of Hilferding's basic formulations: 'The policy of finance capital has three objectives: (1) to establish the largest possible economic territory, (2) to close this territory to foreign competition by a wall of protective tariffs, and consequently, (3) to reserve it as an area of exploitation for the national monopolistic combinations' (Hilferding 1981: 326, Bukharin 1972a: 107).

4. For the Polish social democracy see Lenin (Collected Works, vol. 22: 15 and 320 ff.); for the German social democracy (ibid: 342 ff.); and for the Russian social democracy (ibid.: 360 ff.).

5. Lenin 'I want to recognise only the right of the working classes to self-determination,' says Comrade Bukharin. That is to say, you want to recognise something that has not been achieved in a single country except Russia. That is ridiculous' (Lenin, *CW*, vol. 29).

6. See, for example, 'Critical Remarks on the National Question', December 1913 (Lenin, *CW*, vol. 19).

7. Lenin 'The Discussion on Self-Determination Summed-Up', July 1918, *CW*, vol. 28: 'This is a sort of "imperialist Economism" like the old Economism of 1894–1902 [...] Instead of speaking about the state (which *means*, about the demarcation of its *frontiers*!), [...] they deliberately choose an expression that is indefinite in the sense that all state questions are obliterated!'

8. However, Bukharin remained faithful to Hilferding's schematic conception of 'monopoly predominance' over the capitalist economy, which contradicts some fundamental Marxian theses on capitalist competition and the average profit-rate (for more see Chapter 6).

9. 'Capitals invested in *foreign trade* can yield a *higher rate of profit*, because, in the first place, there is competition with commodities produced in other countries with inferior production facilities, so that the more advanced country sells its goods above their value even though cheaper than the competing countries. In so far as the labour of the more advanced country is here realised as labour of a higher specific weight, the rate of profit rises, because labour which has not been paid as being of a higher quality is sold as such. [...] Just as a manufacturer who employs a new invention before it becomes generally used [...] *secures a surplus-profit*' (Marx 1991: 344–5, cited by Bukharin 1972a: 244–5, who also added the emphasis).

2 Post-World War II 'Metropolis-Periphery' Theories of Imperialism

1. This approach was introduced by Lenin, who spoke of 'the territorial division of the whole world among the biggest capitalist powers' (*CW* vol. 22).

To defend this position Lenin in effect identified the so-called dependent states with colonies. He considered most 'underdeveloped' countries to be 'semi-colonial': 'Not only are the two main groups of countries, those owning colonies, and the colonies themselves, but also the diverse forms of dependent countries which, politically, are formally independent, but in fact, are enmeshed in the net of financial and diplomatic dependence, typical of this epoch' (ibid.: 253). The 'dependent' state is thus considered to be an accessory not only of finance capital but also of other states (the imperialist states). In contrast, Hobson spoke about 'semi-independent States such as Egypt, Afghanistan, Natal, Bhutan, Jehore' (Hobson 1938: 338) in the formal sense, that is referring to their status of political sovereignty.

2. dos Santos (1978).
3. Córdova (1973), see also Cox (1999).
4. Echoes of this problematic are also to be found in recent theories of imperialism, for example see Chapters 3 and 10.
5. Proletarians in the centre not only do not participate in that imperialist exploitation, but, due to the higher productivity of labour 'in reality, these workers are, in general, *more exploited* (in the strict sense of the word) than the workers in the poor countries' (Bettelheim 1972: 302).
6. 'To say that the theory of unequal exchange means that "the workers of the centre exploit those of the periphery" is meaningless, since only ownership of capital makes exploitation possible' (Amin 1976: 196).
7. Amin (1981, 1974).
8. In a recent article John Belamy-Foster (2006) described as follows the way Sweezy assessed *Monopoly Capital* a quarter of a century after its publication: 'Nevertheless, Sweezy on the twenty-fifth anniversary of *Monopoly Capital* saw its analysis as deeply flawed in one respect: the failure to envision the financial take-off that began in the 1970s and accelerated in the 1980s.'
9. 'The economies that are characterized as underdeveloped comprise subsystems whose behaviour cannot be rendered comprehensible without resort to hypotheses to do with the global system that overdetermines them' (dos Santos 1978: 317). 'One should therefore not reason in terms of nations, as if the latter constituted independent entities, but in terms of a world system' (Amin 1976: 358).
10. At the heart of these theories is the concept of wholeness of the *global system*. This wholeness, apart from anything else, is grounded on the structural contradiction between *centre* and *periphery*, which in the contemporary era of capitalism determines the relations between the individual states. The individual states, then, are the units *par excellence* of the global system, the relations between them being subject to a structural centre–periphery relationship, often utilizing the intermediate category of the semi-periphery (see below). However, within this theoretical discussion on global systems two very different sets of assumptions are to be encountered.

On the one hand, there are those who consider that 'something distinctive occurred in (Western) Europe which was radically new somewhere in early modern times' (Wallerstein 1996: 292, Amin 1996), with the result that the world capitalist system is uniquely conditioned not just by capital but by the familiar tendency of imperialism to accompany the expansion of capital (for the same conclusions see Amin 1989). The 'modern world-system' thus dates from around 500 years ago. Its CMP makes it fundamentally different from 'world empires' and all previous world-systems. From this perspective, the '"world system" is not a system "in the world" or "of the world." It is a system "that is a world'". Hence, the hyphen, since "world" is not an attribute of the system. Rather the two words together constitute a single concept' (Wallerstein 1996: 294–5).

On the other hand, there are also those who insist on speaking of a *unique* global system, the basic features of which have remained unchanged for at least the last 5000 years (Frank and Gills 1996). From this viewpoint there are evidently characteristic similarities between the modern world-capitalism and 'other' earlier empires, state systems, or regional economies. There was no historic transition from 'something else' to capitalism because whatever happened in Europe in the sixteenth century was simply a shift within the context of an already existing 'world system', which has existed for several thousand years. It is argued that the essential features of the global CMP should be extended back in time at least 5000 years (ibid.: 11).

11. 'Economic development and underdevelopment are interrelated and the difference between them is qualitative, because they undergo structural differentiations, which are however produced by their reciprocal relation in the context of the global system' (Frank 1969: 27).

12. 'But the proletariat at the periphery assumes different forms. It does not consist solely or even mainly of wage-earners in the large modern enterprises. It also includes the mass of the peasants who are integrated into the world trade system and who, like the urban working class, pay the price of unequal exchange. Although various types of social organization (very precapitalist in appearance) form the setting in which this mass of peasants live, they have eventually become proletarianized [...] through their integration into the world market system' (Amin 1976: 361).

13. It is here that one finds 'the continuity and the relevance of the basic structural features of economic development and underdevelopment. It is for this reason that I place primary emphasis on the continuity of the capitalist structure' (Frank 1969: 30).

14. Also see Hopkins and Wallerstein (1979: 151 ff.).

15. The model of sub-imperialism was first formulated essentially by Marini (1969, 1974), whose investigations are focused on Brazil. Marini supposes that the sub-imperialist economy is incorporated into the economy of the metropolis, on which it is dependent. What is involved is the outcome of a process of dependent development, carried out under the aegis of metropolitan capital and of necessity export oriented and extraverted (production for the global market), supplementary, and not competitive in relation to the metropolitan economy. Sub-imperialist capital thus loses its national character and comes to be considered multinational.

16. In a relatively recent text of theirs, Frank and Gills (1996: 39) confirm their basic thesis that a country's development depends on its specific position 'in the world system'. In a competitive world system 'only a few can win the "development race" at any time; and apparently they cannot even maintain their lead for long.' Since dependence is the major attribute of the world system and 'has existed for millennia' within it, 'eliminating dependence or being/becoming independent of the world system is impossible. Thus,

dependentistas [...] were right in giving structural dependence a central place in their analysis.'

17. The descriptive designation '*Monthly Review* School' was borrowed from the article by Cypher (1979).

18. If we define surplus as 'the difference between what a society produces and the costs of production' we leave out of account the entire scientific theory of Marx, that it is not the society that produces but the working class and/or some other exploited classes. It is therefore logical that 'Baran and Sweezy do not concern themselves with class analysis and the class struggle in the countries of monopoly capitalism. They prefer to become involved with the racial problem in the United States' (Córdova 1973: 150).

19. A thesis which, as we have seen in Chapter 1, was deployed by Lenin in his polemic against the Russian narodniks, and later by Bukharin against Rosa Luxemburg.

3   Theories of Imperialism as Alternatives to Classical and Centre–Periphery Approaches

1. These findings (for alternative summations see Willoughby 1986, Freeman and Kagarlitsky 2004) were in fact to some extent drawn into question in the context of the discussion that developed between the classical theoreticians of imperialism. See in Chapter 1 the theory of Lenin on the imperialist chain, as critique of the theory of global capitalism (whose point of departure was his intervention on the national question and the socialist revolution), Bukharin's critique of the theories of underconsumption and 'surplus capital' (in the context of his polemic with Rosa Luxemburg) and finally Lenin's critical observations on the theory of monopoly capitalism (in the context of his dispute with Bukharin).

2. For more details see Mommsen (1982).

3. 'Imperialism signified both a nationalist ideology devoted to extending the dominion of a particular nation state, and also a policy determined by ceaseless rivalry among the powers composing the international system of states' (Mommsen 1982: 4).

4. For more on this subject see Mommsen (1982: 3–8).

5. 'Every successful imperialist policy of coercing the outside normally – or at least at first – also *strengthens the domestic prestige* and therewith the power and influence of those classes, status groups and parties under whose leadership the success has been attained' (Weber 1978: 920, emphasis added). In one extreme extrapolation of this stance imperialism may be seen as a *strategy for managing* class domination.

6. For the relation between Schumpeter and Kautsky see Kautsky (1961).

7. For more on this issue see Howard and King (1989).

8. For more on this see Kautsky (1961), Howard and King (2000; 1989: 92–4).

9. Kautsky's logic in 1914 is faithfully conveyed in the following extract: 'There is no economic necessity for continuing the arms race after the World War, even from the standpoint of the capitalist class itself, with the exception of at most certain armaments interests. On the contrary, the capitalist economy is seriously threatened precisely by the

contradictions between its states. Every far-sighted capitalist today must call on his fellows: capitalists of all countries, unite! [...] Hence from the purely economic standpoint it is not impossible that capitalism may still live through another phase, the translation of cartellization into foreign policy: a phase of ultra-imperialism, which of course we must struggle against as energetically as we do against imperialism, but whose perils lie in another direction, not in that of the arms race and the threat to world peace' (Kautsky 1914).

10. For similar conclusions see Kautsky (1961), Howard and King (2000).

11. Mommsen (1982: 21–2), for more see Schumpeter (1951: 79–89), Michaelides and Milios (2004).

12. In 1960 criticising the argumentation of Lenin, he remarked: 'here we need only note that, while colonialism is virtually dead, capitalism in the Western Hemisphere, Western Europe and Japan is enjoying an extraordinary surge of growth. It is perfectly evident that, whatever the economic troubles of the capitalist societies, they do not stem primarily from a dependence on imperialism. [...] Domestic demand is not so inadequate as to force attention outward: it is too strong to make it possible for governments to mobilize adequate resources for external affairs' (Rostow 1960: 156).

13. In Schumpeter's own words: 'The social pyramid of the present age has been formed, not by the substance and laws of capitalism alone, but by two different social substances, and by the laws of two different epochs. [...] The nobility entered the modern world in the form into which it had been shaped by the autocratic state – the same state that had also moulded the bourgeoisie. [...] The bourgeoisie did not simply supplant the sovereign, nor did it make him its leader, as did the nobility. It merely wrested a portion of his power from him and for the rest submitted to him' (Schumpeter 1951: 66, 92–3).

14. The 'dilemma' in question may assume a variety of forms. The basic argument is borrowed from the work of Poulantzas (2000: 129) and will be appropriately adapted to the needs of the present text.

15. In our view this is not Marx's mistake but rather his strong point. What Marx really tells us in *Capital* is not that capitalism is lacking in fraud, violence and other predatory characteristics. It is that primitive accumulation does not convey the essence of capitalist exploitation, which is a situation whereby surplus value *is produced* as a 'natural' economic relation supported by the ideological consensus of the exploited. The focus of enquiry in *Capital* is on the 'ideal average' of capitalism, that is the CMP, as a theoretical object corresponding to the 'kernel', the inherent structural components of capitalism. The essence of capitalist exploitation is the production of surplus value, quite irrespective of income distribution, given that the latter is contingent on correlations of power between social classes.

16. 'Feudal relations of production therefore command a dynamic of territorial expansion and state-building. The emergence of the interstate system in late medieval and early modern Europe, therefore, was not simply a consequence of the contingent imperatives of military and political power, as Mann would have it, but arose from what Brenner calls the 'rules of reproduction' specific to feudal property relations –that is, the strategies that classes of economic actors must, within a given system of property

relations, pursue in order to gain access to the means of subsistence' (Callinicos 2007: 541).

17. 'Capitalists need state support for a myriad of reasons, while the relative power of any individual state is dependent on the resources generated by the process of capital accumulation' (Callinicos 2007: 545).

18. A number of examples cited by Callinicos confirm that such a view is latent in his thinking: 'economic rivalries among transnational corporations whose investments and markets are concentrated in one of the three points of the G7 triad – North America, Western Europe and Japan – and that rely on state support in their competitive struggles remain a structural feature of the contemporary global political economy' (Callinicos 2005).

19. Callinicos (2007: 539) in the final analysis fails to assimilate the specific transformations that take place at every level of the CPM from the moment of its constitution (for more on this see Parts II and III).

20. The same line of argumentation can also be found in the work of McNally (2006).

21. As we shall note in detail in Part II of the book, such a view comes into conflict with the Marxist concept of *social capital* pervading a specific conception of the capitalist state.

22. For a similar argumentation see Chtouris (2004: 35–44).

23. For the same argumentation see Carchedi (2001), Freeman and Kagarlitsky (2004). The latter note that 'the rich nations *rule* the poor nations' and that moreover 'this is *why* they are rich. The sovereignty of the rich and the sovereignty of the poor are not, therefore, identical. The first is *unconditional and absolute* and the second is *conditional and relative*' (ibid.: 25). Harvey (2003: 181) expresses exactly the same logic in his analysis: 'Hegemonic state power is typically deployed to ensure and promote those external and international institutional arrangements which the asymmetries of exchange relations can so work as to benefit the hegemonic power. It is through such means that tribute is in effect extracted from the rest of the world. Free trade and open capital markets have become primary means through which to advantage the monopoly powers based in the advanced capitalist countries that already dominate trade, production, services, and finance within the capitalist world.' The same theoretical schema but with emphasis on financial capital is supported by Callari (2008) in the context of the new imperialism of finance.

24. For some useful elucidation of the nuances in the contemporary discussion see Kiely (2006), Brenner (2006), Freeman and Kagarlitksy (2004).

25. Indicatively see Harvey (2003), Callinicos (1994, 2007), Rees (2006), Petras and Veltmeyer (2000), Freeman and Kagarlitsky (2004), Carchedi (2001), Gowan (2003).

26. Panitch and Gindin (2003), Kiely (2005, 2006), Albo (2003), Wood (2005), McNally (2006).

27. As noted indicatively by Panitch and Gindin (2003): 'the vast expansion of direct foreign investment worldwide, whatever the shifting regional shares of the total, meant that far from capital escaping the state, it expanded its dependence on *many* states. At the same time, capital as an effective social force within any given state now tended to include both foreign capital and domestic capital with international linkages and ambitions. Their interpenetration made the notion of distinct national bourgeoisies – let alone rivalries

between them in any sense analogous to those that led to World War I – increasingly anachronistic.'

28. As already mentioned in Section 3.3, it is in this way that an essentialist problematic is implemented. Each historical 'epoch' retains its unique essence with reference to the peculiar property relations. The latter comprises the *causal core* from which all political and ideological forms accrue. In this sense, history is constituted as the succession of different essences and their outer expressions.

29. 'Successful "political accumulation" therefore required that increased military power and/or jurisdictional authority yield returns which more than covered their increased costs, and such costs tended to grow over time. [...] The economic success of individual lords, or groups of them, did tend to depend on feudal state building, and the long-term trend, overall, does appear to have been towards greater political centralization for "political accumulation"' (Brenner 1982: 38–9). In fact what Brenner's followers find interesting is that via the mechanism of political accumulation there is the projection of a process for constituting states prior to the establishment of capitalism (Teschke and Lacher 2007).

30. 'But if the countries of continental Europe, under different forms of absolutism or other non-capitalist forms of political-economic organization, were not capitalist, *they nevertheless pioneered a form of state that continues to influence the organization of political space even today*' (Teschke and Lacher 2007: 573, emphasis added).

31. This argument is not at all hard to find in the writings of the relevant authors. It is, for example, reiterated by Cox (1987: 157–8). We will deal with this particular writer in more detail below.

4   The State as a Vehicle of both Capitalist Expansionism and Decolonization: Historical Evidence and Theoretical Questions

1. 'Along the coasts of Italy, small seaports began to thrive – not only Venice, which was still insignificant at this time, but ten or twenty little Venices. Prominent among them was Amalfi, although there was hardly room for the harbour, houses and later the cathedral, in the little space left between the mountains and the sea. [...] Amalfi was penetrated by a monetary economy: [...] Between the eleventh and the thirteenth century, the landscape of the *valle* of Amalfi was thereby transformed: chestnut trees, vines, olive-groves, citrus fruits and mills appeared everywhere. The Amalfi Tables (*Tavolo Amalfitane*) became one of the great maritime codes of Christian shipping in the Mediterranean, a sign of the prosperous international dealings of the town' (Braudel, 1984: 106–7).

2. See Marx (1991, Ch. 47: 'Genesis of Capitalist Ground-Rent').

3. 'Thus were the agricultural folk first forcibly expropriated from the soil, driven from their homes, turned into vagabonds, and then whipped, branded and tortured by grotesquely terroristic laws, into accepting the discipline necessary for the system of wage-labour' (Marx 1990: 889).

4. 'The advance of capitalist production develops a working class which by education, tradition and habit looks upon the requirements of that mode of production as self-evident natural laws' (Marx 1990: 899).
5. 'In Italy, where capitalistic production developed earliest, the dissolution of serfdom also took place earlier than elsewhere. The serf was emancipated before he had acquired any prescriptive right to the soil. His emancipation at once transformed him into a "free" proletarian, who, moreover, found his master ready waiting for him in the towns [...] When the revolution which took place in the world-market at about the end of the 15th century had annihilated Northern Italy's commercial supremacy, a movement in the reverse direction set in. The urban workers were driven *en masse* into the countryside [...]' (Marx 1990: 876).
6. 'There [in the colonies] the capitalist regime constantly comes up against the obstacle presented by the producer, who, as owner of his own conditions of labour, employs that labour to enrich himself instead of the capitalist. [...] Where the capitalist has behind him the power of the mother country, he tries to use force to clear out of the way the modes of production and appropriation which rest on the personal labour of the independent producer' (Marx 1990: 931).
7. Here Marx agrees with Adam Smith, who pointed out that 'The discovery of America [...] by opening a new and inexhaustible market to all the commodities of Europe, [...] gave occasion to new divisions of labour and improvements of art, which, in the narrow circle of the ancient commerce, could never have taken place [...]' (Smith 1981, IV.I: 348).
8. 'If one compares the rate of growth during the nineteenth century it appears that non-colonial countries had, as a rule, a more rapid economic development than colonial ones. There is an almost perfect correlation. Thus colonial countries like Britain, France, The Netherlands, Portugal and Spain have been characterized by a slower rate of economic growth and industrialization than Belgium, Germany, Sweden and the United States. The "rule" is to a certain extent, also valid for the twentieth century' (Bairoch 1993: 77).
9. Hilferding wrote in 1909: 'The national idea, which found a natural limit in the constitution of a state based upon a nation, because it recognized the right of all nations to independent existence as states, and hence regarded the frontiers of the state as being determined by the natural boundaries of the nation, is now transformed into the notion of elevating one's own nation above all others' (Hilferding 1981: 335).

5 Capitalist Mode of Production and Social Formation: Conclusions Concerning the Organization of Capitalist Power

1. See also Fine and Saad-Filho (2004: 6 ff.).
2. As Marx himself noted in the preface to the first edition of Vol. I of *Capital*: 'What I have to examine in this work is the capitalist mode of production, and the relations of production and forms of intercourse that correspond to it' (Marx 1990: 90); and in Volume III of *Capital* he stated: 'we are only out

to present the internal organization of the capitalist mode of production, its ideal average' (Marx 1991: 970).

3. Productive processes which do not lead to relations of exploitation – production and appropriation of the surplus-product – as is the case with the self-employed producer (simple commodity production), do not constitute a mode of production but a *form of production*.

4. Characteristic is the formation of the Greek nation, in the semi-autonomous Christian territories of the Ottoman Empire. As Eric Hobsbawm aptly notes: 'being Greek had been a little more than the professional requirement of the literate Orthodox Balkan Christian. [...] *In a sense the entire educated and mercantile classes of the Balkans, of the Black Sea area and the Levant, whatever their national origins, were hellenized by the very nature of their activities*' (Hobsbawm 1977: 175, 173–4).

5. 'Class struggle is at the heart of the constitution of nations: the nation represents the form of existence indispensable to the implantation of the capitalist mode of production, in its struggle against the forms of the feudal mode of production. [...] a nation can be constituted only by means of a state – a national state' (Althusser 1999: 11).

6. See Fine and Milonakis (2008: 253, 274).

7. For example see Althusser (1995).

8. The theory of the ideological state apparatuses also stresses the fact that the economy does not constitute the genetic code for *all* ideological forms (such as, e.g. German, US or Greek nationalism, racism, sexism), but an element, which is combined with the political and the ideological element in the complex structured whole of the CMP, playing the *in the last instance determinant* role in this structured whole. Depending on the balance of forces at any given time, ideological constructs derived from the 'economy' or the 'market' are either activated (neoliberalism) or recede into the background (dictatorial regimes of the inter-war period which projected the 'historical commune' or the 'duty of sacrifice in the name of the fatherland').

9. Balibar (1993: 64 ff.).

10. 'Sensible supersensible thing' (Marx 1990: 163).

11. Amariglio and Callari (1989).

6   Capitalist Mode of Production and Monopolies

1. It is however worth remembering that Hilferding completes an analytical direction inside Marxism that had been in the first place set forth by Engels himself during his preparation for the publication of the third volume of *Capital* based on Marx's manuscript. Engels made quite clear his viewpoint that since the time of Marx's writings, 'new forms of industrial organization have been developed' and 'in brief, the ancient and celebrated freedom of competition is at the end of its road and must itself confess its evident and scandalous bankruptcy' (in Marx 1991: 568–69). For an excellent presentation of the Marxist argumentation on the monopoly capitalism of that period see Schumpeter (1951: 79–82).

2. From the moment of Marx's death, it had already become apparent that Marxist theory and Marxist analysis would accommodate more than one

interpretation, and would not evolve within the limits of a single, and unique, theoretical orientation. On the contrary, the history of Marxism is interwoven with the formation of various Marxist trends or schools, which as a rule are constructed on the basis of contradictory theoretical principles, positions and deductions. This phenomenon is universal, and has taken place in all countries where Marxism has acquired a footing (for an analysis see Milios 1995).

3. What is valid for the individual enterprise is much more valid for the persons who man this enterprise (the entrepreneur, the managers …): 'Individuals are dealt with here only in so far as they are the personifications of economic categories, the bearers of particular class-relations and interests' (Marx 1990: 92).
4. This relation manifests itself in the first instance in the commodity character of the economy, in the general exchangeability (through money) of the products of labour on the market.
5. 'With the whole of capitalist production, it is always only in a very intricate and approximate way, as an average of perpetual fluctuations which can never be firmly fixed, that the general law prevails as the dominant tendency' (Marx 1991: 266).
6. There is according to Marx a third possible type of monopoly, this time in the sphere not of production but of circulation of commodities (the market). Marx named this type of monopoly the *accidental monopoly*. The term is applied to certain *individual capitals* which are able to secure extra profit by exploiting conjunctural or more permanent imbalances and fluctuations of supply and demand in the market (Marx 1991: 297). This type of monopoly corresponds to some extent to what in neoclassical theory is described as an oligopoly.
7. For the same line of argumentation see Balibar (1984).

7   Is Imperialism the *Latest* Stage of Capitalism? Reflections on the Question of Periodization of Capitalism and Stages of Capitalist Development

1. For example (as we shall see in Chapter 10), it is thus in no way coincidental that proponents of world system theory regard the historicist analyses of the neo-Gramscians as supplementary and not antagonistic to themselves (Frank and Gills 1996: 36), and the neo-Gramscians too do not seem finally to be very hostile to the latter (Cox 1999: 516).
2. 'The labour process becomes the instrument of the valorisation process, of the process of capital's self-valorisation – the process of the creation of surplus value. The labour process is subsumed under capital (it is capital's *own* process) and the capitalist enters the process as its conductor, its director; for him it is at the same time directly a process of the exploitation of alien labour. I call this the *formal subsumption of labour under capital*' (Marx 1990: 1019, *Results …*).
3. 'The real subsumption of labour under capital is developed in all the forms evolved by relative, as opposed to absolute surplus-value. With the real subsumption of labour under capital a complete (and constantly repeated) revolution takes place in the mode of production, in the productivity of the workers and in the relations between workers and capitalists' (Marx 1990: 1035, *Results …*).

4. 'The technological revolution took place first in textile manufacturing, steel-making and metallurgy [...]. It did however become evident that initially no extensive interlinkages were created between the consumer goods industry and the industry for producing means of production. [...] Around 1840 75% of industrial workers in England were employed in textile manufacturing and of those 50% were engaged in cotton processing' (Schweers 1980: 239–40).

5. Engels, 'England 1845 und 1885', in MEW (21: 191–5), also Schweers (1980: 259) and Hobsbawm (1987: 84 ff.).

6. Panich and Gindin (2004) correctly note the following, critically commenting on the underconsumptionist assumption of classical theories of imperialism, according to which capitalism was constantly being deprived of all forms of domestic demand and foremost popular demand for consumption goods: 'Rather than an exhaustion of consumption possibilities within the leading capitalist countries [...] more and more Western working classes were then achieving increasing levels of private and public consumption.'

7. As Thomas Hurtienne (1981: 120) notes: 'In the context of the predominance of absolute surplus value and extensive capitalist accumulation, the living standards of workers' families up to the time of the First World War remained permanently limited to the level of vital needs for food, clothing, and accommodation (with beer, football and musical gatherings the only recreation for their free time). [...] The revolutionizing of consumer goods production on the basis of large-scale industry first got under way at the beginning of the 20th century [...].'

8. Müller and Neusüss (1971).

9. For more detail see Sotiropoulos (2007). From one viewpoint this is the essence of Marx's *rupture* with political economy. The basic idea of the following analysis is aptly summarized by Althusser (1997: 119) as follows: 'I should like to suggest that, from the theoretical stand-point, Marxism is no more a historicism than it is a humanism [...]; that in many respects both historicism and humanism depend on the same ideological problematic; and that, *theoretically speaking*, Marxism is, in a single movement and by virtue of the unique epistemological rupture which established it, an anti-humanism and an anti-historicism. Strictly speaking, I ought to say an a-humanism and an a-historicism. [...] I have deliberately used this double *negative* formula (anti-humanism, anti-historicism) instead of a simple primitive form, for the latter is not sufficiently imperative to repel the humanist and historicist assault which, in some circles, has threatened Marxism continuously for the past forty years.' We could add to the latter formulation: 'until the present day'.

10. The arguments in this section are based on Althusser's work (1969, 1976, 1997). Also see Milios et al. (2002).

11. In brief, the *overdetermination* 'designates the following essential quality of contradiction: the reflection in contradiction itself of its conditions of existence, that is, of its situation in the structure in dominance of the complex whole' (Althusser 1969: 209).

12. As illustrated by Lenin in *State and Revolution*, CW, vol. 25.

13. We do not intend here to elaborate on the different relevant readings of Gramsci.

14. This observation of Popper (2005: 6–7) is entirely apt.

15. This problematic may be sought out in a number of contemporary hetero-dox analyses, for example: Gills (2001), Gill (2003), Hodgson (1999, 2006), Callinicos (2004).
16. To recall the words of Gramsci (ibid.): 'structures and superstructures form an "historic bloc". That is to say the complex, contradictory and discordant *ensemble* of the superstructures is the reflection of the *ensemble* of the social relations of production.'
17. Many authors, including a number of neo-Marxists, have portrayed classical Marxist thought, and in particular the writings of Marx himself, as the vehicle for a 'progressivist prognosis' of history, according to which all countries will inevitably go through the same stages of economic and social evolution, from pre-capitalist forms to developed capitalism, culminating in socialism (for a brief overview of these approaches see Goodman and Redclift 1982: 24 ff.). Although such formulations can be found in the work of Marx and Engels, particularly in their political writings, there is no 'progressivist prognosis' in the economic writings of Marx's maturity. On the contrary, in these writings Marx simply outlined the *prerequisites* for the transition from pre-capitalist social forms to capitalism.
18. The following statement by Amin (2008), on capitalism and its present economic crisis, is characteristic: 'The current capitalist system is dominated by a handful of oligopolies that control the basic decisions making of the world economy.' Once again, the question, on what grounds and under what conditions or restrictions does this 'handful of oligopolies' make these 'basic decisions', remains unanswered.

8 Internationalization of Capital

1. Lenin criticized, in July 1916, the 'economism' of those conceptions that systematically ignore the state: 'They do not want to think either about state frontiers or even about the state as such. This is a sort of "imperialist Economism" like the old Economism of 1894–1902, [...] Such an apolitical theory is extremely harmful to Marxism' (CW, vol. 22).
2. Only 18 (mostly 'Newly Industrializing Countries' – NICs) of the total of 150 and more non-OECD countries received more than 85% of the direct investments going to non-OECD regions of the planet.
3. FDI denotes export of productive non-loan capital from one country to another. It therefore includes capital exports for the establishment of subsidiary or joint venture companies, for company mergers, etc. FDI is usually identified through ownership of at least 10% of the equity in an enterprise, covering claims that are intended to remain outstanding for more than one year. Loans between an associated company or subsidiary and mother company are in most cases regarded by international statistics as FDI.
4. Also see Petras and Veltmeyer (2001).
5. Also see Busch (1984).
6. Hurtienne (1981).
7. Busch, Schöller and Seelow (1971); Neussüs (1972); Busch (1974); Busch, Grunert and Tobergte (1984). For a similar line of argumentation and more

recent empirical evidence see Fieldhouse (2002), Caves (2007), Goldstein (2007).

8. Marx develops as follows his argument in relation to an individual enterprise possessing a higher-than-average-productivity of labour (less value of inputs needed for the production of one and the same commodity). See section 6.5 and Marx (1990: 434).

9. See Busch et al. (1984: 76–7).

10. We refer here to all 'developing countries' which are sorted by the UNCTAD to at least one of the following categories: *Major exporters of manufactured goods, Emerging economies, Newly Industrialized Economies*. These countries are: Argentina, Brazil, Chile, China and Hong Kong, India, Indonesia, Malaysia, Mexico, Peru, Republic of Korea, Philippines, Singapore, Thailand, Taiwan, Turkey.

11. 'Fifty countries are currently designated by the United Nations as "least developed countries" (LDCs): Afghanistan, Angola, Bangladesh, Benin, Bhutan, Burkina Faso, Burundi, Cambodia, Cape Verde (until December 2007), Central African Republic, Chad, Comoros, Democratic Republic of the Congo, Djibouti, Equatorial Guinea, Eritrea, Ethiopia, Gambia, Guinea, Guinea-Bissau, Haiti, Kiribati, Lao People's Democratic Republic, Lesotho, Liberia, Madagascar, Malawi, Maldives, Mali, Mauritania, Mozambique, Myanmar, Nepal, Niger, Rwanda, Samoa, Sao Tome and Principe, Senegal, Sierra Leone, Solomon Islands, Somalia, Sudan, Timor–Leste, Togo, Tuvalu, Uganda, United Republic of Tanzania, Vanuatu, Yemen and Zambia' (UNCTAD, *The Least Developed Countries Report 2008*, United Nations 2008).

12. Schweers (1980: 173 ff.), Menzel (1988).

13. Busch (1978: 57–74).

14. Busch et al. (1984: 97).

15. Busch (1985).

16. It is true that 'huge chunks of world trade today are managed [...] as a result of a variety of non-tariff restrictions – quotas, production and export subsidies, international strategic alliances, local-content rules and import-limiting agreements' (McNally 2006: 31).

9   Financialization: Market Discipline or Capital Discipline?

1. For example see Palley (2007), Crotty (2005), Smithin (1996), Pollin (1996), Wray (2007), Dumenil and Levy (2004), Epstein and Jayadev (2005), Helleiner (1994), O'Hara (2006).

2. It should be borne in mind that analyses in the post-Keynesian train of thought (Minsky 1993; Palley 2007; Pollin 1996) are closely associated with the approach of the school of institutional economics (Lazonick and O'Sullivan 2000), with the works of the followers of the regulation school (Grahl and Teague 2000), and with some theories of 'financialization' (Froud et al. 2007, Crotty 2005, Dumenil and Levy 2004).

3. See Crotty (2005). In the same line of argumentation O' Hara (2006: 165) argues that: 'the changing structure and dynamics of the US financial system since the 1970s has increased the conflict between finance and industry,

since the real sector has become a sideshow to the main game of capital gains in the equity market.'

4. These analyses are all more or less variations on the same theme and within the same problematic. Shareholders and the managers they hire are conceptualized as *collective economic agents* with distinct economic behaviours and objectives. Managers are supposedly interested in promoting their personal power and status through an infinite expansion in the size of the firm, but not interested in increasing dividends to shareholders. The renewed dominance of rentiers that has come with the resurgence of neoliberalism has forced managers to comply with shareholder demands. They were obliged to abandon the long-term policy of 'retain and reinvest' in favour of a short-sighted practice of 'downsize and distribute'.

5. See also Campbell (2003).

6. It should be noted that despite a fall in growth rates, particularly in developed capitalist economies, throughout the neoliberal period, growth remains at more or less 'satisfactory' levels (Panitch and Gindin 2003).

7. From a more radical political perspective, the powers of labour cannot comprise part of this new regulation, which is directed against their interests. On the other hand, the crisis for the first time in decades gives them the opportunity to intervene so as to change the correlations of power and impose solutions that secure their own interests in the face of those of capital. The point today is that social insurance is dependent on the profitability of the insurance funds, education on the privately funded 'research programmes' and on student loans, work on the international evaluation of the profitability of the enterprise on the world's stock exchanges and banks, food on the smooth functioning of the futures markets, the operations of the municipalities on mutual funds and the international securities markets, the environment on tradable pollution rights and the covering of basic social needs on the level of credit card debt. In present-day conditions the project of de-commodifying needs, that is to say the defence of social organization on the basis of freedom in satisfaction of needs and not the repressive calculus of exploitation of capital, is urgent.

8. Employing their own theoretical resources, Keynesians provide us with a wealth of insights into the workings of the financial markets and so into the great inherent instability of neoliberal capitalism. Minsky's (1982) analysis of capitalist instability is invaluable for comprehending today's financial meltdown (see also Wray 2008).

9. This aspect of Marx's analysis is very pertinently highlighted by Balibar (1984).

10. Marx (1991: 170–240), Milios et al. (2002).

11. See Marx (1990), Marx (1991: 295–300), Busch (1978), Hilferding (1981: 130–50).

12. For the shareholder value maximization strategy see Jensen (2001).

13. It should be noted that the high profitability of a capitalist firm usually translates into high share prices, but at the same time the low risk that goes with being a healthy firm reduces the rate of discount and thus increases the value of the bonds being issued.

14. See Milios (1999b: 196).

15. As frequently noted and mentioned above (section 9.2), the stock market is not the main means for obtaining investment capital. Even in the extreme

case of market-based systems (such as those of the USA., UK and Australia), the main loan sources are retained earnings, bank loans and bond issues (Bryan and Rafferty 2006; Dumenil and Levy 2004; Deakin 2005). At the same time, it is useful to note that in contrast to what is often asserted by heterodox authors, since the beginning of the 1980s joint-stock companies have become steadily less willing to distribute dividends (Fama and French 2001).

16. 'With derivatives, the ability to commensurate the value of capital assets within and between companies at any point in time has been added as a measure of capital's performance alongside and perhaps above the capacity to produce surplus over time. [...] Derivatives separate the capital of firms into financial assets that can be priced and traded or "repackaged", without having either to move them physically, or even change their ownership' (Bryan and Rafferty 2006: 97).

10   The 'Global' Level and the Concept of *Imperialist Chain*

1. For example Cox   (1999, 2004), Gill (2003), Pijl (1998, 2006), Overbeek (2000), Rupert (1995), but also Sklair (2001).

2. At another point the same writer, summarizing the corresponding argumentation of Cox (1999) and Pijl (1998), remarks: 'Global production, exchange and capital flows have widened the basis of this class formation beyond the Atlantic circuits of capital, as industrialization of many parts of the Third World has developed, and as Japan and East Asia have become much more powerful economically. At this "transnational stage" in the development of capitalism, the developing transnational capitalist class or "international establishment" can be said to comprise the segments of the national bourgeoisies and state bureaucracies of a range of countries who have material interests in the relatively free flow of capital, goods and services within the world economy.'

3. For further detail see Sotiris (2005), Thoburn (2001), Bowring (2004).

4. Bensaid (2004).

5. Zizek's (2009: 14) critical comment on the argument of Negri ('the guru of the postmodern left') is rather apt: the latter 'praises digital capitalism as containing *in nuce* all the elements of communism – one has only to drop the capitalist form, and the revolutionary goal is achieved.'

6. Certainly, these ideas are not new in the field of social thought. In the post-war literature, we can find this conception in the texts both of certain early formal exponents of the theory of global capitalism such as Hymer (1976) and of certain traditional Marxist writers such as Mandel (1971). But while Hymer simply reformulates the traditional argumentation (e.g. of Bukharin) in relation to global capitalism, Mandel considers that it is first and foremost the contemporary modes of integration in the context of the European Union that lead for the first time to the formation of international state instrumentalities and functions. The growing interpenetration of capital within the Common Market and the advent of large banks-cum-industrial enterprises, not belonging primarily to any one capitalist class, are the material infrastructure underlying the emergence of supranational instruments of state power in the Common

Market (Mandel 1975: 147). This argumentation concerning internationalization of state functions as a result of internationalization of capital was given its most comprehensive formulation by Murray (1971). Murray maintained that internationalization of capital led to a territorial non-correspondence between the state and (its) capital. *The lack of correspondence between the territory of the state and the area of operations of capital, along with the growing instability of states, results, according to Murray, in the creation of international authorities of a quasi-state type, with corresponding international political functions.* The tendency is for these authorities and these functions to cover the operational terrain, that is to say the actual territory, of the capital. Firstly, it is not necessary for the state economic functions pertaining to any specific capital or cohesive system of capitals to be exercised by only one authority, notwithstanding the fact that usually there is only one sovereign power. Secondly, the instrumentality or instrumentalities that exercises (or exercise) these functions are not necessarily the governmental authorities of national states. Public economic questions of this kind may be an object of attention for a consortium of private capitals, for national governments or for some international public instrumentalities (Murray 1971: 87–8).
7. See Poulantzas (1975).
8. Poulantzas (1973), Balibar (1988), see also Chapter 7.
9. Quite the same argumentation, which of course is entirely in agreement with our analysis in Part II, can be found not only in the interventions of Lenin but also in the theoretical works of Althusser. Lenin, to be specific, thought that in the first phase of the Russian revolution the intervention of 'imperialism', that is to say of the superpowers England and France, significantly *strengthened* the attempt of the bourgeoisie to lead a new power bloc and in this way impose a new regime of political hegemony. Evidently such a 'strengthening' could have no chance if the suitable political forces did not exist that could *also secure the terrain for imperialist intervention.* Nevertheless they ultimately proved altogether incapable of affecting the political outcome and averting the coming revolution (see 'The April Theses', Lenin, *CW*, vol. 24). The theoretical formulation of this reasoning finds finished expression in the texts of Althusser (1969, especially in the essays entitled 'Contradiction and Overdetermination' and 'On the Materialist Dialectic'). The international conjuncture is a determining factor on the terrain of class struggle with a 'special role', meaning that it acts in a multiplicity of different ways, but in a manner always overdetermined. The class struggle, which is internal to every social formation, 'has priority and is the basis for the role of the external unevenness, up to and including the effects this second unevenness has within social formations in confrontation. Every interpretation that reduces the phenomena of internal unevenness (for example, explaining the "exceptional" conjuncture in Russia in 1917 solely by its relation of external unevenness: international relations, the uneven economic development of Russia as compared with the West, etc.) slides into mechanism, or into what is frequently an alibi for it: a theory of the reciprocal interaction of the inside and the outside' (Althusser 1969: 212).
10. Ruccio's argument is interesting in this connection, because he stresses the relation between capitalist exploitation and imperialism (his analysis, however, deviates from our argumentation). He conceives imperialism

neither as a particular stage of capitalism nor as a political choice. Borrowing from Deleuze and Guattari, he thinks of imperialism as a 'machine': 'the machinelike quality of imperialism gives a sense of the ways in which it has various parts that (often but not always) work together, a set of energies, available identities and categories that propel individuals and groups, institutions and structures, to enact designs and to civilize those who attempt to resist its apparent lessons, to make them succumb to the naturalized logic. *Not a stage of capitalism but rather a machine that energizes and is energized by capitalism at various points in its history.* [...] What we call capitalism [...] is that constellation of conditions and effects that are associated (not abstractly or inevitably but concretely and contingently – in other words, historically) with the extraction of surplus labor in the form of surplus-value. *Imperialism, in turn, is the set of conditions that shape and are shaped by the existence of this exploitation'* (Ruccio 2003: 90, 87, emphasis added).

11. In the same line of argumentation Foucault (2007: 379), admitting that the plurality of states entails a *multiple spatiality* (with this plurality of states not being 'a transitional phase between a first unitary kingdom and a final empire in which unity will be restored'), asserts that the 'essential element' in the 'competition between states' is that 'in which, of course, each seeks to turn the relation of force in its favor, but all seek to maintain as a whole' (ibid. 392).

12. As Rubin (1989) correctly argues, Smith's 'invisible hand' as well as the meaning he sometimes ascribes to 'natural' economic phenomena, makes possible the formulation of a theory of the (capitalist) economy and society that goes beyond individuals, focusing on (social and economic) regularities and 'laws' that determine individual action. What emerges is 'a recognition of the *spontaneous law-determined regularity of market phenomena'* (Rubin 1989: 174).

13. See Hirsch (1977), Busch (1978).

14. Busch (1992). In the present analysis we do not intend to investigate the process of European integration, its limitation or the prospects of establishing a united 'European state'. We note only that even if this process of convergence of the European states leads to a new European multinational state along the lines of the United Kingdom of England, Scotland and Ireland, something not yet visible as a dominant trend, the basic structure of the imperialist chain that would emerge from the inter-articulation of social formations is not susceptible to alteration.

15. See, for details of the nature of the regimes and the dynamics of their disintegration, Bettelheim (1975).

16. See Eikenberg (1983).

17. Bond et al. (2006).

18. See Tibi (1973), especially for the Arabic and Islamic countries.

19. See, for example the analysis by Menzel (1985 and 1985a), of the new industrial countries of S. E. Asia.

20. Also see Hirsch (1977: 16–23).

21. Menzel (1986).

22. Pijl (2006: 400).

23. See Sakellaropoulos and Sotiris (2008).

Epilogue Rethinking Imperialism and Capitalist Rule

1. See Lapatsioras, Milios and Sotiropoulos (2008).

References

Abalkin, L., Dzarasov, S. and Kulikov, A. (1983) *Political Economy. A Short Course*. Moscow: Progress Publishers.

Albo, G (2003) 'The Old and New Economics of Imperialism', in L. Panitch and C. Leys (eds) *The Socialist Register 2004*, London: Merlin (pp. 88–113).

Althusser, L. (1969) *For Marx*, The Penguin Press.

Althusser, L. (1976) *Essays in Self-Criticism*, London: NLB.

Althusser, L. (1995) *Sur la Reproduction*, Paris: PUF.

Althusser, L. (1999) Machiavelli and US, London and New York: Verso.

Althusser, L. and Balibar, E. (1997) *Reading Capital*, London: Verso.

Amariglio, J. and Callari, A. (1989) 'Marxian Value Theory and the Problem of the Subject: The Role of Commodity Fetishism', *Rethinking Marxism*, 2:3, 31–60.

Amin, S. (1974) 'Zur Theorie von Akkumulation und Entwicklung in der gegenwärtigen Weltgesellschaft', in D. Senghaas (ed.) *Peripherer Kapitalismus*, Frankfurt/M: Suhrkamp.

Amin, S. (1976) *Unequal Development. An Essay on the Social Formations of Peripheral Capitalism*, Sussex: The Harvester Press.

Amin, S. (1981) 'Interview with Samir Amin', *Monthly Review*, p. 10.

Amin, S. (1989) *Eurocentrism*, London: Zed.

Amin, S. (1996) 'The Ancient World-Systems versus the Modern Capitalist World-System', in A. G. Frank and B. K. Gills (eds) *The World System: Five Hundred Years or Five Thousand?*, London and New York: Routledge.

Amin, S. (2003) *Obsolescent Capitalism*, New York and London: Zed Books.

Amin, S. (2008) 'Financial Collapse, Systemic Crisis? Illusory Answers and Necessary Answers', Paper introducing the World Forum of Alternatives, in Caracas, October 2008 (translated from French by Daniel Paquet, internet http://www.globalresearch.ca/index.php?context=viewArticle&code=AMI20081123&articleId=11099)

Amin, S., Arrighi, G., Frank, A. G. and Wallerstein, I. (1982) *Dynamics of Global Crisis*, New York and London: Monthly Review Press.

Arendt, H. (1951) *The Origins of Totalitarianism*, New York: Harcourt.

Arrighi, G. (1996) *The Long Twentieth Century*, London and New York: Verso.

Arrighi, G. (1999) 'Globalization, state sovereignty, and the "endless" accumulation of capital', in D. A. Smith, D. J. Solinger and S. C. Topik (eds) *States and Sovereignty in the Global Economy*, London and New York: Routledge.

Arthur, C. (2002) *New Dialectic and Marx's Capital*, Leiden-Boston-Köln: Brill Academic Publishers.

Ashman, S. and Callinicos, A. (2006) 'Capital Accumulation and the State System', *Historical Materialism*, 14:4, 107–31.

Bairoch, P. (1993) *Economics and World History. Myths and Paradoxes*, London: Harvester/Wheatsheaf.

Bairoch, P. (2006) *The Economic Development of the Third World since 1900*, London: Routledge.

Balibar, E. (1984) 'Marx et l' Entreprise', *Politique Aujourd'hui*.

Balibar, E. and Wallerstein, I. (1988) *Race, Nation, Class, Les Indentités Ambiguës*, Paris: La Découverte.

Balibar, E. (1993) *La Philosophie de Marx*, Paris: La Decouverte.

Baran, P.A. and Sweezy, P. M. (1968) *Monopoly Capital. An Essay on the American Economic and Social Order*, London: Pelican Books.

Belamy-Foster, J. (2006) 'Monopoly-Finance Capital', *Monthly Review*, http://www.monthlyreview.org/1206jbf.htm

Bensaid, D. (2004) 'Multitudes Ventriloques' (à propos du dernier livre de M. Hardt et T. Negri *Multitude*, Paris, La Decouverte), http://multitudes.samizdat.net/Multitudes-ventriloques

Bettelheim, C. (1972) 'Theoretical Comments', in Emmanuel (ed) *Unequal Exchange. A Study of the Imperialism of Trade*, London: New Left Books.

Bettelheim, C. (1975) *Economic Calculation and Forms of Property. An Essay on the Transition Between Capitalism and Socialism*, New York: Monthly Review Press.

Bond, P., Chitonge, H. and Hopfmann, A. (2006) *The Accumulation of Capital in Southern Africa*, Johannesburg: The University of Kwazulu-Natal.

Bowring, F. (2004) 'From the Mass Worker to the Multitude: A Theoretical Contextualization of Hardt and Negri's empire', *Capital and Class*, 83, 101–32.

Braudel, F. (1984) *The Perspective of the World*, New York: Harper & Row.

Brenner, R. (1976) 'Agrarian structure and economic development in the pre-industrial Europe', *Past and Present*, 70, 30–75.

Brenner, R. (1982) 'The agrarian roots of European Capitalism', *Past and Present*, 97:16–113.

Brenner, R. (2001) 'The low countries in the transition to capitalism', *Journal of Agrarian Change*, 1:2, 169–241.

Brenner, R. (2001a) 'The world economy at the turn of the millennium toward boom or crisis?', *Review of International Political Economy*, 8:1, 6–44.

Brenner, R. (2006) 'What is, and what is not, imperialism?', *Historical Materialism*, 14:4, 79–105.

Brenner, R. (2008) "Devastating Crisis Unfolds", IV Online Magazine: IV396 – January (internet: http://www.internationalviewpoint.org/spip.php?article1417).

Brewer, A. (1980) *Marxist Theories of Imperialism. A Critical Survey*, London: Routledge and Kegan Paul.

Bryan, D. and Rafferty, M. (2006) *Capitalism with Derivatives, A Political Economy of Financial Derivatives, Capital and Class*, New York and London: Palgrave Macmillan.

Bukharin, N. (1972a) *Imperialism and World Economy*, London: Merlin.

Bukharin, N. (1972b) 'Imperialism and the Accumulation of Capital', in R. Luxemburg and N. Bukharin, *Imperialism and the Accumulation of Capital* (ed. by K. J. Tarbuck), London: Allen Lane The Penguin Press.

Busch, K. (1973) 'Ungleicher Tausch-Zur Diskussion uber internationale Durchschnittsprofitrate, ungleichen Tausch und komparative Kostentheorie anhand der Thesen von A. Emmanuel', *PROKLA*, 8/9.

Busch, K. (1974) *Die Multinationalen Konzerne. Zur Analyse der Weltmarktbewegung des Kapitals*, Frankfurt/M: Suhrkamp.

Busch, K. (1978) *Die Krise der Europäischen Gemeinschaft*, Frankfurt/M: Europäische Verlagsanstalt.

Busch, K. (1984) 'Die bundesrepublikanische Weltmarktdiskussion - Eine kritische Bestandsaufnahme ihrer grunlegenden Theorien und Kontroversen', *μehrwert*, no. 25.

Busch, K. (1985) "Mythen Vber den Weltmarkt II," Prokla, n.60.

Busch, K. (1992) *Umbruch in Europa*, Köln: Bund Verlag.

Busch, K., Grunert, G. and Tobergte, W. (1984) *Strukturen der kapitalistischen Weltökonomie. Zur Diskussion über die Gesetze der Weltmarktbewegung des Kapitals*, Saarbrücken - Fort Lauterdale: Breitenbach Publishers.

Busch, K., Schöller, W. and Seelow, W. (1971) *Weltmarkt und Weltwahrugskrise*, Bremen: Gruppe Arbeiterpolitik.

Callari, A. (2008) 'Imperialism and the Rhetoric of Democracy in the Age of Wall Street', *Rethinking Marxism*, 20:4, 700–9.

Callinicos, A. (1994) 'Marxism and Imperialism Today', in *Marxism and the New Imperialism*, London, Chicago and Melbourne: Bookmarks.

Callinicos, A. (2004) *Making History: Agency, Structure, and Change in Social Theory*, Leiden and Boston: Brill.

Callinicos, A. (2005) 'Imperialism and Global Political Economy', *International Socialism*, 108 (http://www.isj.org.uk/index.php4?id=140&issue=108).

Callinicos, A. (2006) Making Sense of Imperialism: A Reply to Leo Panitch and Sam Grindin, International Socialism, issue 11 (internet: http//www.isj.org.uk/index.php4?id=196&issue=110).

Callinicos, A. (2007) 'Does Capitalism Need the State System', *Cambridge Review of International Affairs*, 20:4, 533–49.

Callinicos, A. (2006), Making Sence of Imperialism: A Reply to Leo Panitch and Sam Grindin, *International Socialism,* issue 11" (internet: http://www.isj.org.uk/index.php4?id=196&issue=110).

Campbell, A. (2003) 'Post-WWII Profit Rate Dynamics in the United States, Japan, and Germany: A Classical Perspective', ICAPE 2003 Conference, The Future of Heterodox Economics, June 5–7, University of Missouri at Kansas City.

Carchedi, G. (2001) 'Imperialist Contradictions at the Threshold of the Third Millennium: A New Phase', in R. Albritton, M. Itoh, R. Westra and A. Zuege (eds) *Phases of Capitalist Development*, New York: Palgrave (pp. 215–29).

Cardóso, F. H. (1973) 'Das Brasillianische Entwicklungsmodell', *PROKLA*, no. 6.

Cardóso, F. H. (1974) 'Brasilien: Die Widersprüche der assoziierten Entwicklung', in H. R. Sonntag (ed.) *Lateinamerika. Faschismus oder Revolution. Venezuela, Brasilien, Chile, Peru*, Berlin: Rotbuch.

Caves, R. E. (2007) *Multinational Enterprise and Economic Analysis*, New York: Cambridge University Press.

Chtouris, S. (2004) *Rational Symbolic Networks* (in Greek), Athens: Nissos.

Córdova, A. (1973) *Strukturelle Heterogenitat und Wirtschaftliches Wachstum*, Frankfurt: Suhrkamp Verlag.

Cox, R. W. (1987) *Production, Power, and World Order, Social Forces in the Making of History*, New York: Columbia University Press.

Cox, R. W. (1999) *Approaches to World Order*, Cambridge University Press.

Cox, R. W. (2004) 'Beyond Empire and Terror: Critical Reflections on the Political Economy of World Order', *New Political Economy*, 9:3, 307–23.

Crawford, J. (2006) *The Creation of States in International Law*, Oxford: Clarendon Press.

Crotty, J. (2005) 'The Neoliberal Paradox: The Impact of Destructive Product Market Competition and "Modern" Financial Markets on Nonfinancial Corporation Performance in the Neoliberal Era', in G. A. Epstein (ed.) *Financialization and the World Economy*, Cheltenham (UK) and Northampton (USA): Edward Elgar (pp. 77–110).

Cypher, J. M. (1979) 'The Internationalization of Capital and the Transformation of Social Formations. A Critique of the Monthly Review School', *Review of Radical Political Economics*, 11:4, 33–49.

Davidson, P. (2002) *Financial Markets, Money and the Real World*, Cheltenham (UK) and Northampton (USA): Edward Elgar.

Deakin, D. (2005) 'The Coming Transformation of Shareholder Value', *Corporate Governance: An International Review*, 13:1, 11–18.

Dumenil, G. and Levy, D. (2004) *Capital Resurgent*, Harvard University Press.

Eikenberg, A. (1983) *Die paradigmatische Krise der Theorie ökonomisch unterentwickelter Gesellschaftsformationen*, Marburg/Lahn: Diss. Uni. Osnabrück.

Emmanuel, A. (1972) *Unequal Exchange. A Study of the Imperialism of Trade*, London: New Left Books.

Epstein, G. (2001) 'Financialization, Rentier Interests, and Central Bank Policy', Paper presented at PERI Conference on 'Financialization of the World Economy', 7–8 December 2001 (internet: http://www.umass.edu/peri/pdfs/fin_Epstein.pdf).

Epstein, G. and Jayadev, A. (2005) 'The Rise of Rentier Incomes in OECD Countries: Finanacialization, Central Bank Policy and Labor Solidarity', in G. A. Epstein (ed.) *Financialization and the World Economy*, Cheltenham (UK) and Northampton (USA): Edward Elgar (pp. 46–74).

Fama, E. F. and French, K. R. (2001) 'Disappearing Dividends: Changing Firm Characteristics or Lower Propensity to Pay?', *Journal of Financial Economics*, 60, 3–43.

Fieldhouse, D. K. (1961) '"Imperialism": An Historiographical Revision', *The Economic History Review*, New Series, 14:2, 187–209.

Fieldhouse, D. (2002) '"A New Imperial System"? The Role of the Multinational Corporations Reconsidered', in J. A. Frieden and D. A. Lake (eds) *International Political Economy. Perspectives on Global Power and Wealth*, London and New York: Routledge.

Fine, B. and Saad-Filho, A. (2004) *Marx's Capital*, London: Pluto Press.

Fine, B. and Milonakis, D. (2008) *From Political Economy to Economics: Method, the Social and the Historical in the Evolution of Economic Theory*, London: Routledge.

Foucault, M. (2007) *Security, Territory, Population* (Lectures at the Collège de France), New York: Palgrave Macmillan.

Frank, A. G. (1969) *Kapitalismus und Unterentwicklung in Lateinamerika*, Frankfurt: Europäische Verlagsanstalt.

Frank, A. G. (1984) *Weltwirtschaft in der Krise*, Reinbeck: Rowohlt.

Frank, A. G. and Gills, B. K. (eds) (1996) *The World System: Five Hundred Years or Five Thousand?*, London and New York: Routledge.

Freeman, A. and Kagarlitsky B. (eds) (2004) *The Politics of Empire: Globalisation in Crisis*, London: Pluto Press.

Fröbel, F., Heinrichs, J. and Kreye, O. (1983) *Die Neue Internationale Arbeitsteilung*, Reinbeck: Rowohlt.

Froud, J., Leaver, A. and Williams, K. (2007) 'New Actors in a Financialised Economy and the Remaking of Capitalism', *New Political Economy*, 12:3, 339–47.

Giddens, A. (1981) *A Contemporary Critique of Historical Materialism*, Berkeley: University of California Press.

Giddens, A. (1987) *The Nation State and Violence*, Berkeley: University of California Press.

Gill, S. (2003) *Power and Resistance in the New World Order*, New York: Palgrave Macmillan.

Gills, B. K. (2001) 'Re-orienting the New (International) Political Economy', *New Political Economy*, 6:2, 233–45.

Goldstein, A. (2007) *Multinational Companies from Emerging Economies*, New York: Palgrave Macmillan.

Goodman, D. and Redclift, M. (1982) *From Peasant to Proletarian. Capitalist Development and Agrarian Transitions*, New York: St. Martin's Press.

Gowan, P. (2003) 'Cooperation and Conflict in Transatlantic Relations after the Cold War', *Interventions*, 5:2, 218–23.

Grahl, J. and Teague, P. (2000) 'The Regulation School, the Employment Relation and Financialization', *Economy and Society*, 29:1, 160–78.

Gramsci, A. (1971) *Selections from the Prison Notebooks*, London: Lawrence and Wishart.

Hardt, M. and Negri, A. (2000) *Empire*, Cambridge, Massachusetts and London, England: Harvard University Press.

Hardt, M. and Negri, A. (2004) *Multitude: War and Democracy in the Age of Empire*, New York: The Penguin Press.

Harnecker, M. (1985) *Los Conceptos Elementales del Materialismo Historic*, México: Siglo XXI Editores.

Harris, N. (1986) *The End of the Third World. NICs and the Decline of an Ideology*, New York: Penguin.

Harvey, D. (2003) *The New Imperialism*, Oxford University Press.

Heinrich, M. (1999) *Die Wissenschaft vom Wert*, Berlin: Westfaelisches Dampfboot.

Helleiner, E. (1994) *States and the Resurgence of Global Finance: From Bretton Woods to the 1990s*, New York: Cornell University Press.

Hilferding, R. (1904 [1949]) *Böhm-Bawerk's Criticism of Marx*, New York: Kelley (Printed together with Böhm-Bawerk's essay *Karl Marx and the Close of his System* and edited with an 'Introduction' by Paul Sweezy).

Hilferding, R. (1981) *Finance Capital*, London: Routledge and Kegan Paul.

Hirsch, S. (1977) *Rich Man's, Poor Man's, and Every Man's Goods. Aspects of Industrialization*, Tübingen: Mohr.

Hirschman, A. O. (1976) 'On Hegel, Imperialism, and Structural Stagnation', *Journal of Development Economics*, 3, 1–8.

Hobsbawm, E. J. (1977) 'Some reflections on "The Break-up of Britain"', *New Left Review*, I/105 (September–October).

Hobsbawn, E. J. (1987) *The Age of Empire, 1875–1914*, London: Weidenfeld and Nicolson.

Hobsbawm, E. J. (1993) *The Age of Revolution, 1789–1848*, London: Anacus.

Hobson, J. (1937) 'The Economics of Thorstein Veblen', *Political Science Quarterly*, 52:1, 139–44 (http://www.marxists.org/archive/hobson/1937/03/veblen.htm).

Hobson, J. (1938) *Imperialism: A Study*, London: Allen & Unwin.

Hodgson, G. M. (1999) *Evolution and Institutions*, Edward Elgar Publishing.

Hodgson, G. M. (2006) 'What Are Institutions?', *Journal of Economic Issues*, XL:1, 1–25.

Hopkins, T. K. and Wallerstein, I. (1979) 'Grundzüge der Entwicklung des modernen Weltsystems' in D. Senghaas (ed.) , Frankfurt-M: Suhrkamp (280 ff).

Howard, M. C. and King, J. E. (1989) *A History of Marxian Economics, Volume 1, 1883-1929*, London: Macmillan Education Ltd.

Howard, M. C. and King, J. E. (2000) 'Whatever Happened to Imperialism?', in R. H. Chilcote (ed.) *The Political Economy of Imperialism*, Boston: Rowman & Littlefield Publishers, Inc (pp. 19–40).

Hurtienne, T. (1981) 'Peripherer Kapitalismus und Autozentrierte Entwicklung', *PROKLA*, 44, 105–36.

Hymer, S. (1976) *The International Operations of National Firms: Study of Direct Foreign Investment*, Cambridge, Mass.: MIT Press (Ph.D. Dissertation).

Ioakimoglou, E. and Milios, J. (1993) 'Capital Accumulation and Over-Accumulation Crisis: The Case of Greece (1960-1989)', *Review of Radical Political Economics*, 25:2, 81–107.

Ioakimoglou, E. and Milios, J. (2005) 'Capital Accumulation and Profitability in Greece (1964-2004)', *INEK-2005 Conference on Sustainable Development*, Nicosia July 23–24, 2005 (http://users.ntua.gr/jmilios/en/pc.html).

Jensen, M. C. (2001) 'Value Maximisation, Stakeholder Theory, and the Corporate Objective Function', *European Financial Management*, 7:3, 297–317.

Kautsky, J. H. (1961) 'J. A. Schumpeter and Karl Kautsky: Parallel Theories of Imperialism', *Midwest Journal of Political Science*, 5:2, 101–28.

Kautsky, K. (1892 [1910]) *The Class Struggle (Erfurt Program)*, Charles H. Kerr & Co (internet: http://www.marxists.org/archive/kautsky/1892/erfurt/index.htm).

Kautsky, K. (1898) 'Aeltere und Neuere Kolonialpolitik', *Die Neue Zeit*, 16:1, 769–81, 801–16.

Kautsky, K. (1914) 'Ultra-Imperialism', *Die Neue Zeit* (internet: http://www.marxists.org/archive/kautsky/1914/09/ultra-imp.htm).

Keynes, J. M. (1973) *The General Theory of Employment, Interest and Money*, Cambridge: Cambridge University Press.

Kiely, R. (2005a) 'Capitalist Expansion and the Imperialism-Globalization Debate', *Journal of International Relations and Development*, 8, 27–57.

Kiely, R. (2005b) *Empire in the Age of Globalization, US Hegemony and Neoliberal Disorder*, London: Pluto Press.

Kiely, R. (2006) 'United States Hegemony and Globalization', *Cambridge Review of International Affairs*, 19:2, 205–21.

Koebner, R. (1949) 'The Concept of Economic Imperialism', *The Economic History Review, New Series*, 2:1, 1–29.

Krugman, P. (1997) *The Age of Diminished Expectations*, Cambridge, Massachusetts and London, England: MIT Press.

Lacher, H. (2005) 'International Transformation and the Persistence of Territoriality: Toward a New Political Geography of Capitalism', *Review of International Political Economy*, 12:1, 26–52.

Lapatsioras, S., Milios, J. and Sotiropoulos, D. (2008) 'Marxism, Class Struggle and Ideology. Problems and Opportunities Raised by the Multi-Cleavage of Marxism', Paper presented in the 9th Annual Conference of *Historical Materialism*, University of London, 7–9 November 2008.

Lapavitsas, C. (2008) 'Financialised Capitalism: Direct Exploitation and Periodic Bubbles', Working paper, Department of Economics, SOAS, University of London (internet: http://www.soas.ac.uk/economics/events/crisis/43939.pdf).

Lazonick, W. and O'Sullivan, M. (2000) 'Maximizing Shareholder Value: a New Ideology for Corporate Governance', *Economy and Society*, 29:1, 13–35.

Lenin, C. W. (1977) *Collected Works (CW)*, *Vol. 1, 2, 3*, London: Lawrence and Wishart.

Lenin, V. I. (1964–1977) *Collected Works (CW)*, *Vol. 19, 22, 24, 25, 28, 29, 39*, Moscow: Progress Publishers (internet: http://marxists.org/archive/lenin/works/cw/).

Lipietz, A. (1983) *Le Capital et son Espace*, Paris: La Decouverte/Maspero.

Löwe, A. (1926), 'Zur ökonomischen Theorie des Imperialismus', in R. Wilbrandt, A. Löwe and G. Salomon (eds) *Wirtschaft und Gesellschaft. Beiträge zur Oekonomik und Soziologie der Gegenwart. Festschrift für Franz Oppenheimer*,Frankfurter-Societäts, Frankfurt/M.: Frankfurter-Societäts-Druckerei.

Luxemburg, R. (1925) *Einführung in die Nationalökonomie*, Berlin: Paul Levi.

Luxemburg, R. (1961) *The Russian Revolution* (ed. B. D. Wolfe), University of Michigan Press.

Luxemburg, R. (1971) *The Accumulation of Capital*, London: Routledge and Kegan Paul.

Mandel, E. (1971) *The Formation of the Economic Thought of K Marx*, New York & London: New Left Books.

Mandel, E. (1975) 'International Capitalism and "Supranationality'", in H. Radice (ed.) *International Firms and Modern Imperialism*, Harmondsworth, Middlesex: Penguin Books.

Mann, M. (1986) *The Sources of Social Power, Vol. I*, Cambridge: Cambridge University Press.

Mann, M. (1988) *States, War, and Capitalism: Studies in Political Sociology*, Oxford: Blackwell.

Marini, R. M. (1969) *Subdesarrollo y revolución*, México: Siglo XXI.

Marini, R. M. (1974) *Il Subimperialismo Brasiliano*, Torino: Einaudi.

Marx, K. (1969) *Resultate des unmittelbaren Produktionsprozesses. Das Kapital. I. Buch. Der Produktionsprozess des Kapitals. VI. Kapitel*, Frankfurt/M: Verlag Neue Kritik.

Marx, K. (1990) *Capital, Volume I*, London: Penguin Classics.

Marx, K. (1991) *Capital, Volume II*, London: Penguin Classics.

Marx, K. (1992) *Capital, Volume III*, London: Penguin Classics.

Marx, K. (1993) *Grundrisse*, London: Penguin Classics.

Mattick, P. (1980) *Marx and Keynes*, London: Merlin Press.

McNally, D. (2006) *Another World Is Possible: Globalizaton & Anti-Capitalism*, Winnipeg: Arbeiter Ring Publishing.

Menzel, U. (1985) *In der Nachfolge Europas. Autozentrierte Entwicklung in den ostasiatischen Schwellenländern Südkorea und Taiwan*, München: Simon & Magiera.

Menzel, U. (1985a) 'Die ostasiatischen Schwellenländer. Testfälle für die entwicklungstheoretische Diskussion', *PROKLA*, 59, 9–33.

Menzel, U. (1986) 'The Newly Industrializing Countries of East Asia: Imperialist Continuity or a Case of Catching Up?', in W. J. Mommsen and J. Osterhammel (eds) *Imperialism and After. Continuities and Discontinuities*, London: Allen & Unwin (pp. 247–63).

Menzel, U. (1988) *Auswege aus der Abhangigkeit. Die entwicklungspolitische Aktualitat Europas*, Frankfurt: Suhrkamp Verlag.

MEW (Karl Marx/Friedrich Engels – Werke) (1973) *Vol. 1, 19, 21, 25, 37, 39*, Berlin: Dietz Verlag.

Michaelides, P. and Milios, J. (2005) 'Did Hilferding Influence Schumpeter?', *History of Economics Review*, Vol. 41, Winter: 98–125.

Milios, J. (1988) *Kapitalistische Entwicklung, Nationalstaat und Imperialismus*, Athens: Kritiki.

Milios, J. (1989) 'The Problem of Capitalist Development: Theoretical Considerations in View of the Industrial Countries and the New Industrial Countries', in M. Gottdiener and N. Komninos (eds) *Capitalist Development and Crisis Theory*, London: Macmillan.

Milios, J. (1994) 'Marx's Theory and the Historic Marxist Controversy on Economic Crisis (1900-1937)', *Science and Society*, 58:2, 175–94.

Milios, J. (1995) 'Marxist Theory and Marxism as a Mass Ideology. The Effects of the Collapse of "Real Existing Socialism" and on West European Marxism', *Rethinking Marxism*, 8:4, 61–74.

Milios, J. (1999) 'Preindustrial Capitalist forms: Lenin's Contribution to a Marxist Theory of Economic Development', *Rethinking Marxism*, 11:4, 38–56.

Milios, J. (1999a) 'Colonialism and Imperialism: Classic Texts', in Ph. A. O'Hara (ed.) *Encyclopedia of Political Economy*, London: Routledge (pp. 113–16).

Milios, J. (1999b) 'Diminished Profitability and Welfare Decline (Reflections on the Irreformability of Capitalism in the 1990s)', in J. Milios, L. Katseli and T. Pelagidis (eds) *Rethinking Democracy and the Welfare State*, Athens: Ellinika Grammata.

Milios, J. (2001) 'Hilferding, Rudolf (1877–1941)', in B.R.J. Jones (ed.),*Routledge Encyclopedia of International Political Economy*, London: Routledge (vol. 2, pp. 676–8).

Milios, J. (2003) 'On the theoretical significance of Marx's ambivalences towards Classical Political Economy', *The 2003 Value Theory Mini-Conference*, New York (http://www.greenwich.ac.uk/~fa03/iwgvt).

Milios, J., Dimoulis, D. and Economakis, G. (2002) *Karl Marx and the Classics, An Essay on Value, Crises and the Capitalist Mode of Production*, England: Ashgate Publishing Limited.

Milios, J. and Sotiropoulos, D. (2007) 'Tugan-Baranowsky and Effective Demand', *Science & Society*, 71:2, 227–42.

Minsky, H. P. (1982) *Inflation, Recession and Economic Policy*, Sussex: Wheatsheaf Books Ltd.

Minsky, H. P. (1987) *Securitization* (republished in 2008 with preface and forward by L. Randall Wray by The Levy Economics Institute of Bard College: Policy Note no. 2/2008).

Minsky, H. P. (1993) Schumpeter and Finance, in S. Biasco, A. Roncaglia and M. Salvati (eds) *Market and Institutions in Economic Development: Essays in Honor of Sylos Labini*, New York: St. Martin's Press.

Modelski, G. (1987) *Long Cycles in World Politics*, London: Macmillan.

Mommsen, W. J. (1977) *Imperialismus. Seine geistigen, politischen und wirtschaftlichen Grundlagen. Ein Quellen- und Arbeitsbuch*, Hamburg: Hoffmann und Campe.

Mommsen, W. J. (1982) *Theories of Imperialism*, Chicago: The University of Chicago Press.

Moszkowska, N. (1935) *Zur Kritik moderner Krisentheorien*, Prague: Paul Kacha Verlag.

Müller, W. and Neusüss, Ch. (1971) 'Der Sozialstaatsillusion und der Widerspruch zwischen Lohnarbeit und Kapital', *Probleme des Klassenkampfs*, Sonderheft 1.

Murray, R. (1971) 'The Internationalisation of Capital and the Nation State', *New Left Review*, 67, 84–109.

Neusüss, Ch. (1972) *Imperialismus und Weltmarktbewegung des Kapitals*, Erlangen: Politlanden.

O'Hara, P. A. (2006) *Growth and Development in the Global Political Economy*, London and New York: Routledge.

Overbeek, H. (2000) 'Transnational Historical Materialism: Theories of Transnational Class Formation and World Order', in R. Palan (ed.) *Global Political Economy, Contemporary Theories*, London & New York: Routledge (pp. 168–83).

Palley, T. I. (2007) 'Finacialization: What It Is and Why It Matters', Working paper, No. 525, The Levy Economics Institute of Bard College.

Panitch, L. and Gindin, S. (2003) 'Global Capitalism and American Empire', in L. Panitch and C. Leys (eds) *The Socialist Register 2004*, London: Merlin (pp. 1–42).

Panitch, L. and Gindin, S. (2004) *Global Capitalism and American Empire*, London: The Merlin Press.

Petras, J. and Veltmeyer, H. (2000) 'Globalisation or Imperialism?', *Cambridge Review of International Affairs*, 14:1, 32–48

Petras, J. and Veltmeyer, H. (2001) *Globalization Unmasked*, Delhi: Madhyam Books.

van der Pijl, K. (1998) *Transnational Classes and International Relations*, London and New York: Routledge.

van der Pijl, K. (2006) *Global Rivalries: From the Cold War to Iraq*, London: Pluto Press.

Pleticha H. (ed.) (1996) *Weltgeschichte in 12 Bänden* (Band 9), Gütersloh: Bertelsmann Lexikon Verlag.

Pollin, R. (1996). '"Socialization of Investment" and "Euthanasia of the Rentier": the Relevance of Keynesian policy ideas for the contemporary US Economy', *International Review of Applied Economics*, 10:1, 49–64.

Popov, G. (1984) *Imperialism and the Developing Countries*, Moscow: Progress Publishers.

Popper, K. (2005) *The Poverty of Historicism*, New York: Routledge Classics.

Poulantzas, N. (1973) *Political Power and Social Classes*, London: New Left Books and Seed and Ward.

Poulantzas, N. (1975) *Classes in Contemporary Capitalism*, London: New Left Books and Seed & Ward.

Poulantzas, N. (1980) *State, Power, Socialism*, London/New York: Verso.

Pozo-Martin, G. (2006) 'A Tougher Gordian Knot: Globalization, Imperialism and the Problem of the State', *Cambridge Review of International Affairs*, 19:2, 223–42.

Rees, J. (2006) *Imperialism and Resistance*, London and New York: Routledge.

Rosenberg, N. (1982) *Inside the Black Box: Technology and Economics*, Cambridge: Cambridge University Press.

244   *Rethinking Imperialism: A Study of Capitalist Rule*

Rostow, W. W. (1960) *The Stages of Economic Growth: A Non-Communist Manifesto*, London and New York: Cambridge University Press.
Rubin, I. I. (1989) *A History of Economic Thought*, London: Pluto Press.
Ruccio, F. D. (2003) 'Globalization and Imperialism', *Rethinking Marxism*, 15:1, 75–94.
Rupert, M. (1995) *Producing Hegemony: The Politics of Mass Production and American Global Power*, Cambridge: Cambridge University Press.
Sakellaropoulos, S. and Sotiris, P. (2008) 'American Foreign Policy as Modern Imperialism: from Armed Humanitarianism to Preemptive War', *Science & Society*, 72:2, 208–35.
dos Santos, T. (1978) 'Über die Struktur der Abhängigkeit', in D. Senghaas (ed.) *Imperialismus und strukturelle Gewalt*, Ed. Frankfurt: Suhrkamp Verlag, (243ff).
Schumpeter, J. A. (1950) *Capitalism, Socialism and Democracy*, London: Unwin University Press.
Schumpeter, J. A. (1951) *Imperialism and Social Classes*, New York: Augustus M. Kelly Inc.
Schweers, R. (1980) *Kapitalistische Entwicklung und Unterentwicklung. Voraussetzungen und Schranken der Kapitalakkumulation in ökonomisch schwach entwickelten Laendern*, Frankurt/M: Metzner Verlag.
Senghaas, D. (1982) *Von Europa lernen. Entwicklungsgeschichtliche Betrachtungen*, Frankfurt/M: Suhrkamp.
Sklair, L. (2001) *The Transnational Capitalist Class*, Oxford: Blackwell.
Skocpol, T. (1979) *States and Social Revolutions: A Comparative Analysis of France, Russia, and China*, Cambridge: Cambridge University Press.
Smith, A. (1981) *An Inquiry into the Nature and Causes of the Wealth of Nations*, Indianapolis: Liberty Classics.
Smithin, J. (1996) *Macroeconomic Policy and the Future of Capitalism*, Edward Elgar Publishing Limited.
Sotiris, P. (2005) 'Contradictions of a Democratic Utopia. Notes on Hardt and Negri's *Multitude*' (in Greek), *Theseis*, 91, 61–91.
Sotiropoulos, D. P. (2007) 'Pluralism in Action: A Marxian (Althusserian) Overview. Issues of Theory and Politics', Paper presented at the AHE 9th Annual Conference on 'Pluralism in Action', 13–15 July, University of Bristol (internet: http://www.uwe.ac.uk/bbs/aheconference/Papers/Sotiropoulos.pdf).
Sternberg, F. (1971) *Der Imperialismus*, Frankfurt/M: Neue Kritik.
Stone, N. (1999) *Europe Transformed: 1878–1919*, Blackwell Classic Histories of Europe, Oxford and Malden: Blackwell Publishers.
Szentes, T. (1974) *Politische Ökonomie der Entwicklungsländer*, Frankfurt-Budapest: Europäische Verlagsanstalt.
Szentes, T. (2003) *World Economics: The Political Economy of Development Globalisation and System Transformation*, Budapest: Akademiai Kiado Rt.
Taylor, O. H. (1951) 'Schumpeter and Marx: Imperialism and Social Classes in the Schumpeterian System', *Quarterly Journal of Economics*, 65:4, 611–22.
Teschke, B. (2003) *The Myth of 1648: Class, Geopolitics and the Making of Modern International Relations*, London and New York: Verso.
Teschke, B. and Lacher, H. (2007) 'The Changing "Logics" of Capitalist Competition', *Cambridge Review of International Affairs*, 20:4, 565–80.

Thoburn, N. (2001) 'Autonomous Production? On Negri's "New Synthesis'",
Theory, Culture and Society, 18:5, 75–96.
Tibi, B. (1973) *Militar und Sozialismus in der Dritten Welt*, Frankfurt: Suhrkamp
Verlag.
von Tugan-Baranowsky, M. (1969) *Studien zur Theorie und Geschichte der
Handelskrisen in England*, Aalen: Scientia Verlag.
von Tugan-Baranowsky, M. (2000) 'Studies on the Theory and the History of
Business Crises in England, Part I: Theory and History of Crises', in P. Zarembka
(ed.) *Research in Political Economy, Volume 18, Value, Capitalist Dynamics and
Money*, New York: Jai Press (pp. 53–110).
UNCTAD, FDI/TNC database (www.unctad.org/fdistatistics).
UNCTAD (2006) *Investment Brief*, No. 3.
UNCTAD (2008a) *Investment Brief No 1*.
UNCTAD (2008b) *The Least Developed Countries Report 2008*, United Nations.
Wallerstein, I. (1979) 'Aufstieg und künftiger Niedergang des kapitalistischen
Weltsystems', in D. Senghaas (ed.) *Kapitalistische Weltökonomie*, Ed. Frankfurt:
Suhrkamp.
Wallerstein, I. (1996) 'World System versus World Systems. A Critique', in
A. G. Frank and B. K. Gills (eds) *The World System: Five Hundred Years or Five
Thousand?*, London and New York: Routledge.
Wallerstein, I. (1998) *Utopistics: or, Historical Choices for the Twenty-First Century*,
New York: New Press.
Wallerstein, I. (1999) 'States? Sovereignty? The Dilemmas of Capitalists in an Age
of Transition', in D. A. Smith, D. J. Solinger and S. C. Topik (eds) *States and
Sovereignty in the Global Economy*, London and New York: Routledge.
Weber, M. (1978) *Economy and Society, Volume I and II*, Berkeley, Los Angeles and
London: University of California Press.
Wehler, H. U. (1970) *Bismarck und der Imperialismus*, Cologne: Kiepenheuer und
Witsch.
Willoughby, J. (1986) *Capitalist Imperialism, Crisis and the State*, Harwood,
London, Paris and New York: Academic Publishers.
Winslow, E. M. (1931) 'Marxian, Liberal, and Sociological Theories of Imperialism',
The Journal of Political Economy, 39:6, 713–58.
Winslow, E. M. (1972) *The Pattern of Imperialism*, New York: Octagon Books.
Wolff, R. (2008) 'Capitalist Crisis, Marx's Shadow', http://www.monthlyreview.
org/mrzine/wolff260908.html.
Wood, E. M. (2005) *Empire of Capital*, London: Verso.
Wray, L. R. (2007) 'A Post-Keynesian View of Central Bank Independence, Policy
Targets, and the Rules-versus-Discretion Debate', Working paper, No. 510, The
Levy Economics Institute.
Wray, L. R. (2008) 'Financial Markets Meltdown. What Can We Learn From
Minsky?', Working paper, No. 94, The Levy Economics Institute.
Zizek, S. (2009) *Violence*, London: Profile Books Ltd.

Index